As Sociology Meets History

STUDIES IN SOCIAL DISCONTINUITY

Under the Consulting Editorship of:

CHARLES TILLY
University of Michigan

EDWARD SHORTER
University of Toronto

In preparation

Manuel Gottlieb. A Theory of Economic Systems

Robert Max Jackson. The Formation of Craft Labor Markets

Published

Michael B. Katz. Poverty and Policy in American History

Arthur L. Stinchcombe. Economic Sociology

Jill S. Quadagno. Aging in Early Industrial Society: Work, Family, and Social Policy in Nineteenth-Century England

J. Dennis Willigan and Katherine A. Lynch. Sources and Methods of Historical Demography

Dietrich Gerhard. Old Europe: A Study of Continuity, 1000-1800

Charles Tilly. As Sociology Meets History

Maris A. Vinovskis. Fertility in Massachusetts from the Revolution to the Civil War

Juan G. Espinosa and Andrew S. Zimbalist. Economic Democracy: Workers' Participation in Chilean Industry 1970-1973: Updated Student Edition

Alejandro Portes and John Walton. Labor, Class, and the International System

James H. Mittelman. Underdevelopment and the Transition to Socialism: Mozambique and Tanzania

John R. Gillis. Youth and History: Tradition and Change in European Age Relations, 1770–Present: Expanded Student Edition

Samuel Kline Cohn, Jr. The Laboring Classes in Renaissance Florence

Richard C. Trexler. Public Life in Renaissance Florence

Paul Oquist. Violence, Conflict, and Politics in Colombia

Fred Weinstein. The Dynamics of Nazism: Leadership, Ideology, and the Holocaust

John R. Hanson II. Trade in Transition: Exports from the Third World, 1840–1900

Evelyne Huber Stephens. The Politics of Workers' Participation: The Peruvian Approach in Comparative Perspective

Albert Bergesen (Ed.). Studies of the Modern World-System

The list of titles in this series continues on the last page of this volume

As Sociology Meets History

Charles Tilly
Center for Research on Social Organization,
Department of History, and
Department of Sociology
University of Michigan
Ann Arbor, Michigan

1981

ACADEMIC PRESS, INC.
(Harcourt Brace Jovanovich, Publishers)
Orlando   San Diego   San Francisco   New York   London
Toronto   Montreal   Sydney   Tokyo   Sao Paulo

ACADEMIC PRESS, INC.
Orlando, Florida 32887

United Kingdom Edition published by
ACADEMIC PRESS, INC. (LONDON) LTD.
24/28 Oval Road, London NW1 7DX

Library of Congress Cataloging in Publication Data

Tilly, Charles.
  As sociology meets history.

  (Studies in social discontinuity)
  Bibliography: p.
  Includes index.
  1. Social history. 2. Sociology--Methodology.
3. History--Methodology. 4. Historiography.
I. Title. II. Series.
HN13.T54   907'.2   81-12728
ISBN 0-12-691280-7   AACR2

PRINTED IN THE UNITED STATES OF AMERICA

83 84   9 8 7 6 5 4 3 2

To George Caspar Homans
scientiae armig.

Contents

Preface   xi

EXHORTATION

1

Sociology, Meet History   1

Mercurial Views of the Seventeenth Century   1
Historical Practice   5
Stinchcombe's Challenge   7
History's Place   12
The Historical Zoo   15
Historical Practice as Social Structure   18
Handling the Evidence   21
Reinterpretations and Theories   24
"Social Science History"   27
How Do History and Social Science Coalesce?   29
Is Quantification the Essence?   34
Sociology Reaches for History   37
Historical Analyses of Structural Change
and Collective Action   44
What's Going on Here?   46

2

Computing History   53

A Computational Memory   53
Computers and Social Scientists   55
The Historical Social Sciences   57
Current Countercurrents   59
Is History Computable?   62
Development and History in the Social Sciences   65
Historical Demography as an Illustration   67
Another Personal Note: This Time, Collective Action   70
Richer, More Flexible Records   76
In Sum   82

APPRECIATION

3

Homans, Humans, and History   85

The Poet Scans History   85
Homans's Methods   90
Parallels and Particulars   92

4

Useless Durkheim   95

History in the Newspapers   95
Comparing England and America   96
How the Nineteenth Century Differed from the Eighteenth   99
Durkheim Faces the Nineteenth Century   101
Alternative Accounts of Collective Action   103
Historical Implications of Durkheim's Account   104
Does Durkheim Work?   106

APPLICATION

5

War and Peasant Rebellion in
Seventeenth-Century France   109

Introduction   109
The Burden of Government   115

The Prevalence of War   117
War and the Means of Warmaking   118
Routines of Seventeenth-Century Contention   123
War and the Rhythm and Geography of Contention   137
Appendix: Contentious Gatherings in Anjou, Burgundy,
Flanders, Île-de-France, and Languedoc, 1630–1649   140

6

How (And, to Some Extent, Why) to Study British Contention

How (And, to Some Extent, Why)
to Study British Contention   145
Introduction   145
Studying Contention in Great Britain   150
Additional Collections of Evidence   153
Interaction with Authorities   155
Variations and Changes in Repertoires   160
Interests, Organization, and Action   170
Conclusions   176

EXPLORATION

7

Proletarianization: Theory and Research

Proletarianization: Theory and Research   179
What and Where Is Proletarianization?   179
The Importance of Proletarianization   181
What Sociologists Say, and What They Ignore   184
Can Sociology Comprehend Proletarianization?   187

8

States, Taxes, and Proletarians

States, Taxes, and Proletarians   191
Capitalism and Statemaking Today   191
Proletarianization   195
Proletarianization and Statemaking   201
Taxes and Statemaking   202
Checking the Connections   206

CONCLUSION

9

Looking Forward . . . Into a Rearview Mirror   211

    Carr's Case   211
    Sociology Meets History   214

Bibliography   217

Index   233

Preface

Collectors always take risks. If an author reprints his or her published articles, a reader has a right to wonder why the author thinks they deserve a second airing. If the author assembles unpublished essays, the reader may suspect that there were good reasons for leaving them in the dark. A collection of disparate papers seldom makes a satisfying book. In drawing together the chapters of this volume, I realize that readers may find them less novel and coherent than I do.

In any case, no one can complain that the book's pieces are readily available elsewhere. None of the chapters has previously appeared in print in anything like its present form. Drafts of some have circulated informally as working papers of the Center for Research on Social Organization, University of Michigan. A much earlier version of one chapter ("Computing History") found its way into a professional journal. (Under the title "Computers in Historical Analysis," it appeared in *Computers and the Humanities*, 7 [1973], 323 – 336. I am grateful to the editors of the journal for permission to reprint material from that article.) Otherwise, this is the first time the book's contents have spread beyond the limited audiences for which they were originally prepared.

In one way or another, all the chapters presented here formed as by-products of two long, linked inquiries: (1) into large-scale structural change in Western countries since about 1500; and (2) into changing forms of conflict and collective action in the same countries over the same time span. The large-scale changes that receive the most attention in the book are statemaking and the development of capitalism. The countries in question are most frequently France and England, less frequently other countries of western Europe, only rarely the United States and other countries elsewhere. Under the headings of conflict and collective action, the chapters deal most regularly with revolutions, rebellions, collective violence, strikes, demonstrations, food riots, and related ways of gathering to act on shared interests and grievances.

The two inquiries connect. One big question provides the central connections: In the West of the last few hundred years, how did the development of capitalism and the concentration of power in national states affect the ways that ordinary people could—and did—act together on their common interests? From that central connection, one can move in several distinct directions: toward the general characteristics of capitalism and national states, toward the logic of collective action, toward the problems involved in joining the history and sociology of these large subjects. The book changes course more than once and ends up having moved in all these directions. Its first section ("Exhortation") includes two chapters that deal directly with the interaction between history and sociology; "Sociology, Meet History" sketches the organization and practice of the historical discipline as seen from sociology, whereas "Computing History" examines the impact of electronic computers and associated sociological procedures on historical practice. The book's second section ("Appreciation") again deals with the encounters of sociology and history, but now as represented by the contributions of two important sociologists—George Homans and Emile Durkheim—to historical work. "Homans, Humans, and History" and "Useless Durkheim" match a generally positive appraisal of Homans's contribution with a generally negative appraisal of Durkheim's.

The third section ("Application") of *As Sociology Meets History* presents two different historical problems in whose pursuit a broadly sociological approach helps clarify the crucial processes; "War and Peasant Rebellion in Seventeenth-Century France" and "How (And, to Some Extent, Why) to Study British Contention," however, also identify ways to fortify sociological formulations which lack historical fiber. The fourth section ("Exploration") introduces a larger element of speculation by laying out general ideas concerning the development of Western capitalism, with special attention to the process of proletarianization; "Proletarianization: Theory and Research" surveys the defects of sociological schemes which ought, in principle, to provide coherent accounts of proletarianization, whereas "States, Taxes, and Proletarians" summarizes and illustrates an alternative analysis of proletarianization in the context of hypotheses about the interaction of capitalism and statemaking. Both chapters argue for historically grounded models of large social changes as substitutes for the timeless, unhistorical models sociologists commonly apply to the same changes. The final section ("Conclusion") generalizes that final argument; it simply recapitulates the book's main themes and points up their lessons for sociological and historical practice. The most important is this: that we live in history and cannot escape it by assuming it away; when something happens, what has happened before shapes how it happens, and with what consequences.

The National Science Foundation has long supported the program of research that made this book possible. I am grateful to Robert Fogel, Walter Goldfrank, Lynn Hunt, Theda Skocpol, and Peter Stearns for reviews of an earlier draft of "Sociology, Meet History"; to Randall Collins for a sympathetic critique of the entire manuscript; to Cecilia Brown, Martha Guest, Robert Schweitzer, and Joan Skowronski for assistance with sources; and to Sheila Wilder and Debra Snovak for help in typing the manuscript.

Where sociology and history flow together, rapids form. Four very different men—Samuel Beer, George Homans, Barrington Moore, Jr., and Pitirim Sorokin—pushed me off to start my navigation of those rapids. Now, nearly 30 years after that launching, let me record my debt to them for pointing me toward adventure.

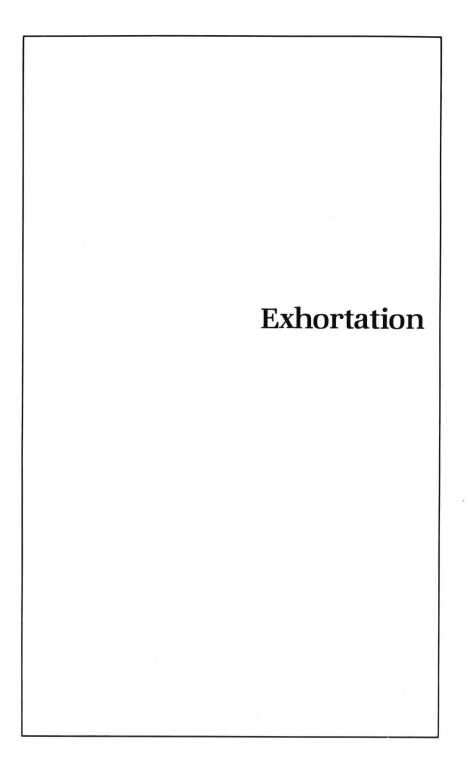

Exhortation

1

Sociology, Meet History

Mercurial Views of the Seventeenth Century

Durant l'Esté de ceste annee le Roy estant à Paris fut adverty par un nommé le capitaine Belin, qu'en Limosin, Perigord, Quercy, & en quelques provinces des environs, plusieurs Gentils-hommes faisoient des assemblées pour relever les fondemens de rebellion, que le feu Mareschal de Biron & ceux qui estoient de sa conspiration y avoient jettez; & ce fut le pretexte ordinaire des rebelles, scavoir, pour descharger le peuple, & pour faire que la Justice fust mieux administrée a l'advenir par ceux qui l'exercaient: & toutes fois leur dessein n'estoit q pour pescher en eau trouble, & sous l'apparence du bien public s'engraisser des ruines du pauvre peuple.

During the summer of this year the King, who was in Paris, was warned by a certain captain Belin that in Limousin, Perigord, Quercy, and other nearby provinces a number of Gentlemen were meeting to restore the bases of the rebellion that the late Marshal Biron and his co-conspirators had laid down. They had the rebels' usual pretext: to lighten the people's burden, and to make sure that those who were charged with the administration of justice would do better in the future. Nonetheless their real hope was to fish in troubled water and, in the guise of the public good, to fatten themselves up at the expense of the poor people [*Mercure françois* 1605: 11–12].

The year is 1605; the king, Henry IV of France; the source, the *Mercure françois*, an ancestor of the daily newspaper. For a twentieth-century reader, it is a curious, exhilirating experience to savor the *Mercure:* to have the noble rebellions, the assassination of Henry IV, the Thirty Years' War coming in as current news.

1

If the twentieth-century reader is a sociologist, this curious experience offers a challenge to reflection on the character of the reader's discipline and on sociology's relationship to history. The *Mercure*'s reporter, after all, is proposing an age-old interpretation of rebellion. The interpretation runs like this:

1. Self-serving, manipulative troublemakers drawn from discontented segments of the dominant classes enlist gullible rebels from the common people.
2. The common people pay all the cost and get none of the benefit — if any — of rebellion.

Elites and authorities often hold that theory today.

In its context, the *Mercure*'s interpretation is not absurd. A major form of rebellion in sixteenth- and seventeenth-century France was, indeed, an alliance between a small group of discontented, self-seeking nobles and a large group of aggrieved commoners. The weight of taxes and the maladministration of justice were, indeed, widespread grievances and frequent justifications for rebellion. The organizers of rebellion, indeed, often decamped with the gains and escaped before royal vengeance struck them down. So far as it goes, in fact, the *Mercure*'s analysis only contains one substantial error: It underestimates the extent to which the "common people" acted knowingly on their interests; it treats ordinary rebels as a shapeless, manipulable mass. That error, many twentieth-century analysts of twentieth-century rebellion have made as well.

The *Mercure* offers many more occasions for sociological reflection. In 1608, for example, we have the story of the Guilleris, three noble brothers from Brittany. During the recent Wars of Religion, the brothers "had followed the League party under the Duke of Mercoeur, and had performed under his leadership as valiant, brave soldiers." On demobilization, they had formed a robber band. "The promenade of all these robbers crossed many parts of France," reported the *Mercure*, "all the way to Normandy, the Lyon region, and Guyenne. On the highways leading to the fairs and markets of Poitou they posted notices on trees, reading PEACE TO GENTLEMEN, DEATH TO PROVOSTS AND ARCHERS, AND THE PURSE FROM MERCHANTS." ("Provosts and archers" were essentially the royal and municipal police of the time.) The governor of the Niort military district called together a force of provosts, besieged the Guilleris' castle, and finally took 80 prisoners. The youngest Guilleri brother was executed (*Mercure français* 1608: 289 – 290).

Shades of Robin Hood! Although we have no evidence that the Guilleri bandits gave to the poor, they certainly assumed the right to take from the rich. In the context of the time, their quick change from valiant soldiers to dangerous criminals was rather more a shift in attitude, name, and coalition than an alteration in their day-to-day behavior. As the people of the ravaged French countryside testified repeatedly, it was often hard to tell the difference between troops and bandits. The transformation from cavalryman to highwayman, the formation of a roving band, the posting of declarations, the siege, and the execution all portray for us a world in which a model of armed conquest was readily available. By no means did the national state have the monopoly on armed conquest.

Not that the state was powerless. The king, his retainers, his clients, and his bureaucracy formed a greater, stronger cluster than any other in France. He who touched the royal person or prerogative paid the price. When Ravaillac assassinated Henry IV in 1610, the king's counselors rolled out the terrible, clanking apparatus of royal justice. In a public execution before the Paris city hall, the hangman assaulted Ravaillac's body with molten lead and red-hot iron. Then it was time for drawing and quartering. "After the horses had pulled for a good hour," reported the *Mercure*,

> Ravaillac finally gave up the ghost without having been dismembered. The executioner having broken him and cut him into quarters, people of all sorts went at the four parts with swords, knives and staves; they snatched the parts from the executioner so eagerly that after having beaten, cut and torn them, the people dragged the pieces here and there through the streets on all sides, in such a frenzy that nothing could stop them [1610: 457].

As was customary on such occasions, the day ended with the burning of the bloody remains in bonfires throughout Paris.

The lurid killing of Ravaillac and the many other public executions recounted in the *Mercure* add two more elements to our understanding of seventeenth-century France. First, we appreciate the importance of exemplary justice and punishment, as opposed to an effort to apprehend all violators of the law. Seventeenth-century authorities did not seek to punish all offenders, by any means. They did not, in general, use jailing as a punishment, although they sometimes incarcerated people as a form of extortion or preventive detention. They lacked the means to send many criminals to the galleys or the gallows. Judges and other officials sought, instead, to deter potential delinquents by the quick and visible chastisement of a few. The mounting of bloody examples dramatized the power of the authorities without overtaxing their limited judicial capacities.

Second, we recognize the participation of ordinary people—as spectators and, to some degree, as critics and participants—in the process of retribution. On other occasions, that popular participation in justice provided a warrant, or at least a model, for the people's taking the law into its own hands. Tax rebellions and attacks on profiteering officials took the forms of assemblies, deliberations, declarations, condemnations, and, sometimes, executions. Exemplary justice and popular participation faded away in later years, as the government's repressive power grew and the separation between accusers and accused increased.

Later in that same year the *Mercure* reported yet another execution at Paris's Place de Grève, in front of the city hall. This time the victims were three gentlemen of Poitou: du Jarrage, Chef-bobbin and Champ-martin. The courts had convicted them of

> preparing a Manifesto which tried to stir the people of Poitou into rebellion, and to induce the people to join [the three gentlemen] in taking up arms, in order (they said) to change the state into an Oligarchy—France, they imagined, not being well governed. Unworthy to die by the sword like nobles, they received the wages of their disgrace: the hangman's rope [1610: 512].

Thus we learn that the law decapitated nobles and hanged commoners. We glimpse the standard routine in which rebels, like highwaymen, posted declarations of intent before striking at their enemies. And we begin to sense the prevalence of rebellion in the early seventeenth century.

These news flashes from 1605, 1608, and 1610 present more than one challenge to the sociologist. The first challenge is to say how the nearly 400 years of experience and thought that have intervened since then have improved our understanding of rebellion and of other sorts of conflict. (The answer, I regret to say, is precious little, and that little comes mainly through (a) conceptual refinements; and (b) clarification of the connections between major conflicts and the routine pursuit of everyday interests.)

The second challenge is to lay out categories within which the general changes occurring in the France of 1605 will make sense: modernization, class struggle, agrarian bureaucracy, something else. (Although any reply we make to that challenge today is bound to be controversial and incomplete, I favor stressing the development of capitalism and the growth of national states as the contexts of seventeenth-century struggles.)

The third challenge is to examine what difference, if any, it makes whether we approach the events of seventeenth-century France as sociologists or as historians—and whether some sort of synthesis is feasible. (My answer is that in practice sociologists and historians approach the analysis of such events rather differently, but in principle there are good reasons for seeking, not one grand Synthesis, but several different syntheses of sociological and historical practice, all having in common a historical grounding of social theory.) For reasons that will become clearer as we proceed, we might call the three challenges the problems of *collective action*, of *structural change*, and of *historical practice*. These three problems have brought the varied chapters in this book into being.

Historical Practice

For the moment, let us concentrate on the problem of historical practice. Although I will yield occasionally to the joy of needling fellow historians, my sermons are aimed at sociologists. More than anything else, I want to dispel the illusion that historical practice amounts to failed sociology. Although few sociologists lay out their belief in quite those insulting terms, a belief in the intellectual feebleness of historical practice lies implicit in sociologists' readiness to capture cases from the historical record without considering the existing historiography, and without grounding their own analyses in systematic knowledge of the contexts from which the cases come. S. M. Lipset offers us a characteristic summary:

> From an ideal-typical point of view, the task of the sociologist is to formulate general hypotheses, hopefully set within a larger theoretical framework, and to test them. His interest in the way in which a nation such as the United States formulated a national identity is to specify propositions about the general processes involved in the creation of national identities in new nations. Similarly, his concern with changes in the patterns of American religious participation is to formulate and test hypotheses about the function of religion for other institutions and the social system as a whole. The sociologist of religion seeks to locate the conditions under which chiliastic religion occurs, what kinds of people are attracted to it, what happens to the sects and their adherents under various conditions, and so on. These are clearly not problems of the historian. History must be concerned with the analysis of the particular set of events or processes. Where the sociologist looks for concepts which subsume a variety of particular descriptive categories, the historian must remain close to the actual happenings and avoid statements which, though linking behavior at one time or place to that elsewhere, lead to a distortion in the description of what occurred in the set of circumstances being analyzed. [From *Sociology and History: Methods* by Seymour Martin Lipset and Richard Hofstadter (eds.) © 1968 by Basic Books, Inc., Publishers, New York: 22–23. Reprinted by permission.]

The division of labor, then, resembles the division between the mycologist and the mushroom collector, between the critic and the translator, between the political analyst and the city hall reporter, between brains and brawn. History does the transcription, sociology the analysis.

Historians have sometimes collaborated in this mystification. As Gareth

Stedman Jones, an outstanding historian of nineteenth-century Great Britain, complains:

> Attitudes toward sociological theory among sociologically inclined historians have often verged on the credulous, and although more critical sociologists might have rejected as naively positivist any distinction between history and sociology which sees the one as "idiographic" and the other as "nomothetic", many of these historians have behaved in practice as if they considered such a division of labour to be legitimate. Defensive about their own subject and repelled by an inadequately understood marxism which appeared to be the only other contender, they have looked uncritically to sociology as a theoretical storehouse from which they could simply select concepts most serviceable for their individual needs [1976: 300].

On the technical side as well, sociologists and historians have often behaved as though historians had nothing to teach and everything to learn. The wholesale application of sociological statistics to historical analyses, the forcing of historical data into computer formats designed for survey results, the adoption in historical work of occupational coding schemes derived from contemporary censuses all embody the idea of raw historical material, ready for processing.

History is not failed sociology, and historical materials are not raw evidence awaiting sociological analysis. Let me divide my arguments on those scores, for the sake of emphasis, into matters of *fact* and matters of *principle*. As a matter of fact, historians conduct their inquiries according to rules that differ significantly from those sociologists follow in their own work, and which may well puzzle or surprise the unsuspecting sociologist who wanders into their territory. Some sections of this chapter will present a sort of primer of historical practice for the sake of puzzled sociologists. As a matter of fact, the materials of history differ, on the average, from those of sociology. Within the limits set by all residues of past behavior, furthermore, historians' current conventions and procedures reduce radically the evidence that is currently susceptible to historical treatment. Again, parts of this chapter will review the character of historical material, for the benefit of sociologists who confront that material.

As a matter of principle, all analyses of social processes are not equally historical. An analysis is historical to the extent that the place and time of the action enter into its explanations: Spengler's fanciful account of Western ills as consequences of the playing out of a particular civilization has more historical bite, in this sense, than Kuznets's more accurate account of the correlates of economic growth in a wide variety of countries. The distinction, then, does not depend on the accuracy of the observation. It has little or nothing to do with the conventional division between "generalizing" and "particularizing" disciplines: Hardly any statement about social processes, for example, could be more general than Sorokin's attempt to sweep all of human history into ideational, idealistic, and sensate phases of specific societies. Yet Sorokin's scheme, in its curious way, builds in place and time; it has historical grounding. Nor does the hoary contrast between the "cultural" sciences and the "natural" sciences—the *Geisteswissenschaften* and the *Naturwissenschaften*—capture what I have in mind. Indeed, "natural" sciences such as geology, paleontology, and evolutionary biology sometimes proceed quite historically. The integration of time and place into the very argument marks off historical analysis. Later on, I will argue that sociological analyses of large-scale change suffer, by and large, from being insufficiently historical. Sociological theory needs more historical grounding. Failed sociology? No, in important ways sociological practice comes down to failed history.

Stinchcombe's Challenge

Traveling a different trajectory, Arthur Stinchcombe has arrived at a similar conclusion. When it comes to "epochal theories of social change," Stinchcombe argues, sociologists have commonly blundered by attempting to force large models onto history, instead of interacting intelligently with the historical evidence. Stinchcombe's *Theoretical Models in Social History* pursues the theme that "one does not apply theory to history; rather one uses history to develop theory [1978: 1]." General ideas are illusory:

> The argument here is that such ideas are flaccid, that they are sufficient neither to guide historical research nor to give the resulting monograph the ring of having told us about the human condition. These ideas are good for introductions and conclusions, for 1-hour distinguished lectureships, for explaining briefly what our profession is all about, and for other functions in which easily comprehensible and inexact ideas are useful. They are not what good theory applied to historical information looks like, and consequently their being psychologically anterior has no epistemological significance. It is the fact that "theories of social change" consist of such flaccid general notions that makes them so much less interesting than studies of social changes [Stinchcombe 1978: 116 – 117].

Later, I will give some reasons for being a bit more enthusiastic about general theories than Stinchcombe declares himself to be. Nevertheless, I cannot help cheering his admonition to ground theories of social change in genuine historical analyses.

Effective studies of social change, according to Stinchcombe, identify deep causal analogies among sets of facts, then build the sets of facts thus established into cumulative causal analyses of the particular processes of change under study. Facts are deeply analogous if they have similar causes and similar effects. Here is a possible example: We might build a deep analogy among different forms of time discipline and work discipline imposed on workers by pointing out that they all result from the same cause—the effort of owners to increase their discretionary control over the factors of production. We would then point to their similar effects: They all tend to sharpen the division between work and nonwork.

Stinchcombe goes farther; he argues that proper causal analogies identify "similarity in what people want and what they think they need to do to get it [1978: 120]." Thus in our analysis of time discipline and work discipline, we might claim that in case after case owners and workers are locked in the same strategic conflict—each side seeking to extend its control over the factors of production but adopting a distinctly different strategy for doing so. By such a deep analogy we anchor a fact in a particular historical situation: These owners and workers in this place and time are locked in a characteristic struggle over time discipline and work discipline. The core of an effective historical analysis, however, is not the establishment of single facts. It is, in Stinchcombe's view, the construction of a sequence of facts (each established as a fact by means of proper causal analogy) into a cumulative causal process in which each fact creates the conditions for the next. Thus we might find a new market opening up, entrepreneurs increasing the work they farm out to local weavers in order to meet the expanded demand, entrepreneurs making profits and accumulating capital, some entrepreneurs trying to increase their volume and their profits by standardizing the product and the conditions of production, those same entrepreneurs inventing or adopting such means of time discipline and work discipline as grouping previously dispersed workers into the same shop, workers resisting by means of sabotage, mutual pressure and strike activity, and so on indefinitely. The mark of a good Stinchcombian analysis is not that the whole sequence repeats itself in many different situations. It is that the causal status of each step in the sequence is established by a deep analogy with other similar situations elsewhere, and that the effects of one step are the causes of the next.

Most narrative history, thinks Stinchcombe, is seductively misleading. It gives the appearance, but not the substance, of such causal sequences. Most narrative history is superficial because the deep analogies are missing; the author substitutes an easy, unverified reading of the intentions of the chief actors or (worse still) a presentation of the sequence of events as the working out of a dominant Force or Plan. Sociologists who stumble into history, Stinchcombe suggests, commonly go wrong because the conventions of narrative history mislead them into thinking they can substitute their own (presumably superior) Forces, Plans, or readings of intentions for the historians' pitiful versions. The sociologists' pretentions convert a harmless, if ineffectual, literary device into a pernicious mishandling of the historical record.

Stinchcombe attaches his provocative arguments to detailed, ingenious exegeses of the work of four historical analysts: Leon Trotsky, Alexis de Tocqueville, Neil Smelser, and Reinhard Bendix. None of the four qualifies as an archive-mongering professional historian—Smelser and Bendix even less so than Trotsky or Tocqueville. For Stinchcombe's main argument, however, it matters little whether the analysts' raw materials are texts or other historians' glosses on texts. In fact, one hears in Stinchcombe's arguments strong echoes of Tocqueville's reflections on the same subject:

> For my part, I hate those absolute systems which make all historical events depend on great primary causes, and link the events into an unbreakable chain, thereby eliminating people from the history of humanity. I find them narrow in their false grandeur, and false beneath their appearance of mathematical truth. Unlike the writers who invent sublime theories to nourish their vanity and ease their labor, I find that many important historical events can only be explained by accidental circumstances, and that many others remain inexplicable. I find, finally, that chance—or, rather, that network of secondary causes which we call chance for lack of ability to untangle them—matters a great deal in everything we see on the world's stage. But I believe strongly that chance does nothing which is not prepared in advance. Previous events, the nature of institutions, states of mind, moral conditions are the materials with which chance devises impromptus that astonish and frighten us [Tocqueville 1978 (1850) © Editions Gallimard 1964: 112 – 113].

Thus Stinchcombe comes out a bit more optimistic—or, at least, a bit more ambitious —than Tocqueville; with proper deep analogies, Stinchcombe argues, we can untangle chance. This is, indeed, his account of what good social historians do. When they are good, Trotsky, Tocqueville, Smelser, Bendix, and other strong historical analysts work effectively with deep analogies. When they try to apply very general models to large historical sequences, conversely, their results are as vacuous and misleading as anyone else's. *Theoretical Methods in Social History* ends with these words:

> The moral of this book is that great theorists descend to the level of such detailed analogies in the course of their work. Further, they become greater theorists down there among the details, for it is the details that theories in history have to grasp if they are to be any good [Stinchcombe 1978: 124].

Now, *there* is a conclusion calculated to offend almost everyone—historians, historiographers, theorists, history-seeking sociologists. Even if it is wrong, any statement that strikes at so many cherished interests with the same blow deserves serious attention.

It is not wrong. There is much truth in Stinchcombe's cantankerous argument. Much supposed application of general theories to history does consist of assigning resounding names—rationalization, modernization, secularization, hegemony, imperialism—to known facts. The search for deep analogies is, indeed, a key to effective historical explanation. Narrative history does commonly give an illusory appearance of causal solidity—an appearance that shatters as we reach out to grasp the connections. Stinchcombe's main points are correct.

Yet those points are only correct within stringent limits. Let us distinguish between two processes: the one by which historians arrive at conclusions, and the one by which they make those conclusions intelligible and convincing to other people. The two processes intertwine, but they are never identical, and they sometimes differ greatly from each other. Stinchcombe's analysis of historical practice deals almost exclusively with the second process—how historians make their conclusions intelligible and convincing to others. The central issues, furthermore, are epistemological; the point is not to say how most run-of-the-mill historians do their work from day to day but to identify the conditions under which we could reasonably accept historical accounts—and instructions for producing historical accounts—as valid.

When it comes to arriving at conclusions, as opposed to validating them, historians can and do rely on broad theories. They do so in two ways: (a) the agenda for any particular subfield of history has a theoretical edge; the student of demographic history, for instance, can hardly escape the influence of the ever-present theory of demographic transition; and (b) haphazardly or rigorously, the search for evidence relevant to the subfield's questions entails a theoretical choice. The American historian who examines the treatment of slaves by undertaking a detailed study of slaveholders' diaries, while neglecting the records of slave auctions, makes an implicit choice favoring a theory in which slaveholders' attitudes are significant determinants of slave experience. Historians may arrive at deep analogies, but they begin with theories, crude or refined.

Even in the area of validation, real historians rarely conform to Stinchcombe's prescriptions. Their practice is narrower in some regards and broader in others. It is narrower in that historians ordinarily require validation that goes beyond logical conviction. The two most pressing requirements are that the analysis be relevant to the existing historical agenda and that it be based on irrefutable texts. It is broader in that historians commonly grant validity to forms of argument that Stinchcombe forcefully rejects — psychologically compelling narrative and effective naming of an era, a group, or an intellectual current. That such practices are widespread does not, of course, make them sound. Still, their prevalence makes it clear that (for all the delightful exegesis of Trotsky, Tocqueville, Smelser, and Bendix) Stinchcombe's main business is not description but prescription.

Within Stinchcombe's chosen limits, however, I have only one substantial objection to his argument. The general theories that Stinchcombe dismisses as irrelevant to historical explanation commonly contain instructions for the identification of deep causal analogies. Theories are tool kits, varying in their range and effectiveness but proposing solutions to recurrent explanatory problems. Some of those instructions are worthless, some are misleading, and some are good. But it is normally better to have a bad tool than none at all.

general theories

Why? Because explanatory problems recur in history as they do elsewhere. When a problem recurs, why make the same mistakes over again? Even a bad theory generates standard ways of solving recurrent problems, reminders of difficulties on the way to the solutions, and a record of past results. Toward the end of the nineteenth century, Emile Durkheim elaborated a theory of social differentiation and its consequences. The theory includes, among other things, a sort of race between differentiation and shared beliefs: If a society's shared beliefs accumulate faster than it differentiates, change is orderly; if differentiation proceeds faster than shared belief, disorder (suicide, industrial strife, protest, sometimes even revolution) results. Durkheim's theory is bad. As Chapter 4, "Useless Durkheim," in this volume indicates, it not only generates invalid historical analogies (for example, between individual crime and collective protest) but also misstates the causal similarities among situations (for example, different streams of rural-to-urban migration) that are, in fact, analogous.

e.g. Durkheim

Yet even this bad theory has advantages as a tool of historical analysis. First, it crystallizes a line of argument that is pervasive in Western folk sociology, and therefore quite likely to turn up when historians confront suicide, industrial strife, protest, and other presumed varieties of disorder. It saves time, effort, and confusion to identify the main lines of the argument at the outset, rather than to have it enter the account piecemeal. Second, it contains instructions for analogizing and marshaling evidence in support of the analogy: The user must at a minimum make a showing that the people detached from existing systems of shared belief have a particular propensity to disorder. Finally, its repeated explicit use produces a record of successes and failures (in the

case of Durkheim's theory, I believe, mostly failures) in arriving at satis-
factory causal analogies. The record should eventually teach the users of
that particular tool kit something about the scope and value of the solutions it contains.

And there are good theories. Leon Trotsky (to take one of Stinchcombe's favorite theorists) proposed a theory of dual power—loosely
stated, that an essential precondition of revolution is the emergence of an
alternative concentration of power, a countergovernment, to which the
bulk of the population can switch its allegiance if the existing government demonstrates its incapacity or intolerability. That is, I think, quite a
good theory. It contains a set of instructions for analyzing a prerevolu-
tionary situation: Look for the dual power, check the conditions for acquiescence of the population to the existing government, watch for de-
fections, and so on. In short, press this particular analogy.

Trotsky's theory of dual power is an especially appropriate example. It
is not just a good theory but also a historically grounded theory. Trotsky
grounds his analysis on an explicit comparison of the English Revolution
of the seventeenth century, the French Revolution of the eighteenth, and
the Russian Revolution of 1917. That sets limits to the theory's domain; as
Trotsky formulates it, the theory is not likely to operate well outside the
world of fairly strong, centralized, and autonomous national states. The
restriction is the price we pay for a theory that works effectively *within*
those limits.

According to this account of the place of theory, and according to
Stinchcombe's treatment of deep analogies, the potential place of the
social sciences in historical work is large. Whatever else they do, the
social sciences serve as a giant warehouse of causal theories and of
concepts involving causal analogies; the problem is to pick one's way
through the junk to the solid merchandise. Stinchcombe rightly scores
the "flaccidity" of our general theories of social change. He wrongly
obscures the significance of good theory to effective historical analysis.
Sociologists and historians alike, however, should be searching for theories that have adequate historical grounding.

History's Place

Before seeking that historical grounding, let us explore the terrain of
history. The word *history* refers to a phenomenon, to a body of material,
and to a set of activities. As a *phenomenon*, history is the cumulative effect
of past events on events of the present—any present you care to name. To
the extent that *when* something happens matters, history is important.

Analysts of industrialization, for example, divide roughly into (a) people who think that essentially the same process of capital accumulation, technological innovation, labor force recruitment, and market growth repeats itself in country after country; and (b) those who think that the process changes fundamentally as a function of which other countries have industrialized and established their shares of the world market before a new section of the world starts industrializing. Only members of the first group can, in good conscience, adopt a common procedure— using a comparison among a number of different countries, ranging from agrarian to industrial, at the same point in time in order to identify the standard correlates of industrialization. Members of the second group should abhor that sort of cross-sectional comparison; they attach greater importance to the phenomenon of history than the first group does.

As a *body of material*, history consists of the durable residues of past (2) behavior. The vignettes from the *Mercure françois* with which we began are misleading in this regard. They perpetuate an easy misunderstanding, one that often wanders into manuals of historiography, that "historical records" consist mainly of narratives of various kinds. Chronicles, confessions, autobiographies, eyewitness reports, and other sorts of narratives are actually a tiny portion of historical material. Most historical material consists of fragmentary by-products of social routines: the remains of stone walls, trash heaps, tools, beaten paths, graffiti, and so on. As it happens, historians have concentrated on the written materials remaining from the past. But the written materials, too, are mainly fragmentary by-products of social routines: birth records, judicial proceedings, financial accounts, administrative correspondence, military rosters, and bills of lading are far more numerous than are narratives of any sort.

All documents are not equally valuable in reconstructing the past. If we are trying to understand the pattern of rebellion in seventeenth-century France, one memorandum from Richelieu will be worth a thousand biblical glosses (or, for that matter, pornographic poems) from the monks of Saint-Germain-des-Prés. Still, coming to terms with the historical record means, among other things, appreciating how much of the seventeenth-century writing went into pious essays and pornography. (3)

What of history as a *set of activities?* The central activity is reconstructing the past. That activity, too, easily lends itself to misunderstanding, to the supposition that the main historical problem is to establish the facts of what happened in the past. Establishing what happened is a hopeless program. It is hopeless for two reasons, which become obvious after a little reflection. First, the supply of information about the past is almost inexhaustible. It far exceeds the capacity of any historian to collect, absorb, synthesize, and relate it. Historians have no choice but to select a small portion of the available documentation.

Second, what matters, among the innumerable things that happened in the past, is a function of the questions and assumptions the historian brings to the analysis. To the historian who concentrates on the histories of regimes, and who believes that in any particular regime the attitudes and decisions of a few statesmen make all the difference, records of births, deaths, and marriages are trivial. Records of births, deaths, and marriages are crucial, on the other hand, to the historian who is trying to explain why industrialization occurred when and where it did, and who believes that fluctuations in the labor supply strongly affect the feasibility of industrialization. Historians therefore select radically among available sources and facts.

Other specialists — geologists, archaeologists, classicists, paleobotanists, for example — also draw selectively on the past. Yet they are not, in general, historians. The distinguishing features of the historical profession are these:

1. Its members specialize in reconstructing past human behavior.
2. They use written residues of the past: texts.
3. They emphasize the grouping and glossing of texts as the means of reconstructing past events.
4. They consider where and, especially, when an event occurred to be an integral part of its meaning, explanation, and impact.

Historians are people who do these four things. Professional historians are simply the people who certify one another as competent to do the four things.

As in other fields, the Ph.D. degree serves as the chief certificate of competence in history. The history Ph.D. is a peculiar experience in one regard: Although the reconstruction of past behavior, the location and transcription of relevant texts, and the analysis of those texts are the historian's distinguishing skills, the average historian-in-the-making has almost no serious practice in these skills until the last phase of his or her training. Very few historians, for example, ever enter an archive before they begin work on their doctoral dissertations. Before that time, they are busy learning other people's syntheses: basic sequences, critical events, rival interpretations, major books. Within a limited number of time — space blocks (Classical Greece, Latin America since 1816, etc.) they are learning what they might later have to teach to undergraduates. They are also, it is true, learning to write expository prose and to criticize other people's arguments. But their teachers only give them serious exposure to the basic historical skills after they, the students, have mastered their share of the discipline's ideas and beliefs. Within any particular specialty, that is, the professionals recognize one another by means of their orientation to a common literature.

In the United States, professional history is a large field, and predominantly a teaching field. At its peak in 1970, the American Historical Association had about 20,000 members. The demographic and economic contraction of the following years brought the number a little below 16,000 by 1977. That was still a great many professionals. History was smaller than the giants among research fields: chemistry, engineering, biology, and psychology. Yet it approached the size of physics and stood in the same range as such fields as mathematics and Anglo-American literature. In 1977, some 17,000 people who had received Ph.D.'s in history from 1934 through 1976 were known to be living in the United States. During the early 1970s, the profession was grinding out about 1000 new Ph.D.'s each year. In 1976–1977, the figure was still 961, with 36% in American history, 27% in European history, and the remaining 37% in a great variety of other fields.

The great bulk of historians who make their livings as historians do so as teachers. In 1976–1977, of all history Ph.D.'s known to be employed, 96% worked for educational institutions. Of all working Ph.D.'s, 79% were in teaching, 6% in research, 6% in management and administration, another 6% in writing and editing, and the final 3% in other sorts of jobs (all figures are from *AHA Newsletter*, December 1978, or National Research Council 1978). Of these thousands of practitioners, most spent most of their time teaching American or European history to young people who had no intention of specializing in history. Many devoted some of their nonteaching time to research and writing. A few hundred of them actually published books and articles reporting their historical work. Those writers were the profession's nucleus. They provided the chief connections among previous work, current research, what students were learning, and what the general public was reading about history. They set the tone of historical practice.

The Historical Zoo

I hope my description does not make the historical profession seem *the too-narrow view* smoothly organized, neatly hierarchical, or deeply coherent. In reality, the practice of history resembles a zoo more than a herbarium, and a herbarium more than a cyclotron. In a cyclotron a huge, costly, unified apparatus whirs into motion to produce a single focused result; history does not behave like that. In a herbarium, a classificatory order prevails;

each dried plant has its own niche. Historians divide their subject matter and their styles of thought into diplomatic, economic, intellectual, and other sorts of history, but the divisions are shifting, inexact . . . and often ignored in practice.

A zoo? Yes, watching historians at work does have something in common with strolling from the polar bears to the emus to the armadillos. Each species of historian is confined to an artificially reduced habitat, fenced off from its natural predators and prey. In the historical zoo, however, the inmates often leap the barriers to run through the spectators, to invade other cages, and even occasionally to change themselves from one sort of beast into another. Intellectual history becomes cultural history, social history edges over into economic. Nevertheless, at any given point in time the boundaries are real and significant: Practitioners on one side of a line or the other have their own journals, their own associations, their own jargons, their own professional agendas. That they should be further subdivided by time and place (Modern American Intellectual History being one recognized specialty, Medieval European Economic History another) only accentuates the fragmentation of historical practice.

What happens in the zoo? Do not trust studies of historiography to tell you. Historiographers rely almost exclusively on the skills of biographers, intellectual historians, and philosophers: They analyze history not as a concrete social activity but as the development and application of general ideas. For every discussion of how Lewis Namier actually did his work, we have a dozen discussions of the possibility, in principle, of contributing to historical knowledge by means of the sort of collective biography that Namier created. Jerzy Topolski's massive *Methodology of History*, for example, begins with the complaint that

> earlier statements by historians on their own research techniques reveal the nature and degree of their methodological awareness. A few decades ago when Marc Bloch was writing his *The Historian's Craft* and the science of scientific method was not so far advanced as now, historians took little interest in explicit problems of methods. Since then, much has been said about the science of history without the participation of historians. Today the practitioners of historiography have to be more aware of methodological considerations [1976: 3].

To remedy earlier oversights, Topolski devotes 600 pages or so to "Patterns of Historical Research," "Objective Methodology of History," "Pragmatic Methodology of History," and "Apragmatic Methodology of History." He energetically reduces the problem of historical knowledge to a special case of the problem of knowledge in general. But he writes nary a page on an actual historian's workaday approach to his or her research.

eg.
mis-reading
Thompson

If we are to believe the historiographers who do portray flesh-and-blood historians, on the other hand, then historians spend most of their time forming, joining, or combating Schools of Thought, focus their analytic efforts on puzzles posed by history, and do most of their own analyses by thinking themselves into the circumstances of historical actors in order to reconstruct the states of mind that led them to act as they did. We might reflect on this characterization of E. P. Thompson's work:

> Attempts to partition society for purposes of analysis often build upon Marx's insight that a group's economic function generates a distinctive class culture and social system as well as particular economic interests. In *The Making of the English Working Class* (1963), E. P. Thompson brilliantly used the Marxist notion of class to analyze the class consciousness or culture of British workers in the eighteenth and nineteenth centuries. Thompson contended that class is not an abstract concept that can be lifted out of context and treated as a static category. If class consciousness is "largely determined by the productive relations into which we are born," he wrote, it still develops over time and is conditioned by particular experiences. Class consciousness cannot be deduced from general principles, but must be studied historically. Thompson insisted that although the rise of class consciousness follows similar patterns in different times and places, it never occurs "in just the same way" [Lichtman and French 1978: 110−111].

Thompson did, indeed, use the Marxist notion of class brilliantly. He did, in fact, emphasize the conditioning of class consciousness by particular experiences. Yet the summary suggests that Thompson chose (for unstated reasons) to study British working-class culture, then chose to set up his study as an analysis of class consciousness, then developed a theory of class consciousness in order to deal with the available evidence.

The intellectual context is missing. Especially lacking are two sorts of controversy—about whether England somehow escaped from a revolutionary situation in the first half of the nineteenth century, about the conditions under which workers develop militant class consciousness. Those controversies entail further questions—about the distinctness of the English experience, about the character of social class, about the extent to which English workers formed a single class with its own autonomous, self-sustaining culture. The questions, furthermore, form part of a contemporary political debate, as well as belonging to the historians' agenda. The Thompson of *The Making of the English Working Class* took a strong stand for class as a process and relationship rather than as a category, for the relative autonomy of working-class culture and consciousness, for the development of a domestic revolutionary tradition within the English working class. A reader of Thompson who ignores this context is likely to be puzzled by his repeated, vigorous, indignant, sometimes dazzling critiques of nineteenth-century observers (such as Francis

Tilly's point in microcosm!

Place and Andrew Ure) as well as of twentieth-century historians (for instance, John Clapham, R.F.W. Wearmouth, George Rudé, and Neil Smelser). Thompson must knock down a lot of bystanders in order to make his own way to the reviewing stand.

E. P. Thompson is not only a talented historian but also an adroit polemicist. With a flick of his pen he can summon an image of an entire worker's movement, or dispatch an opponent to oblivion. Most historians fall short of his accomplishments in either regard. Yet they try. Historiographers tend to ignore, or conceal, how much historical writing consists of documented commentary on previous historical writing. Instead, they give us a historian who dreams up questions and then goes to the sources to find the answers to those questions.

Historical Practice as Social Structure

Real historians behave rather differently. In order to be clear and concrete, let me concentrate for a while on American historical practice. In the United States, by and large, a practicing historian embeds himself or herself in a segment of the profession: modern Latin American economic history, Tokugawa urban history, or something of the sort. The basic differentiation is three-dimensional:

1. Place (Africa, Asia, Brazil, etc.)
2. Time (Medieval, Renaissance, Early Modern, Modern, Contemporary, to take a common way of dividing European history)
3. Subject matter (political, intellectual, diplomatic, social, etc.)

Courses and graduate programs in American universities are divided in roughly the same ways. As a result, most historians work mainly in one time — place — subject subdivision of the profession but are comfortably familiar with one or two more. Someone who works competently in four or five of the hundreds of pigeonholes defined by these dimensions is considered broad indeed.

As a social structure, each historical subdivision has two main elements: an interpersonal network and a shared agenda. The network's nodes consist of major teachers and their former students. The shared agenda has several components: a set of pressing questions, an array of recognized means for answering those questions, and a body of evidence agreed upon as relevant to the questions. Some, but not all, networks formalize their existence by giving themselves a name, an association, a journal, or other professional impedimenta.

American specialists in the history of the family, to take one case, long plied their trade as no more than a particularly well-connected clump in the network of social historians. At the end of the 1960s family historians—encouraged by the success of their European counterparts—began to differentiate themselves more decisively from other social historians. This historical network (like others tainted with social science) connected people who were interested in the same phenomena across a wide variety of times and places; historians of modern Africa talked to historians of ancient Rome. During the early 1970s, American historians of the family created conferences, an association, and a journal of their own. By that time, a well-demarcated subdivision of the profession had come into existence; a college department could say it wanted to hire a historian of the family, and a well-oiled mechanism of communication and validation would whir into action.

Historians with an entrepreneurial flair ordinarily play important parts in this sort of institution building. By these means (as well as by editing, reviewing, refereeing, and other time-honored means of scholarly promotion and control) they help set the intellectual agenda. In history, specialists who are well connected outside their own country—particularly those who are connected with scholars in parts of the world whose history they are studying—carry significant extra weight; even if they have few ideas of their own, they commonly serve as conduits and interpreters of work being done elsewhere. Because of this structure, historians who are already well placed find it fairly easy to reproduce themselves by connecting their own graduate students (and, sometimes, a few other carefully selected clients) to the structure.

The intellectual agenda itself consists of questions, means for answering questions, and a body of evidence. As in many other disciplines, the historians in a given specialty implicitly orient the bulk of their work to a handful of crucial questions. In American political history, for example, whether the War of Independence constituted a full-fledged popular revolution, whether the Civil War was the inevitable denouement of a long struggle between two antithetical ways of life, and why no durable socialist movement arose in the United States stand high on the agenda; they compel much more attention than such questions as whether nineteenth-century changes in suffrage altered the national structure of power. A young historian who wants to make an impact on other historians will pose a fresh answer to part of one of the crucial old questions, will help refute one of the established answers, or will assemble a new body of evidence supporting an answer that is already in competition.

Orientation to a compelling set of questions, however, creates an interesting ambivalence. On one side, the historical profession lies in wait, posing compelling questions, demanding new answers, and insisting on a demonstration of familiarity with previous work in the field as well as with the available evidence. On the other side, a larger public calls for interpretations that are lively, lucid, and self-contained. What is more, professionals reserve a particular admiration for the historian who reaches that larger public without compromising technical standards. In that, they resemble many of their colleagues in the humanities but differ from most of their colleagues in the natural and social sciences. Natural and social scientists tend to doubt the seriousness of anything that reads easily and sells well. Humanists tend to think of the supreme accomplishment as a work that is at once accessible and profound. Humanists and historians are bookish; although they prize the well-turned essay, they cherish the well-read book.

Major book awards reinforce the prestige of accessible history. Biographies and broad new interpretations of American experience dominate the lists. Recent Pulitzer Prizes, for example, have gone to biographies or autobiographies of Dean Acheson, Franklin Roosevelt, Thomas Jefferson, Lamy of Santa Fe, and Leo Baeck, plus a half-dozen general essays on American history. The American Historical Association's Bancroft Prize runs a bit differently:

1973 *Fire in the Lake: The Vietnamese and Americans in Vietnam*
     The United States and the Origins of the Cold War
     Booker T. Washington
1974 *Frederick Jackson Turner*
     The Other Bostonians
     The Devil and John Foster Dulles
1975 *Time on the Cross*
     Roll, Jordan, Roll
     Deterrence in American Foreign Policy: Theory and Practice
1976 *The Problem of Slavery in the Age of Revolution*
     Edith Wharton
1977 *Class and Community: The Industrial Revolution in Lynn*
     Slave Population and Economics in Jamaica
1978 *The Visible Hand: The Managerial Revolution in American*
         Business
     The Transformation of American Law, 1790 – 1860
1979 *Allies of a Kind: The United States, Britain, and the War against*
         Japan, 1941 – 45
     Rockdale: The Growth of an American Village in the Early Industrial Revolution

Biographies still stand out among the prizewinners, but general reinterpretations of American life appear to attract the Bancroft judges less than they do the Pulitzer Prize committees. Fresh answers to old questions on the historical agenda win praise from the insiders. As the inclusion of Robert Fogel and Stanley Engerman's *Time on the Cross* (with its econometric analyses of the profitability of American slavery) indicates, the fresh answers may even be controversial and may even build on the social sciences. Yet on the whole technical *tours de force* take second place to graceful expositions of subjects that interest the literate public. Thus the historical scholar who craves esteem from peers must find a way to surmount the dilemma: solidity versus accessibility.

The newly trained historian faces the dilemma in its extreme form. The doctoral dissertation in which he or she has just invested 4 or 5 years ordinarily addresses a precise subquestion of one of the Big Questions, reviews previous answers to that subquestion meticulously, catalogs and arrays the available sources, and cautiously lays out the evidence for a new reply to the subquestion—in short, situates itself exactly with respect to an existing literature. But now, the dissertation completed, the young historian's career depends on publishing a book. A few fresh Ph.D.'s have the good fortune of access to monograph series that publish books greatly resembling dissertations. Or they have a topic and a dissertation committee that permit them to make light work of the connections with the field. Most of them, however, must think about turning a manuscript heavy with scholarly apparatus into something quite different: a book whose buyers generally care little about the state of the literature but are looking for a rounded, convincing, comprehensible treatment of the subject at hand. As editors and thesis advisors learn to their pain, the transformation commonly requires the dismantling not only of the dissertation but also of the former graduate student's training in documentation and cross-reference. To become working historians, the newcomers must unlearn their graduate educations.

But not completely. The skillful manipulation of acceptable sources remains an essential part of the craft. The problem for the professional is how to convey the insider's signs of authenticity without impeding the outsider's access. The book must contain enough "primary" sources— texts produced as a direct effect or observation of the historical circumstances under analysis—to demonstrate the author's familiarity with the era and its materials. Yet the writer must weave the sources into a coherent argument. The argument, in turn, must differ in some significant way from those proposed by earlier authors. The entire procedure requires a lawyerly handling of the evidence.

Handling the Evidence

What is that evidence? At the borderland of anthropology and history, potsherds, wall paintings, and paving stones serve as the historical record of distant civilizations. Some historians of art and culture work with buildings, sculptures, and pictures. Students of the recent past have tape recordings and films at their disposal. Philippe Ariès and Lawrence Stone have made funerary sculpture speak to us about the family life of earlier centuries. Yet the great bulk of the evidence that historians learn to use—and do use, in fact—consists of texts. Historians are the specialists par excellence in reconstructing social life from its written residues.

Within any particular historical specialty, however, practitioners tend to recognize only a limited range of texts as useful to their enterprise. In most subdivisions of history, ostensibly direct testimonies by major actors—autobiographies, depositions, private letters, and so on—have long held pride of place. In the history of the family, such testimonies complement marriage contracts, birth registers, household property inventories, and other records of routine transactions. A military historian, on the other hand, is unlikely to pay much attention to routine domestic transactions. At least a military historian is unlikely to pay much attention until someone else shows that birth registers and the like yield fresh answers to the questions the discipline is already posing.

A significant part of historical innovation consists, indeed, of showing that new sources will answer old questions better, or differently. During the 1960s, Stephan Thernstrom almost single-handedly reoriented American urban history by demonstrating that with appropriate statistical processing readily available city directories and similar enumerations of the local population would yield estimates of the rates and directions of occupational mobility among different segments of the population. He created skeletal individual biographies by following the same person from one record to the next, summary collective biographies by collating the experiences of all members of a given cohort, class, or ethnic category. Thernstrom modeled many of his procedures on those of sociologists who had been studying twentieth-century mobility patterns and found ways to make them work in a nineteenth-century context with nineteenth-century evidence. He cannily chose to study the very Newburyport, Massachusetts—"Yankee City" in pseudonym—whose twentieth-century class structure Lloyd Warner and associates had examined in such detail, and whose nineteenth-century class structure Warner had sketched from the local people's memory and myth.

Thernstrom's findings countered the notion of a slowing of mobility from a fluid nineteenth century to a rigid twentieth century. They also suggested different *patterns* of mobility for different ethnic groups. His analysis therefore bore on two classic questions of American urban history: whether the nineteenth-century city was a sort of opportunity machine that gradually slowed down, whether the ethnic and racial diversity of the American working class hampered the development of common living conditions, class consciousness, and collective action. Other historians immediately took up Thernstrom's challenge and his model of analysis; not only city directories but also manuscript censuses and a variety of other records suddenly became relevant to pressing questions of the field.

Today's historiography grows from yesterday's history; just as previous historians have set the current questions, they have identified the proper means for answering them. The means vary from one historical subdivision to another. Because so many major questions in American political history turn on the mentalities and calculations of the chief actors—the Founding Fathers, Abraham Lincoln, or, more rarely, The People—the favored means consist either of documenting those mentalities or of rearranging the existing evidence in a new interpretation of mentalities and calculations that appears to be more consistent, economical, and/or plausible than the available interpretations. The conventional means of documenting mentalities proceed through the exposition of correspondence, of public writings, of utterances, or perhaps of the materials of folk culture: songs, slogans, tales, pictures, and the like. Some historians have lavished attention on voting records and have built up large quantitative analyses of the correlates of one voting preference or another. Three of America's most energetic organizers of quantitative electoral studies speak of "the electoral statement as a means of penetrating the outer structure of political life and charting the subterranean arena of conflicting values, interests, and desires that exist in most societies [Silbey, Bogue, and Flanigan 1978: 4]." The persistent secret hope of voting analysts is, I think, not to absorb political history into political science. It is to establish a new, reliable means of documenting popular mentalities.

Reinterpretation, however, scores more points with fellow historians than does documentation. Historians share with artists and literati a deep admiration for the ability to state and defend an "original thesis." An able young scholar must, in consequence, take the greatest care to differentiate his or her arguments from those of his or her mentor; there is nothing worse in history than to be thought imitative—better dull than dependent! That drive to identify a topic and an approach, then to make them your own, accounts for a feature of historians' behavior that frequently puzzles outsiders. If two people discover that they are working on the same topic, instead of competing to solve the problem faster and/or differently (as people in many other fields would do), they tend to divide up the territory: one drops the topic, both redefine, or they work out a division of labor. A "responsible" thesis director will not let a student continue working on a topic if it is discovered that someone else is further along on the same topic.

Historians commonly rationalize this behavior by saying that it takes a long time to become familiar with a topic and that competition for the same unique body of evidence is likely to hamper the work of both investigators; it is therefore doubly inefficient to have two people working on the same problem. But such arguments apply *a fortiori* in fields where research is more expensive and in which no such rule applies. In fact, the rule resembles the rule of serial monogamy: Adultery is unacceptable, but divorce and remarriage are desirable solutions to marital discord. Once Historian A has written his or her book, it is fair play—even high adventure—for Historian B to go back to the sources and tear up A's argument. The stress on originality and the emphasis on reinterpretation dovetail.

Reinterpretations and Theories

This complex social structure helps explain how historians can so easily shrug off work by nonhistorians that, from the outside, looks highly relevant to their concerns. It helps account for the mystique of primary sources and archives. It clarifies why the recurrent call for something like a "general history of civilizations" (e.g., Marrou 1961: 1475) attracts polite applause but no action. Even the "total history" advocated by a Fernand Braudel turns out in practice to be time—place history that broadens the range of sources and processes under examination. Historians recognize fellow specialists by their familiarity with a set of conventional categories and facts concerning a particular ensemble of places and periods, their competence in locating and using a set of sources (usually writings of various sorts) agreed upon as relevant to the events that took place in those periods and places, and their orientation to the current body of doctrine and controversy about those periods and places. The worker who deals familiarly with those categories, facts, sources, doctrines, and controversies, who builds an argument and a body of evidence that reinterpret some or all of the categories, facts, sources, doctrines, and controversies, gains recognition as a genuine historian. The reinterpretation starts from the knowledge that previous practitioners have left behind.

And why not? Any coherent field proceeds by elaboration and criticism of previous work. Even poems and symphonies often define themselves in relation to previous poems and symphonies. I stress the connection between current and previous work in history only because historians have worked out their own distinctive version of that connection: cutting the past into time—place blocks, posing a limited set of questions about each block, paying exceptional attention to the questions the literate public is asking about that period and place, giving priority to politics, being concerned about the didactic, moral, and political implications of the historical experience under analysis, insisting on the virtues of familiarity with a basic set of texts concerning that experience, and valuing the individual mastery, understanding, and interpretation of the available texts. Given this organization of inquiry, we should not be surprised to find historians proceeding in something like the fashion of literary critics: moving, *textes à l'appui*, from reinterpretation to reinterpretation. Not for most historians is the economist's derivation and estimation of a model from neoclassical economic theory, or the sociologist's effort to bring data to bear on two conflicting hypotheses. No, a historical reinterpretation should produce a new understanding of the place, time, phenomenon, and underlying question under study.

Nevertheless, the means of reinterpretation vary from field to field within history. Demographic history, for example, has a technical edge: One shows that the methods by which earlier historians arrived at crucial conclusions were faulty and that other methods produce substantially different conclusions. Thus Thomas McKeown begins his challenging reinterpretation of the causes of modern Western population growth with a modest demurrer:

> Demographers and historians interested in the pre-registration period have attempted to provide a substitute for national records by exploiting the information available in parish registers and bills of mortality. Can we, from such sources, expect to get a reliable national estimate of fertility, mortality and cause of death? I do not think so [McKeown 1976: 7].

This hesitant seed explodes into a giant shade tree, cutting the sun from all its competitors. McKeown systematically sets up the accounting problem, steadily counters alternative accounts of population growth (he is especially deft at cutting down arguments that stress the early contributions of medical improvements to life expectancy), and gradually builds up a case in which better nutrition plays a central part.

Reorientations in political history, on the other hand, rarely spring from methodological innovations. An impressive case in point is quantitative political history. Although dozens of historians have undertaken the measurement and modeling of elections, of legislative behavior, and of political elites, and although the advocates of quantitative analysis have been among the most vociferous critics of narrative and biographical approaches to political history, the field continues serenely to reward studies of Thomas Jefferson and of the American political temper.

The variation in question posing from one subfield in history to another gives the lie to two easy interpretations of the role of theory in historical analysis. (I am not speaking of the role that theory could or should play but of theory's actual place in the routine activities of working historians.) The first easy interpretation is that history is essentially atheoretical—a miscellany of facts and opinions. The second is its contrary—that theory plays about the same part in history as in any other analysis of human affairs, except that historians' general theories are usually commonsense, or poorly explicated, or both.

Neither is correct. The practitioners in each subfield of history create their own agenda and establish a limited number of theories as relevant to the answering of questions on the agenda. Both the agenda and the available theories change in spurts, as new reinterpretations come along. The reinterpretations, in their turn, respond to the internal agenda, to new ideas in adjacent fields, and to events in the world at large. Ultimately, the most consistent points of reference for all these agendas and theories are the political histories of large time—space blocks: Why did European states and their extensions come to dominate Asia and the rest of the world after the eighteenth century? Why did "traditional" China give rise to a far-reaching socialist revolution? Such master questions give rise to the subquestions on which most historical work actually focuses: Why, for example, Great Britain became the dominant colonial power in the eighteenth and nineteenth centuries, or whether the Chinese revolution of 1911 somehow anticipated, or even caused, the struggles that eventually produced a Communist regime. Theories of capitalism, of liberalism, of industrialism, of class struggle ultimately guide historians' inquiries into the multiple subquestions. Elsewhere in history, the master questions and relevant theories are different, but just as well defined.

Many of the relevant theories are themselves historically grounded. "Historically grounded" means embedded in time: focused on some historically specific setting or process, such as the growth of a capitalist world-economy after 1500, or at least postulating some important alteration in a process depending on where it occurs in a time sequence. (Alexander Gerschenkron's discussions of the "advantages of backwardness" in industrialization—the chief advantage being that a latecomer can profit by the successes and failures of early industrializers—provide an example of the second sort of historically grounded theory.) The historical grounding of historians' theories is neither self-evident nor universal; general psychological theories, timeless models of organizational structure, and historical conceptions of political processes show up regularly in historical analysis. Nevertheless, the historical grounding of the historians' master questions also predisposes historians toward historically grounded theories proposing answers to the questions.

[handwritten marginalia: the too-narrow "social science" historic]

"Social Science History"

Yet, something called "social science history" has arisen. There is even a journal by the name *Social Science History*, in addition to journals of economic history, demographic history, social history, and the like. How is that possible? The topics of articles in the first volume of *Social Science History* give an idea:

"The Institutional Context of Crossfiling"
"Urbanization, Industrialization and Crime in Imperial Germany"
"The Evolution of Public Perceptions of Adenauer as a Historic Leader"
"The Congressional Game: A Prospectus"
"Sampling for a Study of the Population and Land Use of Detroit in 1880 – 1885"
"The Social Functions of Voluntary Associations in a Nineteenth-Century American Town"
"Town and Country in Nineteenth-Century Germany: A Review of Urban – Rural Differentials in Demographic Behavior"
"Black Yellow Fever Immunities, Innate and Acquired, as Revealed in the American South"
"The Growth of English Agricultural Productivity in the Seventeenth Century"
"The Changing Context of British Politics in the 1880s: The Reform Acts and the Formation of the Liberal Unionist Party"

This incomplete list shows the variety of topics that crowd in under the name of social science history: elections, public opinion, legislators, urban structure, fertility, disease, and so on. The list does not show the unusual features of the style and contents: full of tables and graphs; frequently summarizing results or hypotheses as equations; self-conscious about techniques of analysis; speaking frequently of models, hypotheses, and problems of measurement; obsessed by comparisons over time and over space. These are the stigmata of social science history. And social science history is flourishing.

Social science history is flourishing for two main reasons: (*a*) a number of social scientists have become interested in working seriously with historical materials, and some of the leaders in American social science history are actually based in departments of political science, sociology, and economics; and (*b*) a few special fields of history have invested heavily in social science approaches to their problems and their evidence. A small proportion of a large discipline, augmented by outsiders, is enough people to create and sustain the institutional apparatus of a subdiscipline. Of the 15,000 – 20,000 professional historians in the United

States, perhaps 1000 consider themselves to be practitioners of social science history.

The subdiscipline of social science history is unusual. It is one of the few specialties in history not defined by a time, a place, and an aspect of social life. Although they come disproportionately from the fields that are otherwise known as social, economic, and political history, the topics that comprise social science history do not form a logically coherent block. Historians have not previously considered most of them to belong together. Nor are they simply the topics that come, in principle, closest to the preoccupations of the adjacent social sciences. The spread of social science practice has not even followed a principle of adjacency *within* history; separate geysers of social science history have erupted through plains of conventional historical practice.

The subdiscipline has other peculiar features. The common literature to which its members are oriented is rather thin and mainly methodological. Since no single, coherent social science exists, the historians involved attend to different literatures within the social sciences, depending on the special historical topics that concern them. Almost all the historians in the discipline have dual or triple allegiances, for in addition to being devoted to social science history as such, they work in specific time—place fields and often seek to make contributions to the social science disciplines—economics, anthropology, demography, and so on—with which they are most closely associated.

People trained outside of history commonly play important roles in social science history. Technical innovations frequently come from outside the subdiscipline; new ways of storing evidence, new statistical techniques, and new models often migrate in from nonhistorical work in the adjacent social sciences. The common ground of social science history, in the last analysis, is not substantive; instead of being committed to common problems, however defined, its members share an attitude, a relationship to the historical profession as a whole, and a small amount of technical lore.

If this shaky common ground were the whole of social science history, one could readily understand the suspicion that greets it elsewhere in history and easily predict its rapid disappearance. What gives social science history its strength, however, is that it is composed of a number of smaller clusters, each of which does share problems, materials, and procedures. As a practical approximation of these clusters, we might take the topics officially represented on the program committee of the 1979 meeting of the Social Science History Association: theory; methods and teaching of social science history; labor history; social structure and mobility; family history; ethnicity; urban history; history of education; economic history; demography; electoral, party and legislative history; bureaucracy; elites; international relations; diplomatic history; violence; public disorder; criminal justice; legal history. (Among the dozen members of the committee, incidentally, six were based in departments of history, four in departments of political science, one in a department of economics, and one in a department of sociology.) The clusters are of two overlapping kinds: historical specialties that have long existed but that have developed close working relationships with one or another of the social sciences; specialties that essentially came into being as a result of the interaction of history and one of the social sciences.

In the first category the most prominent case is economic history. During the 1960s, economic historians began adopting economic models and econometric methods as standard elements of their intellectual armamentarium; it is now hard to enter the field at all without having considerable training in economics. In the category of new specialties, the most dramatic case is demographic history. (Many of its practitioners call the field historical demography; the changed emphasis itself tells us something about the field's character; see Gaunt 1973). Although the specialty's intellectual origins go back to the political arithmeticians of the eighteenth century, demographic history has only existed as a substantial, distinctive body of knowledge since the 1960s.

Somewhere between the cases of economic history and demographic history fall the other major enterprises of social science history: quantitative urban history, the study of social mobility, and so on. Each of these specialties has its own relationship to some portion of the social sciences, and each shares some pool of problems, materials, and procedures. Each has the makings of a distinct subdiscipline.

How Do History and Social Science Coalesce?

Why these areas and not others? From a logical point of view, they are no more obvious candidates for social science work than other subjects that have remained inhospitable to social science — military history, the history of science, the history of popular culture, agricultural history, and biography are cases in point. In all of these fields, there exists a body of related systematic work somewhere in the social sciences, and some scholars have made the effort to apply the approaches of social science to the historical problem. Yet, unlike economic history or the history of the family, these fields have not moved noticeably toward the social sciences.

It is possible, in principle, that the explanation lies in the relative power of the ideas and procedures available inside and outside of history. Fields whose guiding ideas are relatively weak, one might think, tend to succumb to social-scientific enchantment. I think, however, that it has more to do with the compatibility between the existing structure of the historical field and the styles of analysis that prevail in the adjacent areas of social science. The crucial question is this: Will existing social-scientific approaches to a given problem yield fresh and/or superior answers to the questions that historians *are already asking?* If the answer is yes, and if someone with sufficient credentials as a historian to attract other historians' attention demonstrates the way to fresh and/or superior conclusions, others will follow quickly. Graduate students begin proposing investigations to confirm, duplicate, elaborate, or refute the new conclusions. Since revised doctoral dissertations make up the bulk of the monographs published in history, the new approach has a considerable impact on the books historians are reading 5 or 10 years later. The easier and the more general the procedures involved, the more quickly graduate students and junior scholars follow.

The study of American slavery illustrates the point well. The efficiency and profitability of slavery in America's cotton regions before the Civil War are crucial problems because they bear directly on several fundamental questions: whether Southern planters had a strong economic interest in slavery; whether the Peculiar Institution was likely to collapse of its own weight; whether the greater efficiency of Northern agriculture and of free labor were further threats to the economic viability of the South; whether the Civil War was a logical outcome of the confrontation between incompatible sectional interests. These questions stirred American politicians and historians from the time of the Civil War onward. In the late 1950s, however, Alfred Conrad and John Meyer began to redefine the profitability of slavery as a question of formal economics and began to derive estimates of that profitability from evidence on costs, prices, and production in the South. Their estimates portrayed slave-powered agriculture as a relatively efficient and profitable system. That work shifted the terms of the debate and started the stream of econometric research on slavery that eventually included the efforts of Robert Fogel, Stanley Engerman, Gavin Wright, Richard Sutch, and a number of other expert economists. Although noneconomists such as Eugene Genovese and Herbert Gutman continued to play important parts in the assessment of the character and consequences of American slavery, the proposal of an economic answer to an old historical question opened the way to an invasion of that part of history by economists.

The invasion resembled the great migrations of the Mongols or the Normans. Although their arrival deeply transformed the social structure at their destination, eventually the newcomers and the older settlers assimilated to each other. The economists began by acting as if they were simply going to incorporate American economic history into neoclassical economics and leave nothing worthwhile for the historians to do. Eventually, however, the economists began to respond to the peculiarities of the American nineteenth century, even to interest themselves in the historical problems posed by that time and place. At the same time, historians began to learn the strengths and weaknesses of econometric analysis, even on occasion to learn how to do it. As Eugene Genovese once wrote,

> The finest products of the new school have transformed themselves from economists who work on data from the past into economic historians in the full sense—into historians who are primarily concerned with economic processes within larger social processes and who therefore struggle to define the extent to which economic processes are autonomous and the ways in which they are contingent. The better traditional historians, analogously, did not deny a degree of autonomy to the economic sector and did not reject the new methods; they tried to take full account of the new work while reevaluating the relationship between economic behavior and social behavior as a whole [1975: 533].

By 1978—20 years after Conrad and Meyer—Gavin Wright was prefacing an important econometric study of the Cotton South with the declaration that the fruits of econometric economic history "have frequently been valuable and stimulating, but I now believe that it is a mistake for economic history to define itself merely as economics applied to old data. Instead, economic history offers a distinctive intellectual approach to the study of economics, a view of the economic world in which historical time plays a fundamental role [1978: xiii]."

American economic history is in no sense reverting to the status quo ante. Any historian who now wants to be heard on the viability of slavery or any number of other topics in nineteenth-century history has to be familiar with the econometric work on the subject and may well have to undertake his or her own econometric analysis. The basic training in the field now includes a substantial amount of economics; indeed, many of the new people in the field are getting their training in departments of economics. But four further changes have taken the field past the point at which it seemed that economic history might simply vanish into economics:

1. The economists began to act as if the time and place—the historical setting—significantly constrained the operation of economic processes that had previously appeared to be timeless and universal.

2. The economists began to respond to the questions historians in general were asking about the time and place.
3. The historians became sufficiently familiar with the procedures, products, and pitfalls of econometric work that they could assimilate and criticize its results.
4. Historians and economists alike began to identify problems that were crucial but not easily handled by the available economics.

In the process, as Genovese says, a distinct specialty of economic history—neither strictly economics nor strictly history—began to form.

The changing historiography of slavery provides a paradigm for the diffusion of social-scientific approaches into historical inquiry. Similar, less complete transformations have occurred in the historical study of family structure, cities, social class, and a number of other topics. That highly selective coalescence of portions of history with segments of the social sciences accounts for the curious structure of social science history as a whole. Instead of being the edge of the social sciences as a whole with history as a whole, it is a collection of many different edges.

Still, the social science historians have the common ground of prisoners of war—the common ground that results from originating in one broad tradition and being confronted with another. On the one side, there is the historical tradition, with its rooting of analysis in a time and a place by means of a defined set of products, mostly texts, of that time and place. On the other side, there is the social-scientific tradition, with its distinguishing features: explicit conceptualization and modeling of the phenomena under study, a strong emphasis on measurement, the deliberate use of comparison—often quantitative comparison—to establish the strength and direction of important relationships. The attempt to reconcile these two traditions gives social science history a certain methodological unity.

The subdiscipline also bears a paradoxical strain of populism; paradoxical because other historians often resist the numbers and abstractions of the social sciences on the ground that they are inhumane. Yet in field after field the appeal of social-scientific approaches has been that they facilitate the bringing of ordinary people back into the historical record, permit the historian to rescue them from abstraction and to gain a sense of the day-to-day conditions of their lives. Ordinary people leave few diaries, letters, and novels, but their experiences leave documentary evidence nonetheless. The documentary evidence shows up in birth certificates, marriage contracts, notarized transactions, conscription registers, tax rolls, rent books, censuses, catechetical records, and other routine sources. One of the greatest contributions of the social sciences to historical practice has been to suggest means of combining the fugitive mentions of individuals in such sources into biographies—individual biographies, and collective ones as well.

The most obvious example of that populist use of collective biography is one we have already discussed: the systematic study of political militants and revolutionary crowds. In the 1950s, Albert Soboul, Kåre Tønnesson, Richard Cobb, George Rudé, and other students of revolutionary France followed the lead of Georges Lefebvre in attempting exhaustive enumerations and descriptions of different important groups of activists. Their quantitative work was simple and not very extensive, but it demonstrated the existence of abundant evidence concerning ordinary participants in the revolution. Although entirely nonquantitative, the rich essays of E. P. Thompson and E. J. Hobsbawm on the lives of workers likewise displayed the promise of history "from the bottom up." It did not take social scientists long to see that the resulting redefinition of the historical agenda gave them an opportunity to apply their own skills to the available evidence. A segment of social science history devoted to the study of crowds, militants, and ordinary workers grew up.

The growth of demographic history was in some ways contrary to that of crowd studies, yet it produced a similar result. Whereas the urge to study crowds originated within history, the historical study of vital processes grew very largely from the concerns of demographers. French demographer Louis Henry, in particular, sought to pinpoint the conditions under which deliberate fertility limitation became part of a way of life. The search for the origins of unreversed declines in fertility has long been one of demography's dominant preoccupations. Henry's pivotal insight was to realize that the same sorts of materials that antiquarians used for the construction of genealogies would, with great care, yield fine measures of fertility, mortality, and nuptiality. He and his collaborators developed a form of collective biography—"family reconstitution"—using the registers of births, deaths, and marriages the Roman Catholic church had established for its parishioners. The method yielded important results, including indications of much greater variability in preindustrial fertility than had previously been thought to be the case. Other research groups (notably the group working with economic historian E. A. Wrigley and intellectual historian Peter Laslett at Cambridge University) took up similar inquiries. The early agenda was largely demographic; it was, in essence, an effort to modify and refine the theory of demographic transition.

The crossover into history occurred when Wrigley, Pierre Goubert, and other economic historians began to interpret fluctuating vital rates as indicators of welfare and to examine the covariation of demographic fluctuations with swings in the economy. Goubert, for example, traced the devastating effect of periodic food shortages on the death rate in parishes of the Beauvais region, as well as the remarkable recuperation of fertility once the crisis was past. That line of analysis articulated neatly with the already-established interpretation of French economic history as a series of well-defined cycles. In France and elsewhere, the inquiry broadened from there. Some investigators refined the study of demographic processes, others worked at bringing other routinely produced documents into the analysis of everyday experience, still others concentrated on the connections between demographic processes and their economic context. By this time, formal demography, economic modeling, and statistical analysis were becoming commonplaces in this particular branch of historical research. A new variety of social science history was emerging.

Is Quantification the Essence?

In field after field, the leading edge of the change was some form of quantification. Because of that uniformity, many nonquantitative historians mistook the prow for the whole ship: They thought that quantification was the essence of the new movement, that its proper name was "quantitative history," that its practitioners claimed everything could and should be counted. The advocates themselves compounded the misunderstanding. They delighted in showing how much historical reasoning that appears in nonnumerical prose is nonetheless crudely quantitative: More or less, growing or contracting, crisis or continuity recur throughout historical writing. Each of them has an implicitly quantitative content (cf. Fogel 1975). Such arguments invite deliberate quantification.

The point is important, for it provides the demonstration that the quantifiers are not simply amusing (or abusing) themselves but are pursuing significant questions that are already on the historical agenda. Yet the argument is misleading, for two reasons:

1. Available quantitative models and statistical techniques are inadequate to deal with many of the more-or-less statements, which do, indeed, abound in historical argument.
2. Quantification is only the most visible piece of a much larger analytical apparatus—an apparatus of deliberate conceptualization, explicit modeling, painstaking measurement, and self-conscious comparison.

The defense of quantification therefore both oversells and understates the likely impact of social-scientific approaches on historical practice.

Critics of social science history have gradually come around to the realization that quantification is *not* the essence. As quantitative economic history and historical studies of social mobility first lumbered into the light, defenders of history as art stared at the new beasts with distaste . . . and what they saw first was numbers. Jacques Barzun wrote an elegant variant of a standard judgment: "Technical diagnosis or statistical analysis does not amplify understanding or finally explain persons and events, because it abstracts from their particularity in order to put in their place common denominators, mechanisms, averages, or trends [Barzun 1974: 148]." Quantitative history, he thought, violated true principles of historical knowledge.

Later, however, a more explicitly political critique of social science history began to take shape. That critique deflected attention from numbers as such toward the presumptions concerning history which the use of numbers was supposed to reveal: various shades of positivism, an unwarranted confidence in the models and methods of social science, a populism which treated all features of everyday life as equally worthy of investigation, an avoidance of exploitation and class struggle. Even antiquantitative anthropological approaches to history came in for scathing denunciation. As Fox-Genovese and Genovese summed it up:

> As admirable as much of the recent social history has been and as valuable as much of the description of the life of the lower classes may eventually prove, the subject as a whole is steadily sinking into a neoantiquarian swamp presided over by liberal ideologues, the burden of whose political argument—notwithstanding the usual pretense of not having a political argument—rests on an evasion of class confrontation [1976: 214].

Fox-Genovese went on to complain that former leftists and pseudo-leftists were trying to maintain their credentials by clinging to the study of popular culture while abandoning the political struggle a true left perspective entails. Similarly, Tony Judt declared that history is not only about politics, it *is* politics, and that one "consequence of the divorce of political from social history is the insulting denial to people in the past of their political and ideological identity [1979: 68]." In short, by not organizing their inquiries around class struggle, social historians betray the class struggle.

The critique contains some grains of truth. It is true that social history which relies heavily on the social sciences tends to shake the dominance of political history by attributing importance to population changes, to economic transformations, to such esoteric matters as alterations in nutrition. It is also true that populist examinations of political life itself often turn up people who suffered exploitation, yet did not articulate their

Good indication of Tilly's bias — that neither the artistic nor the political critics have scored serious hits on the new forms of history.

suffering in terms of class. But the critique is doubly incorrect. First, social-scientific historians have proved themselves fully capable of following the leads of Rudé, Hobsbawm, Thompson, and other students of class struggle into systematic reconstructions of everyday political and social life; they have not abandoned the study of class or of struggle. Second, social-scientific historians have rendered a great service to political history by making class action simultaneously problematic and accessible to closer scrutiny: identifying circumstances in which ordinary people had an apparent class interest in action and yet acted on bases other than class, or did not act at all; beginning to inventory and connect the concrete means—not only strikes and rebellions but also festivals, mocking ceremonies, and other forms of protest—by which exploited people stated their demands and complaints. That is no mean accomplishment.

... and from the social science perspective itself (e.g. Stone)

Not all the criticism of social science history has come from proponents of class struggle. Partly because of the inevitable discrepancy between early claims and late realities, erstwhile leaders of the movement toward social science have taken to writing disclaimers. The disclaimers commonly say, in effect, "I never promised you a rose garden." Lawrence Stone—an early and influential advocate of quantification in English history—has observed that

> disillusionment with economic or demographic monocausal determinism and with quantification has led historians to start asking a quite new set of questions, many of which were previously blocked from view by the preoccupation with a specific methodology, structural, collective and statistical. More and more of the "new historians" are now trying to discover what was going on inside people's heads in the past, and what it was like to live in the past, questions which inevitably lead back to the use of narrative [1979: 13].

In an earlier statement of the same theme, Stone took a more prophetic tone. He portrayed most of the social sciences as treacherous allies on their way to internal collapse. He deplored the heedless adoption of quantification, especially as the core of large-scale research projects and specialized graduate programs. He castigated the excesses of psychohistory. And he criticized the tendency to apply simple, one-way, causal explanations to the complexities of history.

"The basic objection to these threats to the historical profession," preached Stone, "is that they all tend to reduce the study of man, and the explanation of change, to a simplistic, mechanistic determinism based on some preconceived theoretical notion of universal applicability, regardless of time and space, and allegedly verified by scientific laws and scientific methods [1977: 38]." "It may be," he continued,

that the time has come for the historian to reassert the importance of the
concrete, the particular and the circumstantial, as well as the general theoretical model and the procedural insight; to be more wary of quantification
for the sake of quantification; to be suspicious of vast cooperative projects of
staggering cost; to stress the critical importance of a strict scrutiny of the
reliability of sources; to be passionately determined to combine both quantitative and qualitative data and methods as the only reliable way even to
approach truth about so odd and unpredictable and irrational a creature as
man; and to display a becoming modesty about the validity of our discov-
eries in this most difficult of disciplines [1977: 39].

Veterans of revival meetings will immediately recognize this passage as a
deployment of the "Sinner, Beware!" technique. The preacher fixes his
gaze over the congregation's head, points a prophetic finger, and fore-
casts doom for unrepentant sinners. He names no names, and the sins in
question appear as ominous labels—lust, greed, gluttony—rather than as
concrete actions. Most of the congregation receive the double thrill of
self-satisfaction and righteous indignation, a few thin-skinned souls feel
guilty, and the emptiness of the condemnation passes unnoticed. No
reader, after all, is likely to cheer "quantification for the sake of quantification," much less "projects of staggering cost." The social scientists and
historians who are the objects of these complaints are likely to reply, hurt
and puzzled, "Who, me?" Few readers will dare deny the importance of
the concrete, the value of strict scrutiny of the sources, the attractiveness
of modesty, and so on. Yet Stone's sermon is a disservice to historians. It
is a disservice because it misrepresents how the interaction between
history and the social sciences has usually worked itself out and misstates the choices now before the profession. The critical choice, indeed,
is one I have barely mentioned: whether to help the social scientists make
proper use of historical materials and historical analysis.

Sociology Reaches for History

The choice is more critical today because several social science disciplines that had long operated far from history—notably, anthropology,
sociology, and political science—have reached out to reestablish their
historical connections. Let us focus on sociology. The discipline of sociology grew out of history—especially, I think, out of the nineteenth-
century effort to grasp and control the origins, character, and consequences of industrial capitalism. In this broad sense, such otherwise
contrasting thinkers as Marx, Tönnies, and Durkheim joined in the same
enterprise. The early, self-conscious practitioners of sociology, however,

specialized in large schemes designed to place all historical experience into coherent master sequences. August Comte's Theological, Metaphysical and Positive stages of thought and Herbert Spencer's grand march of human societies along the road of differentiation from "militant" to "industrial" were simply two of the most prominent among many such schemes. Since Comte coined the term *sociology* and Spencer gave it wide currency, however, the two schemes helped define the infant discipline. Quickly the historical content drained out of sociology in favor of an effort to create a timeless natural science of society. Although Weber and some of his successors were zealous historical practitioners, on the whole, twentieth-century sociologists committed themselves to the study of the present; they showed less and less inclination to consider history important, either as a set of influences on contemporary social processes or as a field of inquiry worthy of sociological attention.

Yet in the 1960s and, especially, in the 1970s, sociologists did begin to reach for history. Historical analyses of industrialization, of rebellion, of family structure began to appear in the journals that sociologists read. Departments of sociology began hiring specialists in something called "historical and comparative analysis." Sociological authors began to write as if *when* something happened seriously affected *how* it happened. Some few sociologists actually began to learn the basic historical skills: archival exploration, textual analysis, and the life. History began to matter.

What happened? Among many strands, I see two as strongest. First, the social-scientific work that had been proceeding in history doubled back on the social sciences. The successes of historical demography provided a model for contemporary students of marriage and the family, as well as for other demographers. Historical studies of crime, of voting, of urban structure, of social mobility were sufficiently fruitful and/or provocative with respect to prevailing sociological doctrines that sociologists started to think of them as more than mere *tours de force*. Second (and more important), disillusion with models of modernization and development turned students of large-scale social change toward history.

The disillusion with developmental theories followed a decade or two of enthusiasm after World War II. During the palmy days of developmentalism, Western economists hoped to export the secrets of economic growth to the "underdeveloped" world, and sociologists imagined other forms of development—political, social, educational, urban, and so on—to accompany the economic growth. The reaction against developmental theories had several different origins. Development of any sort proved difficult to engineer. Capital accumulation, family planning, land reform, and other desiderata of development turned out to meet more powerful resistance, and to have more extensive political ramifications, than optimistic Western theories promised. The theories themselves fell on hard times. On the whole, they were inadequate to the task of explaining what was actually happening in the Third World. Their political premises—especially the implication that Western-style party politics was an inevitable, desirable concomitant of other forms of develop-ment—excited the anger of Third World intellectuals and powerholders alike. Among other things, the standard conceptions of political development clashed with the explanation of the disadvantages of poor countries as consequences of Western imperialism; that was, after all, an attractive alternative in the many former colonies that were acquiring statehood and undertaking planned national development. In the course of the widespread opposition to American warmaking in Southeast Asia during the 1960s, many social scientists in the West (including the United States) became aware of, and sympathetic to, the antiimperial and neo-Marxist alternatives to development theories. They even began to contribute to the building of those alternative theories themselves. Developmentalism fell into disrepute.

But why and how were the alternatives to developmentalism *historical?* Largely because, in one way or another, they portrayed the current situation of poor countries as the outcome of a long, slow, historically specific process of conquest, exploitation, and control. Thus André Gunder Frank and other students of Latin America spoke of "underdevelopment," not as the primeval condition from which the still-poor areas of the world had to be rescued, but as a product of the dependency of their economies on those of the world's dominant powers. "The expansion of the capitalist system over the past centuries," wrote Gunder Frank,

> effectively and entirely penetrated even the apparently most isolated sectors of the underdeveloped world. Therefore, the economic, political, social, and cultural institutions and relations we now observe there are the products of the historical development of the capitalist system no less than are the seemingly more modern or capitalist features of the national metropoles of these underdeveloped countries. Analogously to the relations between development and underdevelopment on the international level, the contemporary underdeveloped institutions of the so-called backward or feudal domestic areas of an underdeveloped country are no less the product of the single historical process of capitalist development than are the so-called capitalist institutions of the supposedly more progressive areas [1972: 4–5].

Such an argument denied the idea of a developmental process that repeated itself over and over in different parts of the world, denied the division of the world into "traditional" and "modern" sectors, with the modern transforming the traditional into itself, and denied the validity of any analysis that took a single self-contained society as its unit of analysis. All these denials moved analysts of the contemporary world closer to an explanation of the present as the outcome of a historically specific struggle for power and profit. That Marx and Lenin provided the theoretical linchpins of the whole alternative system of thought further promoted the concern with history.

A prestigious example of the move toward history appears in the work of Immanuel Wallerstein. Wallerstein, an Africanist, published sympathetic studies of decolonization: *Africa: The Politics of Independence, The Road to Independence: Ghana and the Ivory Coast,* and others. As of 1966, he was arguing that

> the imposition of colonial administration created new social structures which took on with time increasing importance in the lives of all those living in them. The rulers of the colonial system, as those of all social systems, engaged in various practices for their own survival and fulfillment which simultaneously resulted in creating movements which in the long run undermined the system. In the case of the colonial situation, what emerged as a consequence of the social change wrought by the administration was a nationalist movement which eventually led a revolution and obtained independence [1966: 7].

In his arguments of the time, history's role was limited. In any particular colony, the past practices of the colonizers accounted for the current political situation. Later, Wallerstein came to see the entire sequence of colonization, exploitation, and decolonization as part of a single historical process: the incorporation of peripheral areas into the expanding capitalist world-system.

Wallerstein tells us that he first explored Western history in a search for parallels with the African experience, in hopes of identifying a standard process of modernization. But the difficulties of drawing boundaries around the societies in question, of identifying the stages in their development, and of making meaningful comparisons of seventeenth-century with twentieth-century states eventually appeared to be more than technical problems to overcome; they grew into fundamental objections to the enterprise. "It was at this point," writes Wallerstein, "that I abandoned the idea altogether of taking either the sovereign state or that vaguer concept, the national society, as the unit of analysis. I decided that neither one was a social system and that one could only speak of social change in social systems. The only social system in this scheme was the world-system [1974: 7]." By this path he arrived at a deeply historical conception of the problem—what happened before made all the difference to what happened next. That new conception drew the onetime Africanist back to a general study of the origins of the capitalist world-system in the European sixteenth century.

As Christian Palloix said of Gunder Frank:

> That emphasis on the capitalist world economy instead of the national economy—the central concept of bourgeois political economy until now—is not new to Marxist thought, since the phrase "capitalist world economy" is due to Rosa Luxemburg, and the concept is ever-present by implication in the work of Bukharin. Rosa Luxemburg was the first to call clearly for the displacement of Marxist analysis from the national to the world level in order to understand contemporary capitalism [1971: I, 8].

Eastern European historians such as Marion Malowist have long used a similar set of ideas to explain the connections between the commercial capitalism of northwestern Europe and the agrarian economies of the East during the fifteenth and sixteenth centuries. Wallerstein takes an extreme Luxemburgian position. He also commits himself firmly to one side of a long-raging debate within Marxist analysis, stressing the relations of exchange, rather than the relations of production, as the distinctive features of alternative modes of production. He therefore rejects the traditional Marxist centerpiece in the tableau of capitalism: the confrontation of a capitalist who owns and controls the means of production with a proletarian who receives wages for the yielding of labor power. "To oversimplify," says Wallerstein in a summary of his argument, "capitalism is a system in which the surplus value of the proletarian is appropriated by the bourgeois [1979: 293]." The bourgeois and the proletarian are often half a world apart, and the complex of relations between them is a complex of unequal exchange. A system of production for exchange, rather than production for use, forges those long, long chains of exploitation. Some significant, controversial conclusions follow: that distant subsistence farmers participate fully in the capitalist world-economy; that so long as a capitalist core sets the terms of international exchange, semiperipheral socialist countries remain integral elements of a capitalist system; and that capitalism did not spread through the world little by little, as one firm, farm, or plantation after another took up wage labor and capitalist control, but took charge in a great, worldwide structural transformation. Thus the history of capitalism occupies a large share of the total history of the last five centuries.

A reader who persists to the end of this book will find that in tracing the development of European capitalism I have seized the other horn of the Marxist dilemma, emphasizing the immediate relations of production as the defining features of capitalism. That choice produces a narrower, later catalog of capitalist development. Wallerstein's broad definition, it seems to me, sacrifices the sort of insight concerning the logic of capitalist social relations that Marx unfolded in his analyses of agrarian change in England—especially the insight into the way in which the capitalist's pursuit of profit helped transform workers into proletarians. For those who, like me, want to examine how the development of capitalism affected the collective action of ordinary people, that insight is essential, its loss critical.

Despite these reservations, let me acknowledge Wallerstein's powerful contribution to sociological practice. For one thing, Wallerstein managed to draw sociologists' attention to a fruitful line of thought they had previously ignored. "Since the publication of Immanuel Wallerstein's *The Modern World System*," Albert Bergesen observes, "there has been an explosion of interest and research on this topic [1980: xiii]." The "explosion" has promoted serious historical work within sociology. Although a number of sociologists have taken world-system ideas as the frame for large, quantitative, cross-sectional comparisons of many contemporary national states (a practice that makes me fear a repetition of mistakes made long since by modernization theorists), time and history have moved onto the practical research agenda as never before.

Not all the sociologists following Wallerstein's lead, furthermore, take his conclusions for granted. In *Labor, Class, and the International System*, for example, Alejandro Portes and John Walton display considerable impatience with Wallersteinian neglect of the concrete connections between world-system processes and the actual workings of such phenomena as international migration. Yet without Wallerstein's forceful posing of the problem, books such as theirs would have been much less likely to appear — and find an audience — within sociology. The dialectic has begun.

Within history as well, Wallerstein's work has made a difference. From the historical perspective, Wallerstein's special contribution is to propose a synthesis — a synthesis between a well-known line of thought about the capitalist world-economy and Fernand Braudel's broad treatment of the entire Mediterranean world during the formative years of European capitalism as a single, interdependent system. Braudel has returned the favor. His sprawling, three-volume *Civilisation matérielle, économie, et capitalisme* explores the history of the entire world during the ascent of capitalism; to the extent that it has a unifying framework, the framework consists of a succession of world-economies, culminating in the capitalist world-economy. He adopts, furthermore, Wallerstein's emphasis on large-scale exchange as the essence of capitalism and likewise places within the capitalist system many people and situations other historians locate outside the system's perimeter. In response to Witold Kula's claim that the landlords who "refeudalized" eastern Europe did not, and could not, calculate as capitalists, Braudel declares:

To be sure, that is not the argument I wish to challenge. It seems to me, however, that the second serfdom was the counterpoint of a merchant capitalism which took advantage of the situation in the East, and even, to some extent, based its operation there. The great landlord was not a capitalist, but he was a tool and a collaborator at the service of the capitalism of Amsterdam and other places. *He was part of the system* [1979: II, 235].

If Braudel has long insisted on the interconnectedness of the world, his latest treatments of the connections have taken on a decidedly Wallersteinian air. Indeed, Braudel's grand synthesis and Wallerstein's magnum opus appear increasingly to be complementary efforts, with the one making unexpected connections in great profusion and the other supplying the long-lacking systematic narrative of the world-economy's historical development. In his swing from single-country studies of political modernization to worldwide studies of capitalism's development, Wallerstein epitomizes the substitution of historical analysis for the developmentalism of the 1950s and 1960s.

Wallerstein's world-system analysis keeps to the enormous scale of the developmental schemes it is meant to replace. He aspires to stuff the whole of human history since 1500 into a single sack. Except when writing textbooks or end-of-career reflections, professional historians almost never work at that scale. Most other sociologists who have taken up historical analyses in recent years have also chosen a smaller scope than Wallerstein. Comparative history has been an important choice; S. N. Eisenstadt's *The Political Systems of Empires* has served as one sort of model, Barrington Moore's *Social Origins of Dictatorship and Democracy* as another. Those are formidable models for emulation, but talented newcomers have met the challenge; Theda Skocpol's searching comparison of the French, Russian, and Chinese revolutions, in *States and Social Revolutions*, is a case in point. Other sociologists have turned down the scale yet another notch or two: Michael Hechter on internal colonialism in Great Britain, Daniel Chirot on the politics of Rumania, Michael Schwartz on a single important farmer's movement in the American South, and so on down to the level of a single community. Some of America's best sociological talent is going into historical studies.

The movement has caught on and is likely to be around for some time. Elsewhere in sociology, historical approaches to crime, collective action, power structures, occupational differentiation, and a host of other topics are becoming commonplace. The sociologists in question are not turning into historians. As a rule, they are not learning to do archival research; nor are they taking their questions from the prevailing historical agenda, or suppressing their inclinations to explicit modeling, careful measurement, and deliberate comparison. They are, on the other hand, edging toward the adoption of genuinely historical arguments—arguments in which where and, especially, when something happens seriously affects its character and outcome. The result, I predict, will not be a general rapprochement of sociology and history but a counterpart to the earlier development of separate social-scientific specialties within history: a highly selective shift of particular topics to historical analyses and historical materials.

Selective or not, the shift is important. It is enlarging the place of historically grounded theories, and challenging the place of theories that disregard time, in sociology: the development of capitalism instead of modernization, the growth of an international state-system instead of political development. It is expanding the opportunities to formulate and test models of long-term change on reliable evidence concerning substantial blocks of time instead of on the sham comparison of presumably "backward" and "advanced" areas of the same point in time. And it is increasing the number of sociologists who, instead of treating the works of historians as if they were raw but solid evidence simply awaiting a sociological gloss, detect what is problematic in existing historical interpretations and know how to go about correcting them. Even if social science history, within history, is reaching a plateau, historical work within sociology is continuing to grow.

Historical Analyses of Structural Change and Collective Action

Two areas of sociological analysis that stand to gain significantly from the swing toward history are studies of large-scale structural change and of collective action. The search for timeless general models of industrialization, rationalization, or political development will yield to twin efforts to identify the master change processes in particular historical eras and to connect specific transformations occurring in those eras to the master processes of change. The attempt to formulate general laws of revolution, of social movements, or of worker organization will give way to a quest for regularities in the collective action of particular historical eras.

For our own era, the two master processes are no doubt the expansion of capitalism and the growth of national states and systems of states. The expansion of capitalism combined the accumulation of capital with proletarianization of producers; increasingly, workers with little or no capital sold their labor power to people who controlled substantial capital and who decided how the capital and labor would be combined for their profit. From a small European base, the capitalists extended their decision-making power to the entire world. Wallerstein's *The Modern World-System* sums up one major interpretation of how that process worked, but there are others — notably, the idea that capitalism was a sort of invention that worked so well that one country after another adopted it. The historical problem is, then, to determine why and how capital accumulation-cum-proletarianization occurred, why and how the system of productive relations expanded, and what were the consequences of that expansion. Time is of the essence, historical analysis indispensable to the enterprise. Yet there remains room for the classic problems that have concerned students of "modernization": why, how, and with what effects production moved into large, capital-intensive organizations; what caused the industrial city to come into being; what happened to the peasantry; and so on. All these follow easily from the historical analysis of capitalism's development.

As counterpoint to that analysis, we have the growth of national states and systems of states. An organization is a *state*, let us say, in so far as (a) it controls the principal organized means of coercion in some territory; (b) that territory is large and contiguous; (c) the organization is differentiated from other organizations operating in the same territory; (d) it is autonomous; (e) it is centralized; and (f) its divisions are formally coordinated with one another. In that sense of the word, states were rare phenomena anywhere in the world before a few hundred years ago. Yet by the twentieth century states had become the dominant organizations almost everywhere in the world. What is more, states struggled with one another, borrowed one another's organizational innovations, formed hierarchies and interdependent clusters, and worked collectively at creating new states, containing old states, and realigning the weaker states to meet the interests of the stronger. In short, not only states but also systems of states came to dominate the world.

Again, the historical analysis begins with the Europe of the Renaissance, fragmented into hundreds of nominally autonomous political units, none of which resembled a twentieth-century national state. For convenience, without insisting stubbornly on the distinction, we can distinguish between the internal and the external history of statemaking — how particular organizations grew up that asserted dominance over their "own" populations and how those organizations established their power with respect to competing organizations outside. Warmaking then becomes crucial on both sides of the divide: internally, as the activity that drove the statemakers to tax, conscript, commandeer, and disarm a subject population, and thus build up their coercive power; externally, as the primary means by which statemakers established their

eg of "nationalism"

the analysis of "collective action"

exclusive rights within their own areas, expanded those areas, and re-shaped the form, personnel, and policies of other states. How states acquired control over education, welfare, marriage, natural resources, and economic activity poses the next round of questions. We move easily to the examination of the central problems of contemporary political sociology: to what extent and how the economically dominant classes control the political apparatus as well; under what conditions a national population is active, organized, and informed with respect to national politics; how riots, rebellions, and revolutions occur; and so forth. But we take up the problems with a difference. We take up the analysis of power, of participation, of rebellion as historical problems, ultimately attaching them to the expansion of capitalism and the growth of systems of national states.

Capitalism and statemaking provide the context for a historically grounded analysis of collective action—of the ways in which people act together in pursuit of shared interests. Grounding the analysis histori-cally, again, means fleeing universal categories. Instead of the eternal behavior of crowds, we study the particular forms of action that people use to advance claims or register grievances. Instead of laws of social move-ments, we study the emergence of the social movement as a political phenomenon. Instead of power in general, we study the modalities of power within a certain mode of production.

Capitalism and statemaking provide another sort of grounding as well, for their rhythms and directions dominated the changes in collective action's three fundamental components: the *interests* around which people were prepared to organize and act; their *capacity* to act on those interests; and the *opportunity* to defend or advance those interests collec-tively. Concretely, we find ourselves examining how and why strikes became standard vehicles for labor—management struggles, the ways in which the expanding intervention of states in everyday life (by taxing, drafting, regulating, or seizing control of crops) excited resistance from peasants and artisans, the conditions under which patron—client net-works lost their political effectiveness, and similar problems. These prob-lems are, to my mind, sufficiently broad and important to compensate sociologists for the fall from timeless universalism that pursuit of these problems entails.

What's Going on Here?

With minor exceptions, the later chapters of this book report ideas and provisional conclusions from the historically grounded study of statemaking, the development of capitalism, and popular collective action in Europe over the last four centuries. Chapters 2 ("Computing History") and 3 ("Homans, Humans, and History") deviate most from that program—the first because it reflects in general about the impact of computers on historical practice before arriving at the specific uses of computers in my group's studies of collective action, and the chapter on Homans because it sketches a style of historical analysis that contrasts with my own. "Useless Durkheim" (Chapter 4), on the other hand, not only presents materials for the study of popular collective action but also examines the weaknesses of standard sociological notions concerning the central problems in the research program.

Chapters 5 and 6 ("War and Peasant Rebellion in Seventeenth-Century France" and "How [And, to Some Extent, Why] to Study British Contention") combine ideas, materials, methods, and provisional results from two inquiries within that research program. Those two inquiries tend to take the processes of statemaking and capitalism for granted and to aim their questions at collective action. Then attention shifts to the historical processes by which capitalism developed and states grew. "Proletarianization: Theory and Research" and "States, Taxes, and Proletarians" (Chapters 7 and 8) follow a somewhat more critical, synthetic, and speculative mode of analysis, in an effort to set priorities for the next round of historically grounded theory and research. And the book's conclusion ("Looking Forward . . . Into a Rearview Mirror") traces continuities among these varied sociological expeditions into historical terrain.

May I mention something else I have found on that terrain? It is, to quote George Homans, "the joy sheer, single facts can give of their own sweet selves." The historically grounded inquiry into statemaking, popular collective action, and the development of capitalism in Europe offers the additional compensation of bringing the sociologist into the rich historical residues of everyday social life. The sorts of residues, for example, that we encountered at the start of the discussion, in the *Mercure françois*.

Let us return to the *Mercure*, to see where a program of historical analysis leads us. Now we can reverse the angle of our approach. Earlier we looked at a text and asked what it could tell us about the era. Now we are in a position to ask how the evidence in the text bears on the analysis of capitalism, statemaking, and collective action. Properly read, the *Mercure* fairly bursts with relevant evidence.

In 1615, Louis XIII (son and successor of the assassinated Henry IV) was 14 years old; his mother, Marie de Medici, was regent. Louis and Marie faced three linked challenges from within his turbulent kingdom. The great sovereign courts, especially the Parlement of Paris, were trying to consolidate their own autonomy by such means as guaranteeing the heredity of offices and to extend their power to review and veto royal actions. The king's close kin and rival princes, including the prince of Condé, alternated between grudging acquiescence and armed rebellion. Protestant consistories in Guienne were organizing to resist by force the very Catholic marriages of the king to a Spanish princess and of his sister to the Spanish crown prince. The resistance of the courts deprived the king of their sanction for new taxes with which to pay the troops required to put down the rebellions. The king and the queen mother turned to cruel old expedients, such as expelling all practicing Jews and confiscating their property. Meanwhile, the rebellious princes faced a parallel problem: how to squeeze the wherewithal for expensive armies from a reluctant population without driving the population itself into rebellion against *them*. On 22 October 1615 the army of the princes

> went to lodge themselves at the little city of Espougny, two leagues from Auxerre. The inhabitants wanted to hold them off, but the city was forced and pillaged. People have written that rape and violence, more than barbarous, took place, in the church as well as elsewhere. Complaints and murmurs reached all the way to the Prince and to the Duke of Mayenne. They had two soldiers, accused of rape and violence, hanged [*Mercure françois* 1615: 260].

When they had to (which was often), the princes let the troops wrest their food, lodging, arms, and sexual satisfaction from the local population; when the exactions threatened to turn the locals into rebels, the military commanders checked their troops by means of exemplary punishment. When they could, the princes established a more regular system of taxation, parallel to that of the king. As the *Mercure*'s writer commented,

> It is very hard on the poor peasants to be trampled by the military, and to pay a double *taille* [the basic property tax] as well; they were obliged to do so by the revenue offices set up by the Princes in the provinces of Picardy, Ile de France, Champagne, Auxerrois, Berry, Touraine and Anjou below the Loire. The officers sent their garrisons to seize the richest peasants, and held them prisoner until they had paid not their own share of the *taille*, but that of the entire village, which they were then supposed to collect from the others [1615: 305 – 306].

That technique, the princes had learned directly from the crown's own tax officers.

Now, it would take a great many more texts to reconstruct the changes going on in the France of 1615. In context, however, these two are enough to identify an unexpected convergence between the interests of

capitalists and the interests of statemakers. Capitalists specialized in set- ‖
ting prices on goods, land, and labor, in exchanging them, and in bringing them into larger and larger markets; that is how they accumulated
capital. Capitalists had a powerful interest in destroying the capacity of
local people to produce for themselves, to barter goods and services, to
keep land off the market. Statemakers needed resources that were embedded in local communities—especially the food, supplies, and manpower required to keep large armies going. To the extent that goods, land,
and labor were being exchanged via a monetized market, and thus had
visible prices, it was easier for the statemakers to seize resources: They
taxed the exchanges themselves, they used market-derived values to
judge the capacity of people to pay, they grabbed the money people
accumulated from selling their goods, and they used the tax revenues to
buy food, supplies, and manpower on the market instead of commandeering them directly from unwilling households. The process had its
converse: The enforcement of taxation in money forced people to sell
goods, services, or land, and thus to expand the market.

Capitalists played facilitating roles at all levels of the process: as local
merchants interested in making a profit on the sale of cattle, as purchasers of tax-collecting offices on which it was possible to make a profit,
as creditors who advanced large sums to the crown in return for the
rights to shares of future tax revenues, enforceable by means of the royal
military power. In other regards the capitalists, too, fought the state's
advance. At these crucial points, however, the interests of capitalists and
statemakers coincided and led to an effective coalition—a coalition that,
for the most part, excluded the statemakers' rivals and victimized the
subject population.

The coalition worked. "Financiers" (as they were called at the time) and
royal officials succeeded in greatly expanding royal revenues, and thus
made possible the building of large, stable, and reliable armies that were
largely independent of the great magnates—the king's rivals. Under that
sort of effort, the French national budget nearly doubled, rising from
about 27 million to about 50 million livres, between 1614 and 1622. The
process of building a regular army occupied a full century, and the fi-
nancing of the army staggered from expedient to expedient up to the
Revolution of 1789. Yet the expedients worked, most of the time, and the
state swelled in size and power.

The statemakers and financiers faced formidable opposition. Ordinary
people resisted the rising taxes, especially when the taxes cut into the
necessities of local life and when they visibly profited the local
bourgeoisie. Nobles, great and small, fought the growth of a rival civil
power and a threat to their own power to tax and exploit the local

population. On the principle that the enemy of my enemy is my friend, the rather different interests aligning both nobles and poor commoners against the crown sometimes produced a powerful alliance. The alliance could mean a regional rebellion far fiercer than the typical noble conspiracy or the commonplace popular resistance to the tax collector. As the *Mercure*'s commentator said back in 1605, the rebels' usual "pretext" was, indeed, "to lighten the people's burden, and to make sure that those who were charged with the administration of justice would do better in the future." If he was also right that "their real hope was to fish in troubled water and, in the guise of the public good, to fatten themselves up at the expense of the poor people," then we can see why the "pretext" had wide popular appeal. Popular rebellions, many of them tied to the conspiracies of great nobles, racked the French seventeenth century. The greatest cluster of them all—the series of popular, noble, and judicial struggles with the crown that we call the Fronde—almost destroyed the monarchy.

With this background, it is easier to understand several puzzling features of France in the seventeenth century: (*a*) the extent to which popular collective action consisted of resistance to someone else's attempt to take something away—the recurrent rebellions against taxation being the most dramatic cases; (*b*) the coexistence of incessant rebellion with successful statemaking; (*c*) the persistent, and ultimately successful, efforts of the crown to neutralize a fractious nobility via cooptation, concession, and repression; and (*d*) the curious coalitions that sometimes sprang up among Protestant zealots, Catholic nobles, and nominally Catholic citizens of the towns. All of these make sense in the light of a vigorously expanding state, seconded by a growing bourgeoisie whose interests coincided temporarily with those of the state.

Consider the province of Quercy in 1623. Bypassing the previous arrangement by which the provincial estates granted tax revenues to the crown, the king had established the Election to collect taxes directly. The officers of the Election had bought their offices and gained their incomes from the taxes they brought in for the crown. Word spread, says the *Mercure*, that the region's powerful people would support a popular rising to abolish the Election. When the new officers came to take office,

a certain Douat, a Quercy native . . . about fifty-five or so (who fooled with horoscopes, was a great physiognomist, and fortune-teller, and had always said he would die in action), having gone from parish to parish secretly agitating the populace, put himself into the field at the head of five thousand men, both peasants and other good-for-nothings who had been discharged from the armies since the peace. The specious pretext of this great rising was the establishment of the new Elections, by which they said the province would be overburdened with *tailles*, and with the salaries, benefits, fees for signing the rolls, and other revenues that had been assigned to the Election officers. Furthermore, that the richest people of the province, who had previously paid the heaviest *taille*, up to three or four hundred livres, having bought the offices for their exemption from the *taille*, they would push the *taille* onto the little people, including the *pro rata* surtaxes which are now due on past and present assessments [*Mercure françois* 1623: 473 – 474].

The rebels attacked the houses of the new officers; their force grew to 16,000 men. But the military governor of Quercy attacked them near Cahors, broke them up, and captured their leaders.

The next day, the 8th of June, the Marshal had Douat and Barau [a second chief] taken to Figeac for trial. The Provost sentenced Douat to have his head cut off, his body quartered, and his head impaled on a post at Figeac, and also that his four quarters would be taken to four of the principal cities of Quercy and suspended there. This was done the same day [*Mercure françois* 1623: 477].

Barau was hanged in his hometown 10 days later. Thus the Quercy rebellion ended like many others, with a few of its leaders punished spectacularly and the fiscal power of the crown (not to mention the privileges of the bourgeois who had bought the royal offices) confirmed by military force.

Except through the presence of the profiteering bourgeoisie, the experience of Quercy in the 1620s does not trace the trajectory of expanding capitalism very clearly. It does, on the other hand, show the interplay of statemaking and popular collective action. Statemaking impinged deeply and directly on the interests of ordinary people. When they could, ordinary people resisted the threat to their interests. But time and military might were on the side of the statemakers; the people tried repeatedly, and lost repeatedly. Before long, their favored allies, the provincial nobility, had been checked as well. From that point on, such popular rebellions as occurred posed a diminishing threat to the state. In fact, as France rolled into the eighteenth century popular collective action against the state declined somewhat, and action against profiteering landlords and merchants became more prominent. Whereas in the seventeenth century the tax rebellion and the attack on occupying troops or grasping officials had been the more visible forms of popular resistance, the eighteenth century brought food riots, occupations of disputed land, and struggles against the landlord's exactions to the fore. Once we see that the food riots acted against merchants and officials who backed merchants and that the landlords who stirred up the greatest dissension were those who bought most eagerly into the expanding cash-crop market, the shift away from statemaking to capitalism as the focus of popular collective action becomes manifest. The changes in collective action responded sensitively to the trends of structural change.

Do not take this sketch of seventeenth-century France as a model for the historically grounded sociological analysis I am advocating. It lacks the painstaking confrontation of the sources with alternative interpretations in which historians excel. It lacks the explicit modeling, precise conceptualization, careful measurement, and deliberate comparison that are the emblems of good social-scientific work. It lacks the essential specification of the forms and changes of statemaking, capitalism, and collective action from one era to the next. Later chapters in this book— "War and Peasant Rebellion in Seventeenth-Century France," "How . . . to Study British Contention," and others—set out fragments of the approach that I have in mind. This preliminary sketch simply evokes the problem—to situate social processes in time and place. The work requires a permanent encounter of sociology and history.

2
Computing History

A Computational Memory

An image of my early days as a graduate student sticks in my mind after almost 30 years. Half a dozen of us are standing around a clanking, whirring machine in a harshly lighted basement room. There in the middle stirs sociologist Samuel Stouffer, talking fast, cigarette swinging from his mouth, ashes showering his vest. Stouffer grabs a deck of punched cards, shoves them into the hopper at one end of the machine, pushes a button, and watches the cards sort themselves into glass-topped bins. He peers at the size of the various piles. Then he says, "OK. Now let's try breaking on religion." He whips each stack of cards from its bin and slaps it onto the glass above the bin. Then he grips the first stack, fans it out, drops it into the hopper again, taps to straighten the cards, sets a weight on top of the stack in the hopper, turns a crank, and pushes the button again.

We, the graduate students, were learning a crude but serviceable way of analyzing data. It consisted of translating arguments about social phenomena into statements about variables and units of analysis. (The units were most often individual survey respondents, and the variables, their responses to standardized questions, but neither was essential to the logic we absorbed with the cigarette smoke.) Then we were supposed to identify the variable to be explained, cast our explanation in terms of differences with respect to other variables, represent obvious alternative explanations as "control" variables, and then carry out a cross-classification of the units that would reveal whether they did, indeed, vary as expected.

We might, for example, have tried to determine whether people living on farms actually said they wanted more children than people in big cities, once we "controlled," or held constant, the present family positions of respondents in the two populations. The machine was not indispensable to this sort of analysis. In principle, one could do it with penciled tallies or with slips of paper sorted on a large table top. (I have done both things myself in emergencies.) Compared with the other alternatives that we knew, however, only the machine made the analysis quick and practical.

The clanking old machine was not, of course, an electronic computer. It was a counter—sorter, a contraption in which electrified metal brushes responding to the presence or absence of holes at different positions in a Hollerith card activated gates along a belt on which the cards were moving, thus shunting the cards into one bin or another, and counted the cards shunted into each bin. Although people who work with punched cards still use the quicker, smoother descendants of our old basement machine in getting their data ready for the computer, the counter—sorter has practically disappeared as a tool of analysis in the social sciences.

Still, the memory is useful. It sums up the predominant experience of social scientists with analytic machines until recent years: The machine has greatly increased the feasibility of procedures that were actually invented without reference to machines, or at least without any necessary connection to them. The analytic inventions occurred more or less independently of the existence of counter—sorters or computers. The diffusion of those inventions, however, depended closely on the availability of the machines.

Something else about that basement scene needs attention. Although Sam Stouffer taught us to admire the classic deductive progression from general theory to specific hypothesis to empirical test against real-life observations, he was a wizard of post hoc interpretation of findings. In the jargon of the time, his "let's try breaking on religion" meant dividing the sample into Protestants, Jews, and so on, in order to see if any new differences, or any new explanations of the old differences, showed up. We learned that part, too. The nature of the data and the implicit or explicit theories the investigator is working with will set limits on how many ad hoc explanatory variables he or she will introduce in this way. Nevertheless, the vaguer and the more variegated the arguments at the investigator's disposal, and the easier the introduction of one more explanatory variables, the greater the likelihood that the investigator will fashion and attach importance to spurious explanations.

The counter—sorter and the tabulating equipment that came with it heightened this risk somewhat by comparison with hand tallying and other such primitive procedures they replaced. Their net effect may still have been to reduce the number of spurious interpretations being seriously entertained by social scientists, because they came into wide use when theories were superabundant, determinate findings relevant to those theories quite rare, and cross-checking of doubtful explanations extremely difficult.

Computers and Social Scientists

The computer compounds the risk. The capacity to absorb, store, and manipulate large bodies of data, the easy introduction of complex, prepackaged statistical routines, the speedy efficiency of the machine (at least on its good days), and the tiny incremental effort ordinarily required to introduce one more analysis, one more variable, or one more observation—all reduce the cost of running vast exploratory analyses. If the self-discipline of social scientists and the determinacy of their theories do not increase at the same rate as the expansion in computing facilities available to them, the net effect is likely to be a growth of the number of spurious explanations of social phenomena having currency.

Depending on one's view of the intrinsic possibility of reliable knowledge about human social behavior, this worry may sound cynical, or it may sound irrelevant. Yet it follows pretty closely from the characteristic relationship of social scientists to their data. The directors of most university computing centers have, for example, had to deal with it in one way or another.

So far as I can tell from personal experience, the university-wide computing facilities that sprang up in the 1950s tended to organize around several interesting assumptions concerning their clientele: (a) that the users were primarily interested in computation as such, rather than in tabulation, compilation, reordering of large files, preparation of descriptive maps and graphs, content analysis of texts, and a variety of other uses to which computers have sometimes been put; (b) that the users would arrive with step-by-step descriptions of the computations they wished to perform and would want to translate each step into a command that the machine could follow; and (c) that the work involved extensive manipulations of relatively small volumes of input data. These assumptions appeared, among other places, in the early emphasis on short courses in FORTRAN (FORmula TRANslation) as the all-purpose preparation for computing, in the physical arrangement of input and output areas to accommodate clients who would ordinarily submit 30 or

40 cards of data and programs, and in the great shortage of facilities for plotting, mapping, reordering files, reading of texts, and the like.

Computation, formula translation, and low ratios of input to analysis do not describe the usual situation of the social scientists who were coming to the computer in the 1950s and 1960s. At the beginning most of us were interested mainly in the sort of reordering and tabulation of data we had previously done with such machines as counter — sorters. We knew little mathematics and found it difficult to transcribe the simple statistical operations we had learned to do with pencil and paper, slide rule, or desk calculator into logical sequences comprehensible to machines. Not much computation there, nor much preparation for programming an entire analysis.

What is more, the computer-bound social scientist most often wanted to do something simple but cumbersome to a large body of data: a rank ordering of all counties in the United States on per capita income, and then on the proportion of the labor force engaged in agriculture, perhaps, or a cross-tabulation by occupation and region of the stated party preferences of 2172 persons in a national sample survey. In short, they desired a high ratio of input to output and a very high ratio of input to computation. A good deal of the extensive development of computing facilities for the social sciences during the 1960s went into redressing the balance: extending the noncomputational capacities of the computer, packaging and simplifying the commands required to get the computer to carry out big but standard routines, and increasing the capacity of computing systems for input, storage, output, and transmission of large bodies of data.

No doubt my description applies least well to the economists of the 1950s and 1960s; although their analyses of national income and related phenomena required simplification of large masses of data, they were already quite accustomed to applying complex models to small numbers of observations. At the other extreme stood the historians. Even the minority who identified themselves with the social sciences, even the smaller minority who were working with material that could, in principle, be placed in machine-readable form, wanted lists, catalogs, tabulations, and other convenient descriptions of their data rather than systematic analyses of patterns, relationships, and correspondence to models. The first textbooks on quantification, statistical analysis, and computing for historians only began to appear, after all, around 1970. My description probably holds best for sociology and political science and loses accuracy as we move away from them.

Now, I am not naive enough to think that the puny demands of university social scientists alone produced the changes in computing that occurred after 1960. Some of them resulted from the increased use of the computer by branches of the natural and physical sciences, such as ecology, whose main need was for the simplification and ordering of large bodies of observational data. More, I think, resulted from business and military applications, which are often quite similar in form (if not in content) to social scientific analyses. In any case, during the later 1960s American social scientists in big centers of research finally began to have at their disposal computing facilities that were well suited to the characteristic approach of social scientists to their data. The 1970s went into expanding the number of people engaged in social science computing, into developing and diffusing large program packages for the handling of social science data, into the creation of systems in which multiple users who were dispersed in space could interact simultaneously with one another and with a large machine, and—at the end of the decade—into the proliferation of small, independent, relatively inexpensive machines with the capacity to do significant and varied computing jobs on their own.

The Historical Social Sciences

Let us look more closely at the experience of the historical social sciences. I mean the conglomeration of specialties that have three things in common:

1. They concentrate on human social relationships.
2. They deal with change over a substantial succession of particular times.
3. Their procedures yield conclusions that are generalizable, at least in principle, beyond the particular cases observed.

Those specialities do not group together in any one major discipline. They exclude most of sociology, even more of anthropology, almost all of psychology, much of economics, perhaps less—surprisingly—of geography, demography, and political science. Demographic history, econometric history, historical studies of social mobility, and long-term analyses of the determinants of political participation illustrate what I have in mind.

Note some common features of this brand of inquiry. First, it commonly involves the systematic accumulation of numerous, more or less uniform individual observations into a general portrayal of the phenomenon under study. Where the observations concern individual people, we call the procedure collective biography or prosopography. Where they concern firms, families, communities, or other units, we have no standard term. But we might call the whole approach collective history. Many American historians have been willing to let the observations of a Tocqueville or the life histories of a few entrepreneurs stand as their evidence of the opportunities for mobility in the nineteenth century, but a number of younger historians have been insisting on the study of occupational mobility for the entire population of whole communities. The most ambitious venture of this kind so far has been Stephan Thernstrom's person-by-person examination of Boston's adult male population from 1880 to 1970 (1973). (Among other things, Thernstrom discovered great stability in the rates of movement from manual to white-collar jobs and in the propensity of new migrants to stay in the city, despite large changes in the rate of in-migration, and an important shift from greater long-distance mobility among manual workers in the nineteenth century to greater long-distance mobility among white-collar workers today.)

Second, this sort of investigation ordinarily includes systematic comparison of standard units—populations, areas, periods, or something else—with respect to both the phenomena to be explained and the explanations proposed for them. Thus in their analysis of the rural uprising of 1830 in England, Eric Hobsbawm and George Rudé tabulate villages that rioted or did not riot by whether land had recently been enclosed, how much of the village population was nonagricultural, and so on. (As it turns out, recently enclosed and semiindustrial villages appear to have had the higher propensity to riot; altogether, the findings lend weight to explanations of the revolt in terms of the defense of particular local rights to land and work and cast doubt on explanations in terms of spontaneous reaction to short-run economic crisis.)

Third, the kind of inquiry I am identifying with the "historical social sciences" tends to rely on the explicit statement of concepts, hypotheses, and models, as well as the self-conscious matching of the observations to them. In his influential study of marketing in rural China, G. W. Skinner begins by laying out the logic of the central-place theory often employed by economic geographers and proceeds to show that the timing, interdependence, and geographical distribution of local and regional markets in pre-Communist China fall into the patterns anticipated by central-place theory. Skinner argues that the market system provided the framework for a wide range of other activities not obviously related to marketing—for example, the choice of marriage partners and the gathering of peasants for recreation—and finally points out the persistence of the fundamental patterns past the revolution of 1949. Skinner's studies launched a whole fleet of analyses of Chinese marketing patterns and their correlates.

Finally, quantification. The aggregation from individual to total population, the reliance on systematic comparison, and the explicit confrontation of fact and theory are not intrinsically quantitative. Yet all three are obviously hospitable to quantification in ways that many approaches to history are not. A case in point: David Herlihy seeks to learn whether, as some theories would lead us to expect, prosperity encouraged the Tuscan population of the fifteenth century to marry younger, have more children, and form larger households. He has enormous documentation at his disposal—notably the *catasto* of 1427, a document resulting from the effort to enumerate and describe every single one of the 50,000 — 60,000 persons eligible to pay taxes in the territory then controlled by Florence. We are not the least surprised to find him casting the crucial questions in quantitative form, by calculating fertility rates, mean household sizes, and the like. (Nor are we surprised to find that computers are doing a major part of the routine work, but let's save that for later.) Once he is committed to checking theory against fact by aggregating thousands of individual observations into comparisons over space, time, and social category, it is hard to imagine how Herlihy could proceed without quantifying a number of his main arguments. Yet dozens of historians before him have written histories of Tuscany and of Florentine families without a trace of quantification.

Current Countercurrents

My reliance on positive examples may obscure this important fact. Most inquiry into history does not fit my description of the historical social sciences. Most historians are not doing collective history, are not making systematic comparisons of standard units, are not self-consciously building models and confronting them with historical fact, are not casting their arguments in quantitative form. Nor do they want to. They are, on the whole, proud to be doing something else. They are often distressed that anyone should be building models, quantifying, and so on. Since the computer is quite unlikely to spread into those areas of history in which investigators lack or reject the habit of putting part of their work into quantitative form, the prospects that the computer will revolutionize historical analysis as a whole in the near future are slight indeed.

The faint possibility of such a revolution has nevertheless called forth indignant roars from some of the profession's strongest voices. The statements on the subject tend to confound computerization with quantification, to trot out examples (real or imagined) of trivial, illegitimate,

and/or misleading quantitative analysis, and then to call for a common
defense against the Huns. The enduring objections, however, do not
appear to center on existing misuses of computers and quantification.
Instead, they concern the possibility that quantitative historians will
abandon the humane depiction of real, whole persons, mistake their
statistical results for the reality, and—worst of all—communicate their
delusions to other historians.

Statements of this view are often written with passion and brilliance.
One of my favorite specimens of the genre comes from Richard Cobb, the
superb portraitist of cops, spies, criminals, rioters, revolutionaries, and
ordinary people of the revolutionary era in France. At one point in the
essay "Historians in White Coats," Cobb describes an investigation then
proceeding in the United States as

> the computerization of 516 urban riots, turbulences, disturbances, *fracas*,
> *prises-de-barbe*, semi-riots, *revolvérisations*, lynchings, stabbings, slaugh-
> ters, massacres, protests, collective threats, abusive slogans, provoca-
> tive songs, in France, for the whole period 1815—1914. The end-product will
> no doubt reveal some highly interesting patterns: that, for instance, market
> riots occur on market days, on or near the market, that marriage riots take
> place after weddings, that funeral riots take place either outside the church
> or near the cemetery or along the course of a funeral procession, that Satur-
> day riots take place on Saturday evenings, between 10 and 12 o'clock in the
> winter and between 11 and 1 o'clock in the summer, that is after the
> wineshops and *bals* have closed, that Sunday riots take place after Mass, that
> rent riots take place on rent days and that they are commoner in April and
> July than they are in January and October, that port riots take place on or
> near ports, that recruitment riots converge on railway stations or on bar-
> racks, that prison riots take place inside or opposite the prison, or both, that
> religious riots, especially in towns or *bourgs* in which there exist two or
> more antagonistic religious communities, favour Sundays, Catholic feast
> days, or St. Bartholomew's Day, or the Passover. Perhaps we thought we
> knew already; but now we *really* know; we have a Model. Riot has been
> tamed, dehumanized and scientificated [1971: 1528].

I had some trouble recognizing my creature in motley. But once I
realized that I was the originator of the investigation in question, I read
Cobb's account with fascination. It proves him a master of historical
fiction. Every detail is invented—the time span, the number of events, the
kinds of action covered, the questions asked, the answers given, the
whole point of the study. (In fact, the study runs from 1830 to the 1970s,
deals mainly with large-scale collective violence, and consists of a number of different efforts to determine the impact of urbanization, industrialization, and political centralization on patterns of collective action
and struggles for power in France, not to mention related work concern-

ing other western European countries. More details come later in this chapter.)

Yet some resemblances to the original are interesting, even disquieting. It is true, for example, that a number of the results of such an inquiry are bound to be trivial, and others, more or less self-evident after the fact. No one is stunned to discover that labor unions became more heavily involved in major French conflicts toward the end of the nineteenth century than they had been 50 years before. Unions had, after all, only existed in the shadows until their legalization in the 1880s.

The main reason for pursuing results that will appear obvious in retrospect is that not all of them are obvious in prospect. Some fly in the face of widely held opinions. In the investigation at hand, the widespread small-town participation in the rebellion of 1851 against Louis Napoleon's coup d'etat (when provincial France as a whole, sickened or disappointed by the course of the 1848 revolution, is supposed to have lapsed into apathy or conservatism) makes us rethink the whole process of political mobilization and demobilization in that period. Other findings help discriminate among several alternative readings of a process, each of which is plausible and therefore obvious in retrospect. Should we, for instance, expect crimes against persons and collective violence to vary together or to follow distinctive patterns in time and space? The latter is the case in modern France. But if we had found the former, there would have been plenty of commonsense rationalizations and sociological theories to make the findings self-evident.

It is also true (as Cobb indicates elsewhere in his essay) that this sort of inquiry is expensive, requires the organization of a research team, and relies relatively little on the traditional lonely encounter of one person with one document. It is true (as Cobb's reasoning suggests, despite the fact that his blurred vision of computing does not allow him to pick out the details) that the combination of high intitial investment and low marginal cost of additional items encourages the builder of a data file, once begun, to pack in all sorts of apparently useless information. It is true that the moving of some of these large machine-readable historical files into the public domain (which is beginning to happen now) facilitates the pursuit of bad hypotheses and meaningless correlations, as well as sound hypotheses and meaningful correlations. It is true, finally, that the scale and complexity of such an investigation produce important periods when the researchers are so preoccupied with problems of coding, file construction, statistical procedure, computer techniques, and coordination of the whole effort that they practically lose contact with the people, events, places, and times they are studying.

These are genuine costs. Nevertheless, it strikes me as perverse to count the costs alone without considering the benefits. Fortunately, working historians pay little attention to exhortations on one side or the other. They respond instead to concrete examples of procedures for getting answers to questions they are already pursuing. The problem is simply to understand why spokesmen for the profession should so regularly emphasize the costs of computing without mentioning the benefits. The answer, I suppose, is that the critics consider the accumulation of systematic knowledge about human behavior either impossible, dangerous, of little value, or a serious diversion from other more worthy pursuits.

Is History Computable?

It is not just that historians are usually impressionistic, belletristic, or just plain cantankerous—although each of these is often the case. By and large, the historical use of computers focuses on problems that include a large element of quantification. A number of traditional and legitimate historical problems simply do not lend themselves to quantification; they therefore remain unlikely prospects for work with computers. The intellectual gain from quantification in history generally rises with (a) the complexity of the models employed; (b) the importance of variation to the arguments at hand; (c) the number of units involved; and (d) the ease with which the phenomenon to be explained can itself be put into quantities. Historians, however, often find themselves trying to account for a single act of a single person by means of some general assertion about that person's character or situation. For my part, I wonder whether there is any means at all of verifying or falsifying statements of that variety. In any case, quantification is not likely to be the means.

Historical work in general has a large component of description, interpretation of texts, reconstitution of sequences, imputation of motives to actors, identification of single connections, pronouncement of judgments, and arrival at moral or political conclusions. In principle, machines do some of these things well. In practice, these capacities of computers are developing slowly, and historians—even historical social scientists—are doing little to encourage their development. Harry Hanham said in 1971 that photocopying machines had to that point exerted a far larger influence on historical practice as a whole than had computers. If he said it now, he would still be right. Photocopying machines do quickly and cheaply something that most historians are already much involved in doing—transcribing and collating texts. The everyday capacities of run-of-the-mill computer installations meet the existing needs of a far smaller group of historians. No substantial increase in the use of computers by historians is therefore likely to occur unless (a) the kinds of problems and explanations with which ordinary historians concern themselves change substantially; and/or (b) the practical capacity of local computer installations to deal with textual analysis, cataloging, indexing, sorting, sequencing, summarizing, and retrieving simply and cheaply expands to a large degree.

The chances that historians will make major changes in the kinds of problems and explanations they favor are slim, at least for the near future. Large technical changes in computing have made the second condition possible in principle but have not so far had much impact on historical work. Word-processing programs, for instance, now greatly simplify textual analysis, cataloging, indexing, sorting, sequencing, summarizing, and retrieving. With unlimited funds, it would not be hard to automate a significant part of the average historian's more routine work. It will not happen soon, in my opinion, because historians lack the power, the funds, and the inclination to make it happen.

We should therefore distinguish between the computer in history as practiced by historians and in the historical social sciences as practiced by people from a wide variety of disciplines. It is in the historical social sciences that we should expect to find rapid increases, and some innovations, in the use of computers. Why? Because it is there that the incentives to quantification are strong; some of the essential facilities, resources, and technical expertise are already available; and the attractiveness of anything that reduces the time, effort, and unit cost involved in dealing with complex analyses and large pools of data is great.

In his *Interessenpolitik und nationale Integration 1848/49*, Heinrich Best gives us a standard example of computer-based work in the historical social sciences. The revolutionary Frankfurt Parliament of 1848–1849, in the course of its efforts to construct a new German government, carried on an extensive debate over a classic nineteenth-century issue: protection versus free trade. Best carries on a careful, nonquantitative analysis of the terms, participants, and outcomes of the debate. One major segment of his discussion closes in on the petitions that different interest groups throughout Germany sent to the Parliament. Seeking evidence concerning the distribution of articulated public opinion on free trade, Best has made machine-readable descriptions of 3775 petitions originated from May 1848 through March 1849—timing, origin, signers, major demands, and so on. Altogether, 3372 of the 3775 petitions followed known exemplars circulated to guide the petition drive; that makes it easier to classify the petitions, although it also makes clear to what extent the petitioning resulted from an organized campaign. This is, as Best says, interest politics, not opinion polling.

Best conducts a variety of analyses of the data: geographic distribution, collaboration of different interest groups, specialization of occupational groups in one demand or another. One of the simpler and more telling tabulations treats the 2757 petitions in which the occupational groups represented among the signers are clearly designated. Here is the distribution of occupational groups among the protectionist and free trade petitions:

Occupational group	Percentage of all petitions in which the specified group appears	
	Protectionist	Free trade
Industrialists	16.4	6.1
Merchants	11.9	68.3
Farmers	20.8	30.1
Independent craftsmen	43.6	20.7
Craft workers	30.0	4.9
Office workers	3.2	2.0
Civil servants	2.9	8.9
Academic occupations	1.1	6.5
Agricultural workers	6.2	15.4
Wine and tobacco growers	33.9	.0
Number of petitions	2511	246

Industrialists, in other words, appeared in 16.4% of all the protectionist petitions, but in only 6.1% of the petitions calling for free trade; the percentages add to more than 100, of course, because more than one group often appeared among the signatories to the same petition. The petition analysis shows a strong tendency for craft workers to line up on the protectionist side, whereas merchants mobilized on the side of free trade—unsurprising after the fact, but useful to have specified. Some of Best's analyses include statistical measurements of the strength and direction of relationships among different characteristics of the petitions. On the whole, however, this treatment of occupations typifies the use Best makes of the computer; the machine performs as a large, precise tabulator. The computer-based analyses lead naturally to closer examinations—both quantitative and qualitative—of the organization of the petition drives within particular trades, of the regional distribution of freetrade and protectionist petitions, of the relationship between protectionism and involvement in long-distance trade, of the fractionation of the German bourgeoisie over trade policy. In short, the computer sums up the evidence for and against conclusions that have nothing blatantly quantitative to them, and which one might have been able to argue without any numbers at all. Despite some glimmers of change, Best's work still represents the typical use of the computer in the historical social sciences. Before examining other applications of computers, let us take a closer look at the character of those disciplines.

Development and History in the Social Sciences

The historical social sciences provide an important object lesson in the responsiveness of scholars to changes in the world about them. The multiplication of new states at the end of World War II turned the interests of a wide variety of Western scholars toward the elaboration of schemes intended to anticipate—and perhaps even to guide—the political, economic, and demographic changes that would take place in the non-Western world. The most popular of those schemes postulated standard paths and processes of "development." We had theories and programs for economic development, of course, but political development, demographic development, educational development, social development, urban development, and still other purported standard processes also came in for a great deal of attention in the social sciences. The models for the developmental schemes came most often from readings of Western history; W. W. Rostow's scheme for stages of economic growth, for instance, began explicitly with an interpretation of English experience. The developmental schemes proposed in the 1940s and 1950s all turned out to have great weaknesses, both in their own terms and as tools for the analysis, anticipation, or guidance of changes in the non-Western world.

The nature of those weaknesses need not detain us here. For present purposes, it is important to realize that dissatisfaction with them drove a number of social scientists back to look more closely at the conceptions of the Western experience that had, implicitly or explicitly, inserted themselves into available theories of development. This happened somewhat independently, and at different points in time, in economics, demography, political science, and other fields, but it happened widely. The net effect of the two moves—first toward formulating theories of long-run development, then toward reexamining the fit between such theories and the historical record—reintroduced long time spans into disciplines that had been concentrating rather heavily on the short run. Julius Rubin describes the situation in economics, while discussing Ester Boserup's *Conditions of Agricultural Growth:*

> It has been a very long time since the last simple, centuries-spanning theory of economic — demographic relations was proposed. After Malthus, Ricardo and John Stuart Mill, economists turned — many with a sense of relief, no doubt — from the problems of the ages to the down-to-earth, short-term analysis of a market economy whose success and stability could be taken for granted. The problems of the long-term, of analytic history, sank into the underground of economics, with rare exceptions neglected in the universities until the Second World War. And though after the war the renewed perception of economic development as a major social problem produced an immense amount of research and generalization, the great economic — demographic framework remained the same: neo-Malthusians are hard to distinguish from paleo-Malthusians. Mrs. Boserup has taken advantage of that research, particularly of the recent advances in our knowledge of agricultural systems, to suggest a modification of the classical framework and has thereby irritated some economists, who are skeptical of all long-term theories and large-scale frameworks, while she has given hope to historically-oriented social scientists who are badly in need of a new Ariadne's thread [1972: 35].

Between John Stuart Mill and Ester Boserup, to be sure, a good deal of economic history was written. Yet economists (with the important exception of Marx and his followers) generally avoided economic history and treated it as an inferior good.

Only after World War II, with the new urgency and respectability acquired by the analysis of economic growth, did any substantial number of people trained primarily in economics turn back to the serious analysis of historical sequences, problems, and materials. But then it happened in a big way. It happened in such a big way, indeed, that by the early 1960s economic historians who received most of their training in history found themselves pressed hard by youngsters who spoke a mathematical language, built models, tried to unearth the buried economic assumptions in older arguments concerning such phenomena as slavery, the building of railroads, or technological change in agriculture, and employed considerably different standards of evidence from those of their elders. What is more, the youngsters frequently used computers to collate their data or to perform their computations.

Thus important parts of economic history became econometric history, or "cliometrics." Economists were precocious in all these regards. But similar processes created new specialties at the meeting points of history with demography, sociology, geography, and other social sciences. In all of them there was at least one moment of sharp confrontation between the oldsters who were accustomed to offering comprehensive, sympathetic, narrative accounts of their material and the newcomers with their models, their jargon, their numbers, their computation — and, many oldsters said, their arrogance. Their ideas and procedures crystallized into new specialties: the historical social sciences.

Historical Demography as an Illustration

Historical demography illustrates the current situation of the historical social sciences. Demography has a reasonable claim to have been the first of the social sciences to take something like its contemporary Western form. From its seventeenth-century emergence in England as "Political arithmetic," demography has recurrently dealt with historical materials and long spans of time. In the nineteenth century, however, the development of censuses and related means of collecting detailed data at particular points in time shifted the study of population away from historical concerns. As the standard data, procedures, and theories of demography crystallized, they converged on short-run processes and on the comparison of different populations at the same point in time. Even today, two-thirds or more of the average demographic textbook deals with those ahistorical matters. The substantive chapters of George W. Barclay's standard *Techniques of Population Analysis*, for instance, cover:

- Rates and ratios
- Accuracy and error
- The life table
- The study of mortality
- Measurement of fertility
- Growth of population
- Migration and the distribution of population
- Manpower and working activities

The longest span of continuous observation for any particular population discussed in the book, furthermore, is 10 years. Demography crystallized as a nonhistorical social science.

Nevertheless, a nice dialectic was working. The very accumulation of censuses in the nineteenth and twentieth centuries and the very improvement in the measurement of fertility, mortality, and related processes made it increasingly clear that Western countries were undergoing long-run demographic transformations that could be plausibly related to the industrialization and urbanization of the West after 1750. In the 1920s and 1930s Western demographers formulated the idea of a standard "demographic transition" occurring country by country throughout the world. In David Eversley's neat summary:

> This "theory" shows that countries go through various stages of population change: beginning with high birth and death rates allowing a low fluctuating rate of increase (if any), they pass through a phase of increasing death control which leads to very high rates of growth, and finally into the last stage where the pressures set up by fast growth produce some control of the birth-rate which results in a considerable slowing down of the increase. Though this is exactly what happened in all western countries some time between 1800 and 1900, and in Japan rather later, and is beginning to happen in some of the more affluent third world countries, it really tells us very little. The "transition" may last 100 years, and indeed in some countries we do not yet know whether it will ever occur at all, or whether their problems will not after all be "solved" by Malthusian disasters [1971: 1151].

The last two or three decades of effort to refine this argument, check its applicability to the actual patterns of change in particular Western countries, verify the alternative explanations conventionally given for the declines in fertility and mortality, and judge if and how such a transition is likely to occur in the rest of the world have shaken demographers' confidence in all simple versions of the theory. They have not yet produced an acceptable substitute. But they have stimulated an important series of investigations in the demographic history of England, France, and a half-dozen other countries, mainly in western Europe. These investigations have created a new discipline: historical demography.

The computer played no important part in the creation of the new discipline. (As we shall see later, however, it is playing an important part in the discipline's current work.) Historical demography grew apart from demography, economics, and history by refashioning elements drawn from each of them. The most significant elements, as I see them, were (a) basic descriptive schemes and models of "stable populations" drawn from demography; (b) econometric tools adopted from economics for the purpose of testing the applicability of alternative models to actual historical observations; and (c) creation of new procedures for extracting demographic measurements from registers of births, deaths, and marriages, old enumerations of population, and other such bulky sources long known to historians but long neglected for lack of any effective way of exploiting them.

The invention of the procedure called "family reconstitution" probably made the largest difference. The most important contributions came from Louis Henry, a demographer at the Institut National d'Etudes Démographiques in Paris, who began with relatively little interest in history as such, but with a strong desire to get at long-run population dynamics.

Family reconstitution is one of those bright ideas that is perfectly obvious once stated. It consists of accumulating the individual, scattered records of births, deaths, and marriages occurring in a locality into family dossiers relating the events to one another. If the registration is fairly complete, if the population does not move too much, and if it is usually possible to match a person mentioned in a given record with a family and with other mentions of the same person, the dossiers will yield tolerably good estimates of the vital rates prevailing in the population as a whole. The record of a wedding, for example, may not include the ages of the spouses. But if we also have birth records for them, we can calculate their ages at marriage. Again, if the bride has her first child 2 years later, we can calculate her age at first birth without difficulty.

To the extent that registration is incomplete, the population mobile, and the identification of individuals uncertain, the job gets harder and the estimates become less trustworthy. The procedure is possible in important parts of Europe from the seventeenth century onward only because almost everyone invoked religious ceremonies for births, marriages, and deaths, and the parish clergy kept comprehensive registers of the baptisms, weddings, and burials at which they officiated. In those rarer places where civil registration was equally complete before the nineteenth century, it is of course possible to follow a similar procedure.

Hand reconstitution of families is tedious. It takes a long time. It requires numerous small judgments. It produces large files. And calculating vital rates from those large files is a fairly complicated operation. This is where the computer can come in. In fact, the extensive use of the computer in family reconstitution is just beginning. Although scores of scholars, especially in France, have reconstituted the populations of individual parishes over substantial periods of time, none of them seems to have done the major part of his or her work by machine. The two research teams that have done the most extensive analyses of multiple communities are the one founded by Louis Henry at the Institut National d'Etudes Démographiques in Paris and the collaborative venture of Peter Laslett, E. A. Wrigley, and R. S. Schofield at Cambridge University. The Paris group does not employ computers for any of its main tasks. The Cambridge group has experimented with computers for years; at this point, however, it has not completed the reconstitution of a single parish by machine. Other research teams doing related work in Tuscany, Quebec, Iceland, Normandy, and elsewhere have all reached about the same stage: having experimental runs or successful programs for part of the whole inquiry complete, but not having put into operation a true computer-based system for family reconstitution. The basic cataloging, collating, and computing now present no insuperable difficulties. The process seems to encounter immovable obstacles, however, when it arrives at the points at which the investigators now use their own judgment to manage uncertainties and gaps in the evidence.

One of the more interesting difficulties in setting up such a system results from the uncertainty involved in matching different records with the "same" person. The difficulty appears in all sorts of collective history, not just in family reconstitution. In his study of Boston, for example, Stephan Thernstrom calls it the Michael Murphy problem. When dozens of Michael Murphys are born every year, and the supplementary information supplied with birth or marriage certificates is sparse, how do you decide *which* Michael Murphy got married 20 years later? What about misspellings, or variant spellings, of the same name: Are Michael Murphy, born in 1874 (birth record), and Michal Murphey, born in 1874 (marriage record), and Michael Murphey, 60 years old in 1935, the same person? Every one of the simple and obvious solutions is susceptible to introducing systematic errors into the analysis: dealing only with uncommon names, throwing away all uncertain matches, matching with the first plausible fit, matching randomly, and so forth. Every investigator faced with the problem so far has adopted some sort of hand solution that requires subjective judgment. Here is a problem worth giving to the computer: applying an explicit set of decision rules to all such matches, tagging each completed record as to the degree of certainty in its matching, identifying all unmatchable observations and their characteristics, calculating the possible effects of different kinds of matching errors on the demographic parameters being estimated from the whole body of data. In fact, most of the research teams that are using computers for family reconstitution or related operations are also working seriously on computer-based solutions to exactly this set of problems.

Does all this mean that the use of the computer for historical demography is all promise and no accomplishment? No. At this moment historical demographers are using computers to collate the material from huge sources, such as the Florentine *catasto* of 1427, to perform a wide range of time-series analyses for detecting the relationships between demographic and economic fluctuations, testing models proposed for the explanation of regional differences in fertility, and dozens of other purposes. Few students now learning the specialty will enter their professional lives without some competence in computing.

Another Personal Note: This Time, Collective Action

Early in the 1960s, I began some research that has continued to this day. It is the same research to which Richard Cobb responded with such spirit and imagination in the quotation reproduced earlier in this chapter. At the start, I thought my subject was "political upheaval" and that my evidence concerned "political disturbances" in France from 1830 to 1960. Both terms turned out to be unfortunate: vague and tendentious at the same time. The adoption of that maladroit vocabulary followed from my being clearer about the negative side of the problem than about the positive—having grave doubts about standard ideas that treated political conflict as a consequence of the disorganization and disorientation produced by rapid, extensive social change, but having only an uncertain sense that existing interests and social organization played a significant part in "protest," "disorder," and "upheaval." That uncertainty led me to organize the research as a mirror image of the ideas I was combating. In brief: I began assembling a large catalog of violent events in France from 1830 onward and began organizing a body of evidence about changes going on in different periods and regions within that frame. Together, the two bodies of information would, I thought, permit a sort of epidemiology of violent events, by means of comparisons between rapidly changing and slowly changing places, and so on.

It is hard to describe that research program without breast-beating, nail-biting, and special pleading. After all, for a long time much of my effort has gone into criticizing and correcting my initial errors. Let me settle for two statements, one negative and one positive. The plans I laid out in the early 1960s had important defects: an implicit acceptance of the epidemiological analogy; the sharp focus on violent events, to the near exclusion of the nonviolent collective action out of which group violence ordinarily flows; the weak representation of power and struggles for power in both the questions and the materials. They did, however, have some compensating virtues: a large, dense, carefully assembled body of evidence extending over a substantial range of time, space, and social settings; a deliberate provision for comparisons among times, places, and settings, including those in which little or no visible conflict had occurred; the extension of the analysis to other forms of collective action—notably, strikes—which were not intrinsically violent; a design that allowed significant reformulations of the guiding questions and easy incorporation of new evidence as it became available.

Why be so compulsive? Certainly not because given enough facts, the facts would speak for themselves. From the start the inquiry required a continuous interweaving of theory, concept, and fact. The problem was, indeed, that it was all too easy to pluck promising facts from the historical record and string them together in an ample, plausible, and yet fallacious account of a sequence of collective action. Exactly that has happened repeatedly in the reconstruction of "social movements" such as socialism and feminism. Suppose we wanted to take seriously the investigation of the ways in which the expansion of capitalism and the growing hegemony of national states affected the ways that ordinary people could and did act together on their interests? Then, presumably, we would want reliable evidence concerning the impact of statemaking and capitalism on the interests of ordinary people; concerning the influence of statemaking and capitalism on the means of collective action that were, in principle, available to those same people; concerning the processes by which people gained, lost, or failed to acquire the means, the will, and the opportunity to act together; concerning the actual varieties and circumstances of collective action. Presumably we would want that evidence to permit comparisons among different phases and modes of statemaking and capitalism, among different constellations of interests, among different sorts of people, among alternative forms of action—and, for that matter, of inaction. There was no way to single out the crucial interests, actions, and transitions without collecting a great deal of information about ostensibly trivial matters—about the day-to-day context within which crucial events occur. From the start, in short, a serious commitment to the problem entailed (a) concern with detailed, systematic comparison; and (b) willingness to examine a great deal of evidence that would ultimately turn out to be uninteresting, inconsequential, or even boring in itself. The research on France represented a compromise between these desiderata and the practical need to have some results to stay up the inquiry before it collapsed of its own weight. Thus my research group focused on one country, on a mere thirteen or fourteen decades, on strikes and violent events. Thus the group created a research design that selected only a small portion of the available evidence.

From the perspective of computing, what was that design? Essentially to build and merge two large sets of files—of *contexts* and of *events*. The first set described the contexts: for the most part, characteristics of geographical areas of France at different points in time. The most common data set within this class provided a numerical description of some feature—the population's age—sex distribution, the industrial composition of the labor force, or something else—for all of the 86 to 90 *départements* into which France was divided during our period. Other sets contained limited amounts of information for all large cities, for major categories of workers, for France as a whole in a series of years, or for other units of observation. Much of the information in these files simply transcribed entries from the census and from similar national compilations. The material was voluminous, straightforward, and mostly numerical. As a result, it was not hard to devise punched-card transcriptions of the data. The real difficulties only began with the attempt to synthesize evidence from different sources; there, competing definitions, changing geographical boundaries, and inconsistent categories wreaked the ruin they always do. The structure of the evidence usually made it much easier to portray variations in social conditions at the same point in time than to examine *changes* in those social conditions. We could not blame the computer for that; the evidence itself presented the problem.

The second large set of files described the events: strikes, on the one hand, occasions involving collective violence, on the other. The strike files did little more than transcribe our basic sources (such as the *Statistique des Grèves et des Recours en Conciliation* for the years 1890 – 1935) in numerical codes, following the order of the source. But files concerning violent events went farther. They broke the description into chunks corresponding to a simple dramaturgy: several collective actors (*formations*) carried on a sequence of actions and interactions (*formation sequence* and *event sequence*) in one or more places (*communes*); meanwhile, a chorus, or *coder*, offered inferences, summaries, and comments. Stated as a series of punched cards, the record of an event looked like this:

One card describing each *commune* in which the event took place

Two cards describing each *formation* taking part in the event

One card describing the sequence of up to 34 *actions* for each formation or subformation (subset of formation who acted separately at some point in the event)

One card describing the sequence of up to 34 *general states of the action* for the event as a whole

Two cards describing the event as a whole

One card identifying the sources and characterizing the coding of the event

Up to 9 cards containing general English-language comments on the coding of the event as a whole

Up to 99 cards, keyed to specific locations in the previous cards, containing English-language comments explaining, elaborating, or qualifying the coding decisions

The peculiar numerical limits to various items resulted from the need to produce a standard-format, standard-length record, identical in form from one event to the next. And why that? Because we were heading toward the use of computer program packages, designed for social science analyses, that required just such a succession of standard records.

We set down the comments and a few other pieces of information in ordinary English, for easy retrieval of qualitative material concerning the event and our coding of it. But for the rest we adopted the standard social science process: inventing numerical codes for each category of information we wanted to record, with a separate number representing each distinction we wanted to make within the category. Many distinctions took judgments, sometimes difficult or idiosyncratic judgments. In the case of some unhappy codes, two coders making the same judgment of the same event tended to arrive at different conclusions. Here, for example, is an unreliable code:

COORDINATION OF THE DISTURBANCE AS A WHOLE

0 Insufficient information
1 No evidence of response to each other's commands by formations participating in the disturbance, and no indication that the interaction of the formations followed a known, established pattern
2 Some response to each other's commands, but in general the interaction of the formations neither responded to commands nor followed a known, established pattern
3 No evidence of response to each other's commands, but in general the interaction of the formations followed a known, established pattern
4 A significant part of the interaction of the formations consisted of response to each other's commands, but another significant part of it was uncoordinated
5 A significant part of the interaction of the formations consisted of response to common norms, but another significant part was uncoordinated
6 In almost all respects, the interaction of the formations was coordinated by established rules and/or deliberate commands
9 Other: MANDATORY COMMENT

In 37 pairs of independent applications of the code to randomly selected events, the coders only agreed 22 times, and 13 of those agreements said 0 = insufficient information. In designing that code, I obviously missed my mark. For a relatively reliable code, we may turn to our recording of the "detailed occupation" of members of a formation:

0 Insufficient information or not applicable
1 Peasants
2 Ouvriers (unspecified)
3 Artisans: COMMENT if maitres, compagnons, or apprentis are specified
4 Combination of workers and artisans: COMMENT encouraged
5 Low white-collar workers: clercs, commis, employes
6 Intermediate managerial: direction, cadres, responsables
7 Patrons, chefs
9 Others and combinations: MANDATORY COMMENT

Coders agreed on these judgments 94% of the time.

What differentiates the two codes? The first not only requires a synthetic judgment but also makes that judgment rather abstract. The second comes much closer to material likely to appear directly in the texts being coded. Almost none of our sources ever discusses coordination and established patterns of interaction as such, whereas many of them name peasants, workers, and others as actors in just those terms. The difference in quality between the two codes follows an important general principle: The more abstract the code, and the greater the judgment it requires, the worse the code will be. A bad code has multiple disadvantages: It is unreliable, its results are often inaccurate, and it places crucial analytic decisions in the hands of coders rather than in the hands of those who will actually carry out the analysis.

By these standards, *neither* of the codes reproduced in the preceding paragraphs actually has much to be said for it. Even the more reliable code requires substantial judgment, employs some abstract categories, and hides analytic decisions in the descriptions of the evidence. Yet codes of this general sort were, and are, common in the preparation of historical material for machine processing. The desire to contain the choices within the 10 positions available in a single column of an 80-column punched card leads to a reduction of the actual observations into a small number of categories, few or none of them corresponding exactly to material in the texts being coded. The bending of the code to the likely needs of quantitative analysis suggests the use of numerical tags and their array in something like the headings of a table or the intervals of a scale.

Plenty of information disappears through the cracks in such a scheme. Sometimes, for example, our text told us that a given formation consisted of *garçons charpentiers:* roughly, 'carpenters' helpers.' In the preceding code we would designate them as artisans, adding the label *garçons* as a comment. In another code, they would show up as belonging to the *industries du bois*, the wood-handling industries. In other codes, we would designate them as being male, as having no stated political affiliation, as bringing with them "insufficient information" to decide whether they were local or nonlocal, and so on through a dozen different items. The whole procedure touches on the ludicrous. We have a single item of information: our source's identification of one set of actors as carpenters' helpers. On the one hand, we take a dozen different codes to describe them and reify a whole series of judgments in the process. On the other hand, we never quite get the exact information at hand into the record: We have no precise, differentiated code for *garçons charpentiers*. An ineffectual effort, at best.

In the days when we relied on the old counter—sorter as an analytic instrument, the reduction of rich evidence to 10-position numerical codes representing the categories of a table or a scale had a certain logic. Without that reduction, the task soon became unmanageable. But counter—sorter rigidity has long since disappeared from computing. Whatever excuse I might have had for devising those awkward codes in the early 1960s, the excuse has lost its plausibility.

Richer, More Flexible Records

For the sake of contrast, let us look at a broadly similar effort that is now going on. My research group is now transcribing information about "contentious gatherings" that occurred somewhere in Great Britain during the years from 1828 through 1834. We are also following the contentious gatherings of the London region—Middlesex, Kent, Surrey, and Sussex—back to the 1750s. A *contentious gathering*, according to our definition, was an occasion on which 10 or more people gathered in a publicly accessible place and visibly made claims that, if realized, would affect the interests of some person(s) outside the group. The definition obviously requires a number of further specifications: rules for judging whether 10 or more people were present, and so on. Carefully applied to the available historical materials, it captures almost all events that historians commonly label "protests," "riots," "disturbances," "strikes," "demonstrations," and the like, plus a considerable number of orderly gatherings in the course of which people made demands, prepared petitions, or otherwise voiced their will. The materials available for any given year yield hundreds, sometimes thousands, of contentious gatherings in one part of Great Britain or another.

Nowadays we need not reduce our information on complex, various events to stark numerical codes. Existing computer facilities and routines make it feasible to do one of two things: (a) make the entire body of texts that we are examining machine-readable, and then proceed through machine-assisted searches and summaries of the texts; and (b) ask standard questions of the texts but record the answers as verbal transcriptions or paraphrases of material in the texts themselves. For the sake of economy and discipline, we have taken the second course in our study of Great Britain. The dramaturgy still resembles that of the French events: Various files describe whole contentious gatherings, places, individual formations, action phases, sources, and comments. We can now accommodate an unlimited number of any of these subdivisions, merely by adding another record, and then another. (The most complex event we have discovered in the years 1828 and 1829—a large rally against Catholic rights held on Penenden Heath, Kent, in October 1828—involved, by our count, 28 formations and 51 action phases.) Thus the machine-readable description of the event as a whole grows with the event's complexity and with the volume of available detail.

The most important break with our practice of the 1960s, however, is this: writing the machine-readable description as a series of standardized, English-language responses to a sort of questionnaire presented on the screen of a computer terminal and monitored instantly by the computer for internal consistency and for correctness of format. After we have collated all the material we have concerning a given event, decided whether the event qualifies as a contentious gathering, and organized the material into a series of answers to the questions we know will come from the computer, one of us sits at the terminal keyboard, calls for the questionnaire, and begins to type in answers to the items on the screen.

A simple, unimportant event will illustrate the procedure without flooding the discussion with detail. London's *Morning Chronicle* carried the following article on 4 February 1828:

> On Monday night, George Wiltshire, and two other men went into a public-house in this town for refreshment, where they met about thirty soldiers (Fusileers) and several other persons. Wiltshire, by accident, trod upon the foot of one of the soldiers, but immediately apologised for having done so. The soldier, however, insisted that it was an intentional insult; some of the company thought the matter should be passed over, others instigated the man to violence, and a general uproar ensued. Not thinking their party sufficiently strong, the soldiers sent for a number of their companions from an adjoining room. A desperate scuffle took place, in which Wiltshire had his head laid open in a dreadful manner with a quart pot, it is supposed by the soldier in question. The officer on guard at the Castle, and the constable, were immediately sent for, and tranquillity was soon restored. The soldier who was the subject of the disturbance has been placed in confinement, under the supposition that he committed the assault on Wiltshire, which is partly confirmed by the fact of his giving him six shillings and a sixpence to compromise the matter, and it is understood he will be punished for the offence. The wounded man received prompt surgical aid from the Dispensary, and is in a fair way of recovery.—These drunken brawls, or, as *The Post* more politely terms them, "irregularities," are becoming the most regular affairs possible, being of almost nightly occurrence—*Windsor Express*.

The following day's London *Times* carried an almost identical story, without the attribution to the *Windsor Express*. Windsor's barroom brawl barely made it into our category of contentious gatherings. The clear division between soldiers and civilians, the claim of an intentional insult, and the indications of a degree of deliberation among the soldiers combined to tip the event into the sample.

The mention of "Monday" made a date of 28 January probable, so we numbered the contentious gathering 828 01 28 03—the third event enumerated for 28 January 1828. We listed the formations involved as:

01 Fusileers
02 Wiltshire, George
03 Someone [the person who sent for the constable]
04 Constable
05 Soldier [the one who was arrested]

We then read into the computer those formation names, the place (a public house in Windsor), and other information about the event and our sources. Figure 2.1 shows an approximation of the action-phase section, as we fed it into the computer. In each case, we list:

Two sequence numbers, the second number running 01 . . . 02 . . . in cases of two or more simultaneous actions
The identity of the "subject" formation(s)—the formation(s) performing the action in question
The identity of the "object" formation(s)—the formation(s), if any, serving as the object of the action in question
An action verb, stated as a present-tense version of the verb in the text when possible, otherwise marked # and inferred from the text
A transcription, as long as necessary, of the relevant text

In this way we standardize the form of the machine-readable record yet retain much of the original text's richness. As we proceed, the computer screens the entries to make sure that they are internally consistent and within established limits.

Our procedure avoids most of the difficulties of abstraction, judgment, and omission of detail illustrated by the codes for French events I presented earlier in this chapter. Instead of recording separate codes designating a formation as "artisan," "male," and so on, the equivalent of our British codes would simply record *garçons charpentiers* once and leave it at that. To be sure, at some point we are likely to want to classify our formations as artisan, peasant, and so on, to sort them by sex, or to aggregate them in some way. That works neatly. Instead of going back to the individual records to add new codes, we call up a machine-generated "dictionary" listing all variants of the replies given to a certain question over a specified set of records—including, if need be, all records we have ever coded. For example, the names of all formations enumerated 10 times or more in the events of 1828 are:

benefit society (10 times)	mob (15)
committee (15)	officials (18)
Common Council (14)	parishioners (17)
Friendly Society (19)	Parliament (326)
gameskeeper or gameskeepers (15)	poachers (20)
government (18)	Protestant Dissenters (163)
inhabitants (38)	Select Vestry (18)
magistrate or magistrates (23)	someone (31)
mayor (13)	Wardmote (14)

For many purposes, we might want to combine one or another of these formation names with others that appeared less frequently: for example, the Catholics (8), Irishmen (9), King (8), Lord Mayor (6), officers (9), or Vestry (7). For the year 1829, the comparable list looks like this:

Congregation (10 times)	men (12)
constables (14)	mob (30)
crowd (25)	parishioners (12)
deputation (10)	Parliament (259)
gentlemen (12)	persons (38)
government (19)	police (16)
inhabitants (52)	Protestant Dissenters (64)
King (13)	Select Vestry (16)
magistrates (37)	someone (30)
manufacturers (14)	weavers (46)
masters (15)	Wellington, Duke of (11)
mayor (22)	

For some purposes, one might want to combine the police and the constables on the list; for other purposes, one might want to add less frequent formations, such as Dissenters (4) or Unitarians (7). The virtue of the machine-readable dictionary is to make the combinations easy and flexible.

Note that the dictionary itself contains useful information. The prominence of religious groups on the 2 years' lists, for example, reflects the agitation over Catholic Emancipation and the repeal of the Test and Corporation Acts. The greater number of industrial names—manufacturers, masters, weavers, and so on—in 1829 reveals the rising frequency of industrial conflict in that year. In order to use these clues for analytical purposes, we have only to sort the items in the dictionary into the categories we have in mind; the computer will then sort and tally the individual records as we wish. When we have a useful set of categories, we store it in the machine for future reference.

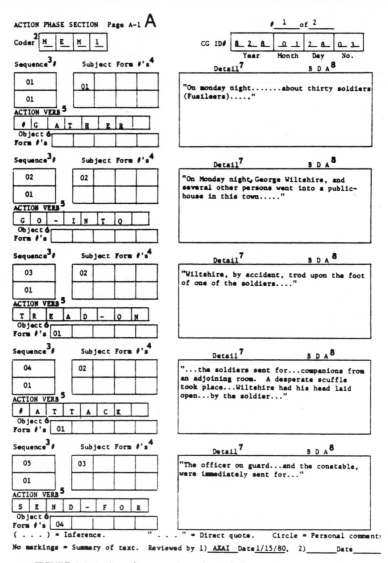

FIGURE 2.1. Action-phase section of a coded contentious gathering.

As compared with the stiff procedures of our work on France, these techniques add greatly to both the precision of our machine-readable records and the power of our analyses. Yet the basic computer routines resemble inventory-control procedures that are already in common use among libraries, parts departments, and auto-rental agencies. For some reason, they have not caught on quickly as approaches to social science

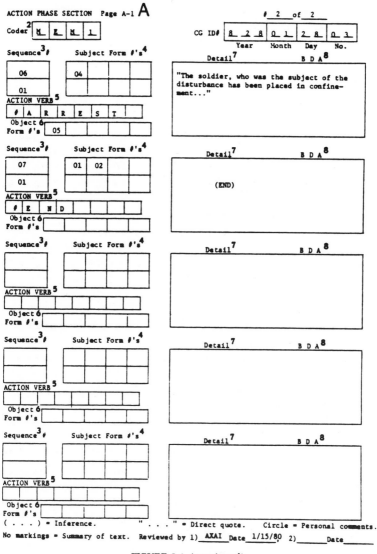

FIGURE 2.1. (*continued*)

research and have barely appeared at all in historical work. Social scientists, including historical researchers, cling to numerical codes and to records in standard, fixed-length formats. That the most widely available program packages for social science data analysis require numerical data and fixed-length formats encourages researchers to cling to those ways of the 1960s. As news of interactive, direct-entry, alphabetical, variable-length coding spreads, however, more and more historical researchers will surely take it up.

In Sum

I have concentrated my review of computing on the two fields with which I am most familiar: historical studies of population processes and of collective action. If we were to direct the same sort of survey to work in economic history, we would discover a routine use of more complex models, smaller data files, less emphasis on description, and a higher ratio of computation to input and output. If we turned instead to the systematic historical study of elites, class structure, and social mobility, the prevalence of essentially descriptive work would increase; we would find computers being used primarily for collating, sorting, aggregating, and providing statistical descriptions of large numbers of individual observations. *Mutatis his mutandis*, the other historical social sciences have reached roughly the same point as historical demography.

In these fields the computer's chief impact so far has been to decrease the effort and unit costs involved in procedures for which hand routines were already well established, and thus to increase the scale of analysis to which those procedures could be applied. The critical innovations (such as family reconstitution) have so far occurred more or less independently of the computer, but the computer is making their diffusion easier. In each field, a few investigators are demanding more of the computer: building complex files with extensive cross-referencing, testing complex mathematical models against large bodies of data, simulating social processes in order to rule out assumptions that produce implausible results, performing content analyses of texts. In each field, no more than a handful of investigators learn much about computing itself; the great majority content themselves with a knowledge of prepackaged programs, with perhaps a rudimentary competence in FORTRAN, COBOL, or some other standard language for emergencies. And many are willing to let others handle their access to the computer.

There lies a danger. In these days of the computer it is easy, tempting, and relatively cheap to run large statistical analyses that are appropriate neither for the data at hand nor for the arguments that the investigator is really prepared to make. So long as the computer is being used simply to collate and describe large bodies of data, the main costs of freehandedness are likely to be wasted effort, boredom, and excessively long manuscripts.

When it comes to fitting statistical models to data, however, the potential costs are much more serious. The ease with which historical social scientists can run a hundred multiple regressions, carry out a large factor analysis, or compare every vote in a given legislature to every other one makes it easy to coax striking pseudoresults from almost any substantial collection of data. The danger is that investigators will use the easy procedures to explore the whole terrain instead of to follow a map already prepared on the basis of well-reasoned theory and previous findings. If that were to happen without a compensating strengthening of our theories of social processes and without a complementary increase in our ability to articulate and test the more complicated notions we have about those social processes, then, alas, the many critics who see the computer as the harbinger of mindless empiricism would be right.

Appreciation

Homans, Humans, and History

The Poet Scans History

"The Law of civilization and decay," writes today's poet, "Decrees each culture its memorial/And travelers through history shall say/ Discovering a carving on a wall

> *No army but the desert could have stormed;*
> *"This shows a race by no means as they were*
> *But as they saw themselves. This legend warmed*
> *The remnant that outlived defeat. O stir*
>
> *Gently the dust these crevices to clear.*
> *Our epitaph will be such food for weather*
> *Soon, for in time's perspective we are near*
> *These others. We shall spend the dark together."*

The poet, himself of that "remnant that outlived defeat," goes on to sketch the house and the garden in which four generations of the race dreamed and grew. The sketch has the suffused brilliance of a Turner painting: object, percept, and precept at one with one another. "Such is the spring," our poet says, "and by this cycle span

> *The longer cycle of the family.*
> *The processes of nature measure man*
> *Last and most surely. He himself may be*
> *Only a world's reply to entropy.*

In George Caspar Homans's poem about the Adams mansion in Quincy, Massachusetts, the themes of his kinsman Brooks Adams—entropy, civilization, and decay—touch the entire Adams lineage, then mankind as a whole. The poet links the particular time and place on two opposite sides: to himself, and to all of history.

Yet Brooks Adams is not the poet's true guide. For all his searching after generality in other pursuits, our poet scans history in the manner of a historian: He scans history for continuities and particularities. Henry Adams comes closer. Henry Adams summed up a coherent, believing age in the architecture of Mont-Saint-Michel and Chartres. The poet epitomizes that same age in the English village. Henry Adams begins our inspection of Mont-Saint-Michel on the parvis. There we are, he says, "looking out over the sea and sands which are as good eleventh-century landscape as they ever were; or turning at times towards the church door which is the *pons seclorum*, the bridge of ages, between us and our ancestors [1933 (1905): 5]". The poet likewise takes us across the bidge of ages. The village is his cathedral. Like Will Langland, however, he prefers a field full of folk to a basilica bursting with bishops.

Not that our poet—historian settles for the impressionism of Henry Adams. After all, Henry Adams tells us that when he first faced a class in Harvard College, as its new assistant professor of medieval history, "he had given, as far as he could remember, an hour, more or less, to the Middle Ages [1931 (1918): 300]". Our poet—historian, by contrast, early made it his business to become expert in the materials and methods of medieval history. Under his scrutiny, the English village becomes an object of painstaking documentary reconstruction, rigorous comparison, ingenious structural analysis.

The village also becomes two other things. It serves as a microcosm of an entire social order, and even of all social orders; the closing pages of *English Villagers of the Thirteenth Century* bear the title "The Anatomy of Society." They lay out a general scheme in terms of institutions, organization, interaction, sentiment, and function. Here we find the author seeking to synthesize ethnography and historiography.

The English village also serves as a point of reference for the present. Although *English Villagers* barely alludes to those connections with the present, the author mentions them elsewhere. In voyaging from New England to Old England, the Yankee retraces his own origins, seeks his own identity. This particular Yankee's historical explorations, indeed, lead back from the present to pre-Revolutionary Massachusetts, to the English Puritans, to medieval England, to the settlement of East Anglia. In the frank and graceful memoir that opens his book *Sentiments and Activities*, George Homans says as much. The silver thread that attaches him to an old house in Quincy is centuries long; it winds back to the Frisians who inscribed their *ploegs* and *leets* on the landscape of Norfolk. Happily, the thread does not lead through the swamp of genealogy and self-justification, but across the plains of human existence. The subject, to paraphrase our author, is not Homans but humans.

How does this poet — historian — ethnographer carry on his work? We notice first of all that he seems to enjoy it. "No one who works in modern sociology," he confides at one point, "where data are so plentiful they become mere statistics, can know the joy sheer, single facts can give of their own sweet selves [Homans 1962: 13]." His historical work conveys that pleasure. It consists for the most part of tracing the hidden connections among small arrays of large facts. A paper on the Puritans and the clothing industry in sixteenth- and seventeenth-century England, for example, draws on the *Calendar of State Papers* and a few other publications to argue a three-way correspondence: woolen manufacturing, Puritanism, emigration to America. Recurrent depressions in the clothing industry, according to this analysis, operate as a pump driving Englishmen across the Atlantic. Rich Winthrops and poor weavers alike join the stream. The evidence comes mainly in the form of geographical correspondences. The early immigrants and place names of New England reveal the influence of East Anglia and the West Country, the clothing districts stand out among those origins of migrants, and so on. The similarity of patterns argues for connections among the patterns.

The method is quite general: Identify a characteristic pattern in one setting; locate a homologous pattern in another setting; use the homology to argue a relationship between the settings. The relationship may be one of historical continuity, or diffusion, or of functional similarity. In the historical work, it is usually either continuity or diffusion.

An even more formidable exercise of scholarship appears in "The Frisians in East Anglia." The title itself must be one of the most esoteric in the bibliographies of major contemporary sociologists. We could make it compete with the most recondite historical titles by adding dates and a subtitle. What about "The Frisians in East Anglia, 400 – 500 A.D.: Further Reflections on Dr. Siebs' Analyses of Friesland"? Indeed, the preparatory work for the article required an impressive array of knowledge and skills. The crucial parallels to East Anglia turned up in an obscure German study of Frisian land systems — that of Dr. Siebs. The basic sources require a knowledge of Medieval Latin, Middle English, and Frisian. (Not long after the article appeared, I walked into the author's office to congratulate him. Struggling with the technical demands of a much easier body of material, I was greatly impressed with the skills he had deployed. After talking about the more salient and important features of the work, I got to the question that really intrigued me. "How in the world," I asked, "did you ever learn Frisian?" "Oh, Charlie," he replied, "It's *easy* if you know Anglo-Saxon!") As a matter of fact, a number of people have had the necessary technical skills. A few have also had the requisite knowledge of English field systems, inheritance patterns, and local structures of power. But no one, to my knowledge, had previously seen the homologies in these regards between Frisia and East Anglia.

The argument of "The Frisians in East Anglia" runs through a careful comparison, cluster by cluster, of the local institutions on both sides of the Channel. On the English side, the documentation issues from the whole of George Homans's previous work on the medieval period. On the Dutch side, Siebs's *Grundlagen und Aufbau der altfriesischen Verfassung* summarizes the evidence. Thus we encounter similarities at the level of the basic tenement, a compact body of land that appears to have borne collective responsibility for legal duties and to have owed 10 men to the military service. On both sides, we find suggestions of lineage control over those tenements, compromised by well-defined systems of partible inheritance. We discover similarities in the vocabularies applied to inheritance and to the major classes of the population.

The demonstration moves on. The parallels accumulate. At the end, our author is saying:

> As Frisian is the language most closely related to English, so Frisian institutions are the institutions most closely related to East Anglian ones. The conclusion must be that Frisians invaded East Anglia in the fifth century. The similarity of institutions, in spite of the fact that something like adequate written records about them begin to appear only in the eleventh century, at least six hundred years after the new Frisians must have separated from the old, seems to me to strengthen this conclusion rather than weaken it. How much more eloquently do the institutions speak for a common origin when they had so much time, opportunity, and reason to diverge [Homans 1962: 181].

The method of argument recalls the ethnologist who retraces the movements and divisions of a common culture, the linguist who reconstructs diffusion and elaboration of a family of languages. Both reason from distributions observed long after the processes in question.

Plenty of the same sort of analysis appears in George Homans's first and largest examination of medieval history, his *English Villagers of the Thirteenth Century*. Now 40 years old, the book is still a standard authority. Contemporary scholars pay it the compliment of contesting its interpretations as they pass on to their own. For example, Alan Macfarlane, on his way to challenging the treatment of medieval England as a classic peasant society, speaks of "the formidable and widely accepted work of Homans, Kosminsky, Postan and Vinogradoff which rest on the strong assumption that this was a classical 'peasant' society [1978: 101]." That is strong company for a mere sociologist.

True, some features of *English Villagers* mark it as a product of the 1930s. Nowadays, such a book would almost certainly include more extensive observations on climate, on *conjoncture*, on demography, on the structure of marketing, on the findings that have come in from the archaeology and aerial photography of village sites. In the face of later evidence concerning medieval shifts in production as a function of market conditions and labor supply, the book's emphasis on subsistence farming and the predominance of custom might well be qualified. (Given the author's character, however, we would not be surprised to find the contested arguments stated all the more firmly).

In any case, the last few decades' changes in medieval historiography bear mainly on the context of village life rather than on its internal organization. *English Villagers* deals chiefly with that internal organization. As compared with such an essay as "The Frisians in East Anglia," the book relies more heavily on the study of concomitant variation. We begin with the grand contrast of woodland and champion country, enclosed-field and open-field landscapes. That gives us the means to see the special properties of open-field areas, which are to be the chief object of study. From there on, the book proceeds like an ethnography. First the land, agriculture, and villages. Then the family, marriage, kinship and inheritance. Later, the manor, class divisions, and power structure. At last, the yearly round, the church, a vision of life as a whole.

Throughout, we find our author scrutinizing the meanings and origins of common terms, making comparisons, posing hypotheses concerning the sources of standard institutions. In the course of his illuminating exposition of the logic of the scattered, intermingled fields in the champion country, for instance, he speculates:

> There is the stronger reason to guess that there was once in England a system of laying out the strips of the different holdings in a regular order of rotation, and that the order was related to a conventional conception of the direction and course of the sun, in the fact that such a system is known to have been in force until recent times in villages of Denmark and Sweden which had the general characteristics of English champion villages [Homans 1941: 96—97].

But the most extensive and characteristic arguments of the book relate one well-defined institution to another. In an example which has since become commonplace, *English Villagers* identifies the intimate connection of marriage opportunities to inheritance of land:

> The working of the rule, no land, no marriage, had two aspects. First, men and women who were not to inherit a family tenement did not marry unless they could secure land for themselves. Second, in many places, the man who was to inherit the tenement did not marry until its last holder was ready to turn it over to him. In this manner the sentiments and customs of men secured a stable adaptation of society to its economic conditions. Despite the logic of Malthus, they limited the number of persons who pressed on the land for subsistence [Homans 1941: 159].

Homans's Methods

In *English Villagers* and the other writings on medieval history, we discover two complementary methods at work. The first takes one piece of social behavior, identifies its dependence on another piece of social behavior in the same setting, and so on, until a coherent, interdependent pattern of social behavior is in view. The second matches patterns in different times, places, or realms of behavior, then accounts for the match through continuity, diffusion, or functional interdependence. Readers of social anthropology will find both methods familiar.

Perhaps this sounds like what everybody does. Much as Kingsley Davis once told us that all sociologists search for functional relationships, someone might object that all historians search for matching patterns. They do not. Consider Henry Adams. He declared that "historians undertaken to arrange sequences,—called stories, or histories—assuming in silence a relation of cause and effect [1931 (1918): 382]." Adams was describing the historian as Narrator, who is still with us today. Toward the end of his life Adams came to think that the sequences would take on meaning if they measured the distance from—or to—some fixed point in history. In his own case, as he said, he "might use the century 1150—1250, expressed in Amiens Cathedral and the Works of Thomas Aquinas, as the unit from which he might measure motion down to his own time, without assuming anything as true or untrue, except relation [H. Adams 1931 (1918) 435]." Although High Medieval Culture has lost its popularity as a reference point, many contemporary historians attempt to "measure motion" with respect to the Industrial Revolution, twentieth-century states, or some such marker.

Or think back to Brooks Adams, who tried to discern great cycles and giant laws in history. It was Brooks Adams who asserted "the exceedingly small part played by conscious thought in moulding the fate of men." At the moment of action, he wrote, "the human being almost invariably obeys an instinct, like an animal, only after action has ceased does he reflect." It was he who claimed to have found "that the intellectual phenomena under examination fell into a series which seemed to correspond, somewhat closely, with the laws which are supposed to regulate the movements of the material universe [B. Adams 1943 (1896): 58, 59]."

Universal history of this sort has lost favor in the twentieth century, but other modes that avoid George Homans's pattern matching abound. Some historians seize on a single person and hope at best to find a distinctive formula that will characterize and illuminate that person's life. Others attempt to apply the same, essentially biographical, procedure to a whole people or a whole era. Still others attempt to trace some momentous event to the peculiarities of its immediate context. These modes of argument do not exhaust the possibilities. Historians have found a number of ways of doing history which do not consist of point-for-point comparisons between patterns.

When sociologists move into history, furthermore, they do not ordinarily take up comparison of patterns in the manner of our ethnographer, historian, and poet. They more often dig into history to locate samples that they then truck out for use as cases in multivariate analyses; the analyses typically bear on arguments cast so generally as to have little bearing on the settings from which the samples were originally drawn. Or the sociologists use the softer version of the same procedure, which consists of ransacking readily available historical sources to find support for a nonhistorical argument. There is the working up of history that fills the obligatory dull first chapter on the past in textbooks on cities or stratification. And there is the occasional sociologist who takes on an established historical problem by applying the standard sociological estimation procedures to materials that have never before been so insulted. Only the last of these approaches the Homansian effort to identify and match patterns. Even there, in most cases the difference between pattern matching via statistical estimation and via simple, salient correspondences remains enormous.

Stop. Following the plodding routines of everyday scholarship, I have thoughtlessly stuffed a noble hawk into an ordinary pigeonhole. The hawk bats his wings in the pigeonhole and eventually smashes it to smithereens. Who ever heard of relegating a poet, sailor, sociologist, historian, ethnographer, and stentor to mere pattern making? Why, it almost sounds like . . . pattern maintenance. You probably know Joseph Turner's 1840 painting, *Slavers throwing overboard the Dead and Dying*. It once belonged to John Ruskin and now belongs to the Boston Museum of Fine Arts. Sun and sea are both aflame as the ship pitches in the middle left, and gulls flap around the chained leg thrust above the waves in the right foreground. At the painting's first showing, Turner displayed with it these lines from the *Fallacies of Hope* (Turner's own poem):

> *Aloft all hands, strike the top-masts and belay;*
> *You angry setting sun and fierce-edged clouds*
> *Declare the Typhon's coming.*
> *Before it sweep your desks, throw overboard*
> *The dead and dying—n'er heed their chains.*
> *Hope, Hope fallacious Hope!*
> *Where is thy market now?*

Reviewing the show, Thackeray wrote, "The sun glows down upon a horrible sea of emerald and purple. . . . If Wilberforce's statute downstairs were to be confronted with this picture, the stony old gentleman would spring off his chair and fly away in terror!" The *Art Union* called the painting "a gross outrage on nature." But Ruskin wrote of "the noblest sea that Turner has painted and, if so, the noblest certainly ever painted by man [Tate 1974: 144–145]." Today we look back at that painting and its companions to see the savage color and daring form breaking through the academic order, anticipating the impressionists by 50 years. To approach historical materials as an ethnographer is now so commonplace that we easily catalogue George Homans as no more than an early exemplar of a well-established style. Such are the perils of success. If you go back to the Jolliffes, the Stentons, the Stubbs that one read to learn medieval history in the 1930s, however, you will see instantly how brash and disrespectful it was then to treat the English village as an anthropologist's domain, pipe rolls as field notes, field systems as patterns of culture.

Parallels and Particulars

Not that our author labors alone, a quirky original. Some of the masters of social history have displayed the same bent for argument from patterned correspondence. Marc Bloch assembled much of his great synthesis of French rural history in that manner. Fernand Braudel commands our admiring assent precisely by his ability to pick up two historical shards and fit their edges together. G. William Skinner's remarkable analysis of Chinese marketing systems depends on an ingenious, unexpected identification of correspondences. Need I mention Michael Ventris and the decipherment of Linear B? Models of the style are available in history, but the style is not obvious, easy, or common.

George Homans's style extends to the way he reports his findings. What a pleasure it is to read historical work in well-made sentences and coherent paragraphs! The prose is all bone and sinew. It knows where it goes. A close reader notices that every sentence identifies its agent, that weak verbs and passive voices rarely appear, that if a complication or reservation arises, it occupies a separate statement instead of dragging down the initial sentence. He also senses the absence of neologisms, the sparing use of metaphor, the unembarrassed employment of *I* when the author speaks for himself. Many students of sociology and history have the right to roar with Caliban at their professorial Prosperos: "You taught me language, and my profit on't/Is, I know how to curse. The red plague rid you/For learning me your language!" George Homans knows how to curse but does so in plain language. That sociological prose seldom has these qualities is notorious. For some reason, the writing of academic historians has never achieved the reputation for drabness that it generally deserves. The vigor and clarity of a veteran versifier show up in our author's historical writing.

You probably know the advice that another veteran versifier prepared for a Harvard commencement years ago. Part of W. H. Auden's "Hermetic Decalogue" runs:

> *Thou shalt not do as the dean pleases,*
> *Thou shalt not write thy doctor's thesis*
> *On education,*
>
> *Thou shalt not worship projects nor*
> *Shalt thou or thine bow down before*
> *Administration.*
>
> *Thou shalt not answer questionnaires*
> *Or quizzes upon World-Affairs,*
> *Nor with compliance*
> *Take any test. Thou shalt not sit*
> *With statisticians nor commit*
> *A social science.*

If we read only our author's historical work, we could easily interpret it as an expression of Auden's hermetic creed.

Unsettling, but true. The zealous generalizer of *Social Behavior: Its Elementary Forms* is also the meticulous particularizer of "The Frisians in East Anglia." The theoretician of "Bringing Men Back In" also wrote, "History had never needed a Newton; from the beginning it had known its principles, at least in their vulgar form as the characteristics of human nature [Homans 1962: 34]."

The contradiction is manifest. Yet it resembles the contradiction of sailing east or sailing west to get to the other side of the world. The antipodes for both voyages are the elementary, universal traits of individual human behavior. Unfortunately for our understanding, the historical flotilla stops short of its destination. If *English Villagers* closes with broad reflections on the structure and importance of small social units, such subsequent essays as "The Rural Sociology of Medieval England" settle for analyzing the interdependence among inheritance arrangements, field systems, migration patterns, and other features of local social life. It is up to us—or up to our author's as-yet-unpublished writings—to drive historical analysis back to elementary social behavior.

4
Useless Durkheim

History in the Newspapers

The *Annual Register*, the *Gentleman's Magazine*, and the *South Carolina Gazette* are much more fun to read than most serious historical sources. The run-of-the-mill archival assignment consists of plodding through 2132 police reports of arrests for vagrancy, public drunkenness, or prostitution to find the three scattered records of "seditious crimes." Interesting in principle, dreary in practice. Or it consists of combing 655 birth registrations, puzzling out the handwriting, then taking from each entry four pieces of information, if they are there: data, sex, name, parents. Drearier still. Small wonder that historians prefer archives with coffee shops close at hand. Most archival work is a bore.

That is why reading such sources as the *Annual Register* gives me a feeling of joy, and faint puritanical guilt: if it's this diverting, can it be good for you? The *Register*, *Gentleman's Magazine*, and *South Carolina Gazette* correspond to one common, but generally mistaken, image of historical sources; they are composed largely of reports and interpretations of events that people of the time found interesting. All three began publication in the eighteenth century and continued into the nineteenth. The *Annual Register*, as its title implies, summarizes the notable events of the year in the form of chronicles, tables, and essays. The *Gentleman's Magazine*, as its title does not imply, contains miscellaneous items snipped from other publications, essays and letters volunteered by the journal's correspondents, book reviews, lists of such memorable elite happenings as knightings, presentations to livings, marriages, or royal appointments, and a monthly chronical of newsworthy events. The *South Carolina Gazette* differs from the others in being a weekly published in North America rather than in England, in devoting a major part of its space to paid advertisements of slave sales, of arrivals of ships and merchants, or of established retail businesses, and, unsurprisingly, in giving extensive sympathetic attention to American affairs.

Actually, the two British publications also display a lively concern for American affairs in the period I have been reading, which runs from 1755 to 1785. For example, one of the first articles in *Gentleman's* January 1755 issue deals with "A General View of the Conduct of the French in America, and of our Settlements there." In retrospect, we find the topic a natural one; after all, England went to war with France the next year and wrested Canada away from France in the 7-year struggle that followed. The article begins with a geographic survey, including such items as this:

> South Carolina lies in 32 deg., is very hot, and has but very little winter. Its produce is the same with that of North Carolina; but its principal product is rice, with which it supplies all Europe; and if the article of indigo, which they have lately fallen on, will succeed, this will soon become one of the richest colonies we have; and we shall save vast sums which we pay France annually for that article.

> Charles Town is the capital of this province, and is about as big as the city of Gloucester. The inhabitants are very genteel and polite. All this country has every necessary, and most of the conveniences of life. Many fine rivers, and good harbours. All the goods they consume, they have from England, and pay for them in rice, pitch, tar, deer skins, and fur [*Gentleman's Magazine* 1755: 17].

Other news from the American colonies in the 30 ensuing years contained many such surveys. The news emphasized the English, French, and Spanish competition for political and mercantile power on the Continent, the constant play of alliances and hostilities with different groups of Indians, the resistance of the colonists to the taxation and military force imposed directly from England after the Seven Years' War, and, of course, the events which (after the fact) we string together as the American Revolution. It took the participants themselves a while to realize that they were making a revolution—a fact that a sizable minority of them were rather upset to discover.

Comparing England and America

I confess that an unexpected fit of bicentennial piety led me to start looking systematically at such publications as the *Annual Register*. It has also taken me to such archives as the Public Record Office, the South Carolina state archives, the Michigan's own Clements collection of eighteenth-century manuscripts. The point of these peregrinations is to compare the evolution of collective action in England and its American colonies during the eighteenth century.

In reality, the problem is both broader and narrower: broader in that the implicit comparisons set off America against western Europe as a whole—and in that I hope to stagger toward explanations of the changes and differences—narrower in that the work concentrates on contentious gatherings rather than on all forms of collective action. (I defined *contentious gatherings* and gave some idea of how my group goes about describing them in Chapter 2.) Meetings, petition marches, land occupations, seizures of food, movements against conscription, and other contentious public gatherings comprised an important part of the eighteenth-century repertoire of popular collective action in Europe and America, but by no means all of it.

The comparison of eighteenth-century England and America is a busman's holiday. The people who usually ride the bus include a number of graduate students at the University of Michigan, a smaller number of faculty members elsewhere, and a variable number of researchers who actually get paid for riding with us. Our full program of research concerns the evolution of collective action in Europe under the influence of capitalism and statemaking. That program takes us back to the sixteenth century and up to the present. We have concentrated on Italy, France, Germany, and Great Britain. The seventeenth-century tales from the *Mercure françois* with which this book began illustrate the French equivalent of the material that I am taking from the *Gentleman's Magazine* for eighteenth-century Britain; other evidence from seventeenth-century France will appear, in a somewhat more systematic guise, later in the book. Likewise, organized versions of the evidence from nineteenth-century Britain showed up in my discussion of computing and will reappear several times later on.

Our bus travels in two directions. The first direction takes us from (a) general arguments concerning the effects of capitalism and statemaking and about the determinants of different forms of collective action; through (b) problems of conceptualization and measurement; to (c) the analysis of specific streams or instances of collective action. Thus different members of the research group have tried out general arguments about the determinants of strike activity on long, large blocks of evidence from France, Italy, the United States, Great Britain, and Sweden. The second direction starts from some particular set of groups, settings, or events and attempts to formulate and test alternative explanations of their complexities. Thus we have attempted to deal with the June insurrection of 1848 in Paris, the May insurrection of 1898 in Milan, the patterns of repression and working-class collective action in nineteenth-century Lancashire, and the mobilization of different groups of workers in nineteenth-century Marseilles and Toulouse.

Our largest current enterprises are a comparison of structural change and contention in five major regions of France from 1600 to the present, an analysis of the changing geography of contention in the London area from 1750 to the 1830s, and an examination of collective action in the whole of Great Britain from 1828 through 1834. Compared with those massive collections and analyses of data, my personal exploration of eighteenth-century England and America is a trivial enterprise. I have no plans to spoil the fun by turning it into a voluminous project. The advantage of doing both sorts of work at the same time is to be aware of the variety and complexity of the available sources and of how abundant they are.

For anyone interested in making comparisons across the eighteenth century and across the Atlantic, the difficulty is not shortage of evidence. It is the selectivity, inaccuracy, heterogeneity, and superabundance of evidence. We have, for instance, report after report in the vein of this one from the *South Carolina Gazette* (Charleston) of 31 October 1765:

Early on Saturday morning (October 19th) in the middle of Broad Street and Church Street, near Mr. Dillon's (being the most central and public part of the town) appeared suspended on a gallows twenty feet high, an effigy, with a figure of the devil on its right hand, and on its left a boot, with a head stuck upon it distinguished by a blue bonnet, to each of which were affixed labels expressive of the sense of the people unshaken in their loyalty but tenacious of just liberty. They declared that all internal duties imposed upon them without the consent of their immediate, or even virtual, representation, was grievous, oppressive, and unconstitutional, and that an extension of the powers and jurisdiction of admiralty courts in America tended to subvert one of their most darling legal rights, that of trials by juries.

Another sign attached to the gallows read LIBERTY AND NO STAMP ACT and threatened anyone who tore down the structure. That evening a crowd arrived with a procession of wagons to dismount gallows, signs, and effigies. They paraded to the house of George Saxby, the designated stamp distributor. There the crowd broke a few windows and opened the house to ask for stamped papers. None were in the house. The paraders moved to the town green, then to the barracks, where they burned the effigies. Someone rang the bells of St. Michael's Church. Then people went home.

The report is captivating in its own right—colorful, exotic, full of life. A lot more fun than arrest records and birth certificates. It also requires its own interpretive apparatus. For example, we need to know that the boot on display was a commonplace pun for Lord Bute, the king's chief minister; the same symbolism of boot, devil, and gallows appeared in similar events throughout the American colonies. We need to know that eighteenth-century statements of grievances often took on the air of street theater: tarring and feathering, shivaree, mock trials, riding the stang. Most of all, we need to know something of the struggle over the Stamp Act, which was shaking the colonies, and Great Britain, in 1765. Those first large protests over taxation via stamped paper, after all, are the standard beginning for accounts of the American Revolution.

About the same time, London Radicals and the followers of John Wilkes were attacking the ministry and its American policy from their side of the Atlantic. Wilkes's first jail sentence for criticizing royal policy came in 1763. In 1765, during the American protests against the Stamp Act, he was on the Continent, in exile to avoid another prosecution. Three years later, however, he was back in London leading great petition marches, then mass celebrations of his election to Parliament and mass protests against Parliament's denial of admission to him. In those mass marches through the streets of London, something like the modern demonstration came into being. We see a similar transformation occurring in the American Stamp Act protests. The public assembly of a large number of people around a well-defined grievance, demand, or program is beginning to detach itself from the specific direct action to achieve that object: the lynching, the petition, the people's court, the food riot, machine breaking, tearing down the customs barrier, invading the enclosed common fields.

How the Nineteenth Century Differed from the Eighteenth

Nevertheless, if we move forward to the nineteenth century either in England or in America, we discover significant further changes in the prevailing forms of contentious gatherings. We notice the food riot, machine breaking, invasions of common fields, and their companion forms of collective action peaking and then disappearing. We find the demonstration, the strike, the election rally, the public meeting, and allied forms of action taking on more and more prominence. And we find that the interpretive apparatus required to follow the specific content of the Charleston gallows theater or the Wilkite petition marches fails us utterly when applied to their nineteenth-century successors.

The straightforward comparison of English and American collective actions in the eighteenth and nineteenth centuries poses some strictly historical problems. They are strictly historical in that they consist of attaching the events to their temporal and geographical contexts. The first set of problems, indeed, consists of identifying the issues, interests, symbols, groups, and structures of power immediately involved in the action and connecting the one event with others in its immediate setting. The second set of historical problems consists of accounting for the dramatic changes in the repertoire of collective actions and for the trans- formations of the individual performances within it: Why and how did the demonstration and strike supersede the shivaree, tax riot, and inva- sion of fields? Why and how did the demonstration itself shed those eighteenth-century elements of direct action and street theater?

That is where the sociologists come in—or at least would like to come in. When we edge over from strictly historical questions into the effort to provide accounts, and even explanations, of large social changes, we blunder into the common ground of history and sociology.

I am *not* talking about something called "historical sociology." I would be happier if the phrase had never been invented. It implies the existence of a separate field of study—parallel, say, to political sociology or the sociology of religion. There are, I concede, a group of sociologists who work mainly on the relatively distant past and a smaller group who deal regularly with the archival materials that are the historian's stock-in- trade. There are a body of lore, a set of procedures, and a fund of informa- tion concerning particular places, times, and people that are indispensa- ble to the analysis of many types of historical evidence. There probably is something special about analytic problems in which time and place figure specifically and indissolubly—as they do, for example, in analyses of the origins and expansion of capitalism and as they do not in most analyses of economic development. There probably is even a distinctive historical style or cast of mind which produces a variety of work different in feeling from that prevailing in other brands of sociology. Nevertheless, I object to having subdisciplines emerge from techniques and approaches rather than from theoretically coherent subject matters. Not that my objections will deter others who like to distinguish between sociologists who "do history" and all the rest.

In any case, the English and American events we were discussing before my diatribe provide legitimate material for plenty of sociologists who have no great interest in eighteenth- or nineteenth-century England and America as such. I imagine that as I reminded you of the contrast between the eighteenth and nineteenth centuries, a half-dozen sociolog- ical schemes flashed through your minds, most of them involving that execrable word *modernization*. The comparison of these eighteenth- and nineteenth-century means of acting together raises at least three standard, major sociological problems: First, what determines how and when people *ever* act collectively? That is the sort of question James Coleman addressed in his *Mathematics of Collective Action*. Second, what impact does the pace or character of large-scale structural change have on the form, personnel, intensity, and outcome of collective action? That is the sort of question Neil Smelser addressed in his *Social Change in the Industrial Revolution* and, to some extent, in his *Theory of Collective Behavior*. Third, what are the standard processes, if any, of large-scale social change, and what produces them? That is the sort of question myriad contemporary students of "modernization" and "development" have addressed. Its standard phrasing was already present in Durkheim's *Division of Labor in Society*.

Durkheim Faces the Nineteenth Century

Indeed, I think Durkheim crystallized a widespread nineteenth-century view of what industrialization was doing to the world and fashioned it into a set of arguments that have remained dominant in sociology, especially American sociology, up to our own time. Talcott Parsons said essentially the same thing, albeit with much greater enthusiasm about the outcome, when he declared that

> it was the problem of the integration of the social system, of what holds societies together, which was the most persistent preoccupation of Durkheim's career. In the situation of the time, one could not have chosen a more strategic focus for contributing to sociological theory. Moreover, the work Durkheim did in this field can be said to have been nothing short of epoch-making; he did not stand entirely alone, but his work was far more sharply focused and deeply penetrating than that of any other author of his time [1960: 118].

In *Division of Labor* and *Suicide*, Durkheim laid out a view of something called a society differentiating unsteadily in response to a variety of pressures. Speaking abstractly, Durkheim sums up those pressures as a growth in the volume and density of society. Speaking concretely, he discusses occupational changes. The pressures emphatically include the internal logic of industrialization. On the first page of *Division of Labor*, Durkheim tells us

> we need have no further illusions about the tendencies of modern industry; it advances steadily towards powerful machines, towards great concentrations of forces and capital, and consequently to the extreme division of labor.

> Occupations are infinitely separated and specialized, not only inside the factories, but each product is itself a specialty dependent upon others [1933: 39. This quotation and subsequent quotations cited to Durkheim 1933 are from *The Division of Labor in Society* by Emile Durkheim, translated by George Simpson (Copyright © 1933 by Macmillan Publishing Co., Inc.)].

That "society," according to Durkheim, exerts its control over individuals via their participation in a shared consciousness. As Durkheim puts it, "The totality of beliefs and sentiments common to average citizens of the same society forms a determinate system which has its own life; one may call it the collective or common conscience [1933: 79]." The advancing division of labor, he says, threatens the shared consciousness based on the essential similarity of individuals and thereby threatens the primacy of the needs and demands of the society as a whole over the impulses and interests of the individual. A new shared consciousness based on interdependence and common fate is both problematic and slow to emerge. Into the gap between the level of differentiation and the level of shared consciousness moves *anomie*.

To be precise, *anomie* is Durkheim's name for that gap between the degree of differentiation and the extent of regulation of social relations; from it he derives a series of undesirable results: individual disorientation, destructive social life, extensive conflict. His concrete examples again come almost entirely from the industrial world; they are the economic crash, the conflict between management and labor, the separation of work and family life, and so on, through the standard concerns of nineteenth-century reformers. In *Suicide*, Durkheim sketches the consequences of a rapid growth in power and wealth:

> Time is required for the public conscience to reclassify men and things. So long as the social forces thus freed have not regained equilibrium, their respective values are unknown and so all regulation is lacking for a time. . . . Consequently, there is no restraint upon aspirations. . . . With increased prosperity desires increase. At the very moment when traditional rules have lost their authority, the richer prize offered these appetites stimulates them and makes them more exigent and impatient of control. The state of deregulation or anomy is thus further heightened by passions being less disciplined, precisely when they need more disciplining [1951: 253].

We begin to see that Durkheim not only propounded a theory of social change but also proposed a theory of collective action.

In fact, he proposed two or three of each. When it comes to the link between large-scale social change and collective action, we find Durkheim distinguishing sharply between the orderly pursuit of shared interests that occurs when the division of labor is not outrunning the shared consciousness and the free-for-all that results from *anomie*. And later, in *The Elementary Forms of the Religious Life*, we find Durkheim analyzing the solidarity-producing consequences of ritualized, approved forms of collective action.

Alternative Accounts of Collective Action

Durkheim's views of social change and of collective action became sociological commonplaces. The standard analyses of industrialization, urbanization, deviance, social control, collective behavior, and social disorganization that emerged in the twentieth century were all heavily Durkheimian. Yet several important alternatives were available in Durkheim's time and have remained operable since then. We can identify the main alternatives loosely with John Stuart Mill and the Utilitarians, Karl Marx and the historical materialists, Max Weber and the historical idealists.

On the analysis of collective action and its relation to large-scale social change, we find each school taking a rather different view from Durkheim's. In Mill is an analysis of the aggregation of interests into decisions through sets of rules, or constitutions, which vary in the extent to which they place the general interest ahead of the particular. Thus large-scale change transforms collective action mainly by affecting interests and constitutions. These days the literature of collective choice has a strongly Millian tone.

In Marx are two relevant analyses: one of the transformation of class divisions and interests through the changing organization of production, the other of readiness to act on those interests as a function of the internal organization, external relations, and self-consciousness of the classes in question. In our own time, historians such as E. J. Hobsbawm and John Foster have made the most effective applications of this Marxian line to the analysis of social change and collective action.

Weber, like Durkheim, provided at least two separate accounts of collective action and its links to large-scale social change. In the first, routine collective action expresses the interests of an organization constrained by a powerful, well-defined set of beliefs and changes gradually as a function of changes in those beliefs and interests. In the other, a new group forms around a distinctive set of beliefs, acts in order to implement those beliefs, but responds to external pressures and internal exigencies by routinizing its organization, procedures, and interpretations of the belief itself. Through this process of routinization, to be sure, the group comes to approximate the condition described by the first model: routine collective action on the basis of organizational interests constrained by well-defined beliefs. The literature of social movements draws heavily on this Weberian line of thought.

With these alternatives available, it is a pity that Durkheim's models prevailed. Yet they did. Turn to the study of crime, and see the fundamental role of arguments treating it as a product of social disintegration. Turn to the study of urban dislocation, deviance, and social disorganization, and find the very definition of the problem based on a Durkheimian view of the world. Turn to the study of collective behavior, and discover a redefinition of important varieties of collective action as expressions of the gap between the level of social differentiation and the extent of shared consciousness. Because Durkheim and his successors are ever present, we will do well to ask two questions: What sorts of historical arguments and analyses follow from Durkheim's thinking? When can we translate them into terms consonant with the historical material, how useful and valid are Durkheim's theories?

Historical Implications of Durkheim's Account

Durkheim's discussions of differentiation, *anomie*, and conflict lend themselves to three historical arguments. First, where traditional social controls weaken, the unbounded pursuit of individual interests—the war of all against all—breaks out. "It is this anomic state that is the cause," declared Durkheim, "of the incessantly recurrent conflicts, and the multifarious disorders of which the economic world exhibits so sad a spectacle. For, as nothing restrains the active forces and assigns them limits they are bound to respect, they tend to develop haphazardly, and come into collision with one another, battling and weakening themselves [1933: 2]." If we can wrench this statement out of the tautology into which it cramps almost as a reflex, we find it suggesting that relatively small, homogeneous groups having extensive shared beliefs will experience lower levels of conflict, and perhaps struggle less with other groups, than relatively large, heterogeneous groups which have few shared beliefs. In the history of industrialization, we might expect these effects to show up as a cross-sectional difference in the involvement in conflict of groups having different bases of organization and a more or less continuous increase in the level of conflict.

In a second line of reasoning, Durkheim indicates that short-run disruptions of the balance between morality and organizational structure result from rapid change, accelerated economic growth, or industrial crisis and likewise incite disorder in the groups most affected by them. In our historical material, we might reasonably expect to find rapid rural-to-urban migration, massive industrialization, and major economic fluctuations producing exceptionally high levels of conflict and protest.

Thirdly, Durkheim says that the forms of disorder—individual and collective, "egoistic" and "anarchic"—vary together. "The abnormal development of suicide and the general unrest of contemporary societies," he writes at the end of *Suicide*, "spring from the same causes [1951: 391]." Historically, a Durkheimian view leads us to look for crime, suicide, conflict, and protest in the same settings and circumstances.

These three arguments are rash extrapolations of what Durkheim actually said and are therefore open to the objection that their truth or falsehood does not really bear on the validity of Durkheim's own scheme. That we have to choose between rash extrapolation and no historical implications at all is, however, a serious criticism of such widely used analyses of social change. In any case, contemporary followers of Durkheim *have* made all the applications to large-scale industrialization and urbanization that I have attributed to the Master. Neil Smelser's language, to take just one important case, could hardly be more Durkheimian:

Rapid industrialization . . . bites unevenly into the established social and economic structures. And throughout the society, the differentiation occasioned by agricultural, industrial, and urban changes always proceeds in a see-saw relationship with integration: the two forces continuously breed lags and bottlenecks. The faster the tempo of modernization is, the more severe the discontinuities. This unevenness creates *anomie* in the classical sense, for it generates disharmony between life experiences and the normative framework which regulates them. . . . *Anomie* may be partially relieved by new integrative devices, like unions, associations, clubs, and government regulations. However, such innovations are often opposed by traditional vested interests because they compete with the older undifferentiated systems of solidarity. The result in a three-way tug-of-war among the forces of tradition, the forces of differentiation, and the new forces of integration. Under these conditions, virtually unlimited potentialities for group conflict are created. Three classic responses to these discontinuities are anxiety, hostility, and fantasy. If and when these responses become collective, they crystallize into a variety of social movements—peaceful agitation, political violence, millennarianism, nationalism, revolution, underground subversion, etc. There is plausible—although not entirely convincing—evidence that the people most readily drawn into such movements are those suffering most severely under the displacements created by structural change. . . . Other theoretical and empirical data suggest that social movements appeal most to those who have been dislodged from old social ties by differentiation without also being integrated into the new social order [1966: 44].

With minor alterations in the text's vocabulary, a hoaxer could easily pass off Smelser's statement as a long-lost fragment of Durkheim's own writings. So, we have some evidence that Durkheim's arguments are still relevant to today's sociological theorizing. (I insist on a point that is obvious to me because of a vivid recollection. George Homans once broke up a long, agitated debate on the place of history of theory in the sociological curriculum by groaning ostentatiously, "Who *cares* what old Durkheim said?")

Does Durkheim Work?

The first historical argument we extracted from Durkheim concerned the relationship between the level of conflict and the scale, homogeneity, and ideological unity of the groups involved. So far as the level of violent conflict is concerned, there seems to be nothing to it. There is no general tendency for conflict to become more widespread as differentiated organizations become prevalent. Nor is there any notable sign that conflicts within small-scale groups are less acute than those within large-scale groups. Perhaps Durkheim and his successors drew their mistaken conclusions from some trends that *did* appear in the modern European experience: a widening of the scale at which conflicts were fought out as politics nationalized, power centralized, and communications among dissident groups improved; an increasing importance of large associations such as trade unions and political parties as the vehicles of conflict; a corresponding decline in the significance for conflict and protest of communal groups such as youth abbeys and guilds. These changes in the locus and organizational bases of conflict, however, do not conform at all to the basic Durkheimian reasoning.

The second historical argument associates disorder with rapid social change—the rapider, the more disorderly. Again, the idea appears to have no historical validity whatsoever. When we look at the correlates of accelerated urbanization or industrial growth in the modern European experience, we simply discover no tendency for periods or areas of rapid change to be more turbulent. Indeed, we gather some signs of the opposite effect: for example, that mass migration to cities withdraws people from the organizations within which they were previously able to act together, and thus depresses their capacity and propensity to struggle. It looks as though this second Durkheimian idea has gained credence through a double confusion. Observers have confused the emergence of new forms of struggle based on urban—industrial organization with an overall increase in the level of disorder, while disregarding the decline of old, important forms of struggle. They have also labeled some features of the rapid social changes they are experiencing as disorder and have thereby fallen victim to a simple, neat tautology: rapid social change causes . . . rapid social change.

Argument number three treats the various forms of "disorder" as equivalent and associated. They "spring from the same causes" and blend into one another. The modern European historical experience negates this idea as well. For example, through much of the nineteenth century the frequency of serious property crimes declined as suicide rose. Durkheim brushed off the French version of the trend as a statistical aberration, but I think it is real and largely a consequence of intensified policing. Looking at year-to-year fluctuations in strikes, violent conflicts, crimes against property, suicide, and other supposed indicators of disorder, my group has been unable to detect any significant tendency of the individual and collective forms of disapproved behavior to vary together, positively or negatively. We do, on the other hand, discover some covariation of strikes and collective violence; after all, the two phenomena overlap considerably at some points in time. We do find considerable relationships between fluctuations in collective conflicts and such solid organizational and political variables as unionization, national political maneuvering, and governmental repression. Cross-sectional comparisons on the large scale and the small yield the same negative conclusions concerning the Durkheimian formulation: no reliable connection between crime and collective conflict.

A close examination of the actual structure, personnel, and social backgrounds of contentious gatherings in the Europe of the last few hundred years likewise leads to profound skepticism about the three basic Durkheimian arguments. Seen close up, the conflicts that blur into "disorders" at a distance turn out to concern serious disagreements over the collective rights of well-defined groups and to represent only the most visible segments of a continuous stream of action in pursuit of those rights. Even the summary accounts we find in *Gentleman's Magazine* or a *South Carolina Gazette* emphasize the clash of rights and claims to common lands, employment, food, and just taxation. They portray real interests of established groups articulated in specific grievances and demands. In the Charleston of 1765 – 1775, crowds are sacking houses and seizing tea, all right, but in intimate connection with the continuous struggles which set the royal governor against the provincial assembly and the Sons of Liberty against the Loyalists. Mill, Weber, and, especially, Marx are far superior guides to what we actually see on the ground.

When I began my long inquiry into conflict, protest, and collective action, I hoped to accumulate the evidence for a decisive refutation of the Durkheimian line. Since then my ambitions have moderated. For good reason. It turns out that sociologists always have one more version of Durkheim to offer when the last one has failed. It develops that many of the key ideas in Durkheim are either circular or extraordinarily difficult to translate into verifiable propositions. It happens that in the last analysis the Durkheimian corpus concerning the impact of large-scale social change on collective action yields few fruitful, or even interesting, historical hypotheses. The challenge of refuting Durkheim becomes more difficult and less engaging. Isn't that outcome in itself a serious condemnation of a major sociological tradition?

Application

5

War and Peasant Rebellion
in Seventeenth-Century France

Introduction

Despite appearances, seventeenth-century France was not a land of peasant rebellions. To be sure, most years of the century brought at least one substantial attack on authorities and powerholders somewhere in the country. To be sure, from the 1630s to the 1650s it was rare for fewer than 2 or 3 of France's 20-odd provinces to be up in arms against the crown. To be sure, the French fought a tumultuous civil war, the Fronde, from 1648 to 1652. To be sure, the bulk of the seventeenth-century French population consisted of peasants, however we use that elusive term. To be sure, when Roland Mousnier writes a comparative study of peasant revolts, he does not hesitate to begin with seventeenth-century France, and to include the rebellion of Montmorency (1632) or the rebellion of Bordeaux (1635) along with the big rural uprisings of the Croquants (1636 onward), the Nu-Pieds (1639), and the Torrében (1675). To be sure, peasants often took part in these insurrections, and in the frequent smaller-scale struggles which complemented them. Yet it would be misleading to call any of France's seventeenth-century conflicts a peasant rebellion. Or, to put the matter more cautiously, the conflicts and rebellions that involved seventeenth-century French peasants do not conform to the models that twentieth-century analysts have fashioned for peasant revolts.

To clarify what is at issue, let us look at Jeffery Paige's characterization of peasant revolts. Paige considers peasant revolt to be the characteristic collective action of cultivators where the landed upper class "depends directly or indirectly on land-starved laborers or small farmers for its labor, expands its income through extralegal land seizures, and discourages improvements in agricultural technology which would increase agricultural income [1975: 44–45]." "Thus when peasants do act," continues Paige,

> the only way in which they can improve their economic position is through the seizure of the lord's lands. The intransigence of the landed upper class and its inability to make economic concessions limits conflict to disputes over property. Thus the actions of landed estate cultivators are invariably focused on the redistribution of property. . . . The political consequences of the landed estate . . . suggest that an agrarian revolt is likely whenever the upper class is weak or the lower class can obtain organizational support. It is agrarian because the presence of a landed upper class focuses conflict on the distribution of landed property, and a revolt because moderate action will be repressed and revolutionary action is restrained by the political weakness of the peasants.[From Jeffery M. Paige, *Agrarian Revolution, Social Movements and Export Agriculture in the Underdeveloped World*: 45. Copyright © 1975 by The Free Press, a Division of Macmillan Publishing Co., Inc. Reprinted by permission.]

Paige's characterization of peasant revolts corresponds to the usual opinion in two important regards. First, the word *peasant* stretches to include all sorts of rural cultivators. Second, the interests around which they are likely to organize and act—if they organize and act at all—concern control of land.

Gerrit Huizer's *Peasant Rebellion in Latin America* differs from Paige's *Agrarian Revolution* in emphasizing frustration, resentment, desires for vengeance, and other states of mind. When it comes to the definition of peasant rebellion, nevertheless, the two books converge. Like Paige, Huizer adopts a broad definition of the peasantry and centers his analysis on control of the land. After a review of many concrete cases of agrarian conflict in Latin America, Huizer concludes:

> On the whole it seems that the means used by the peasants were usually such that, with a minimum of extralegality, a maximum of concrete benefits of security could be achieved, mainly the possession of the land which they tilled. As soon as the peasants' demands were satisfied, and the land they worked was in their possession, in most cases they lost interest in the political movement as a whole. . . . It seems, however, that the landlords have so much fear of change that they take a stand which provokes the peasantry to use increasingly radical means. Thus the peasant movement became in some cases a revolutionary factor in the society as a whole, in spite of originally limited demands and the moderate attitude of the peasants. In those areas where the peasants took to radical forms of action, their civil violence occurred generally as a direct response to landlord intransi-

gence and violence, and because no other ways were open to them [1973: 140–141].

Thus land and the behavior of landlords become the pivots of peasant rebellion. Even Henry Landsberger (1974), in his cautious, comprehensive, classificatory approach to "peasant movements," takes essentially the same line. Most writers on peasant rebellion have something such as this in mind: Land-poor cultivators band together and carry out sustained, large-scale, violent attacks on people who control local land, or who are making visible efforts to gain control of the land.

If that is peasant rebellion, then seventeenth-century France had no significant peasant rebellions. Attacks on landlords were rare, and the theme of access to land was virtually absent from the major movements which did involve cultivators. The closest approach to a full-fledged peasant rebellion was the series of conflicts in Brittany called the Bonnets Rouges (Red Caps). From April and, especially, from June to July 1675, the rural movement coupled with a series of urban struggles that came to be known as the Révolte du Papier Timbré ('Stamped-Paper Revolt'). Seeking to raise the funds for armed forces sufficient to battle Spain, Lorraine, and the German Empire while intimidating Holland and England, Jean Baptiste Colbert had tried a whole array of fiscal expedients, including the imposition of stamped paper for official transactions, the establishment of a profitable tobacco monopoly, and an inspection tax on pewter ware. In Brittany, quite plausibly, word spread that a salt tax was next. Unlike the innumerable other rebellions that reacted somehow to fiscal pressure, however, the revolt of the Bonnets Rouges involved rural attacks on landlords and tithe collectors. As two historians of the revolt sum things up:

> Under the influence of a collective feeling, and in holiday excitement, people went off to attack a variety of objects—castles, offices or monasteries—which gave immediate, concrete satisfaction to their anger, and sometimes ended in orgy. It was only later, when the movement had spread contagiously in the void left by the weakness of repressive forces, that some parishes tried to coordinate their efforts better, and even started conceiving a measure of strategy under the leadership of improvised chiefs [Garlan and Nières 1975: 206].

At a certain point, some local rebels were able to impose treaties involving such matters as abolition of corvées and feudal rents, limitations on legal and ecclesiastical fees, freedom to hunt on noble land, and abolition of the tithe; abbots, lords, and bourgeois signed in fear of their lives. The rebel victories were brief, the repression, terrible. Although the Bonnets Rouges did not seize the land, they did sound some of the standard themes of peasant rebellion and did anticipate some of the issues that emerged as salient rural grievances during the French Revolution, twelve decades later.

Yet the revolt of the Bonnets Rouges is marginal to the category of peasant rebellion as described by most twentieth-century analysts. And it stands out as an exception in seventeenth-century France. Why? If we take the structural approach adopted by Paige, Huizer, and many others, we will stress how rarely seventeenth-century French landlords ran their estates as large farms and how little cultivation involved the labor of land-poor cultivators on other people's large estates. To find the conditions for peasant rebellion in seventeenth-century Europe, following this line of thought, we would have to move out of France and into Spain, England, southern Italy, or, preeminently, Russia and eastern Europe. If we take the expansion-of-capitalism approach adopted by Eric Wolf, Eric Hobsbawm, and many others, we will stress the tardiness of French landlords in adopting capitalist strategies for the use of their land. We will then call attention to the proliferation of land invasions, struggles over common-use rights, and attacks on landlords during the eighteenth century as the landed classes did, indeed, take up the capitalist game. Either way, we arrive at a rationale for treating seventeenth-century France as a negative case.

Why waste time on a negative case? Partly because it is useful to think through why and how seventeenth-century France, despite its rebelliousness and its large peasant base, failed to produce peasant rebellions—at least in the narrow twentieth-century sense of the word. Partly because the processes of conflict and rebellion that did occur in seventeenth-century France illustrate major ways in which the development of capitalism and the expansion of the national state affect the interests of agrarian populations and bring ordinary people into collective action. Partly because the frequency with which French peasants mobilized in response to fiscal pressure suggests that conceptions of peasant rebellion that concentrate on control of land are too narrow. And partly, I admit, because I was well into my analysis before I saw clearly that, by conventional definitions of *peasant rebellion,* I was examining a negative case.

The analysis that follows concentrates on the effects of war. It sketches the impact of warmaking, and preparations for warmaking, on the dominant forms of contention in seventeenth-century France. The analysis not only neglects peasant rebellion but also treats the peasantry as but one of several classes affected by the French state's monumental effort to build a war machine. In compensation, it draws attention to a phenomenon that students of peasant movements have neglected unduly: the strong impact of the effort to gather the resources for warmaking on the interests of ordinary people, including peasants.

One brought out into the open, the strong impact of war on peasants is not hard to understand. It is not just that seventeenth-century armies ravaged the countryside on their way to besiege the cities. Far more important, in the long run, is the fact that the bulk of the resources required for the waging of war were somehow embedded in the land. Directly or indirectly, the men, animals, food, clothing, shelter, and money committed to armies came largely from the countryside. The great majority of the seventeenth-century French population lived in villages. Although a substantial number of industrial workers, landless agricultural laborers, rentiers, priests, notaries, and other nonpeasants plied their trades in the countryside, a comfortable majority of the villagers were probably peasants in a narrow sense of the word: members of households which drew their main subsistence from working land over which they exercised substantial control and for which they supplied the bulk of the essential labor. When authorities stepped up the demand for men, animals, food, clothing, shelter, and money in order to build armies, somehow the wherewithal had to come mainly from peasant stocks. Some peasants yielded some of the warmaking requisites willingly, just so long as they fetched a good price. But on the whole the following details were true of those requisites:

1. They were not so fully commercialized and readily supplied as to allow the everyday operation of prices within the market to make them available to warmaking authorities.
2. Those that were under the control of peasant households were entirely committed either to the maintenance of the household or to the household's outside obligations.
3. Both households and communities invested those commitments and obligations with moral and legal value.
4. The conditions under which landlords, priests, local officials, and other authorities could claim resources that were under the control of peasant households were matters of incessant bargaining and bickering but were also stringently limited by contracts, codes, and local customs.
5. Authorities who sought to increase their claims on those resources were competing with others who had claims on the same resources and threatening the ability of the households involved to meet their obligations.
6. At the extreme, demands for resources threatened the survival of the households involved.

7. Ordinarily, demands for cash required households to forgo crucial purchases, to sell more or different resources than they were accustomed to doing, to borrow money, and/or to default on their cash obligations.

The impressment of a peasant's son for military service deprived a household of essential labor, and perhaps of a needed marriage exchange. The commandeering of an ox reduced the household's ability to plow. The collection of heavy taxes in money drove households into the market, and sometimes into the liquidation of their land, cattle, or equipment. Existing claims on all these resources were matters of right and obligation. We begin to understand that expanded warmaking could tear at the vital interests of peasant households and communities. We begin to understand that conflicts of interest could easily align peasants against national authorities as well as against landlords. We begin to understand why local powerholders, with their own claims on peasant resources threatened, sometimes sided with rebellious peasants. And we begin to understand why seventeenth-century rebellions could begin with disputes over something so amoral as taxation and yet proceed with the passionate advancement of legal and moral claims.

All these are justifications for taking a circuitous path to the analysis of conflicts involving the seventeenth-century French peasantry. In this chapter, I propose to trace out the connections between the French crown's strenuous and growing involvement in war and a series of standard forms of conflict. Peasants will appear and reappear in the analysis, if only because they comprised such an important share of the total French population. But the analysis itself centers on the confrontation between French statemakers and the whole population from which they were striving to wrest the means of warmaking. That analysis will, I think, clear the way for a consideration of forms of rebellion that do not fit twentieth-century conceptions of peasant revolts but nevertheless involve peasants vitally.

The scattered evidence presented through the rest of the chapter comes from a general study of the impact of statemaking and the development of capitalism on the character of contention in France from 1600 to the present. By *contention* I mean the making of claims that bear on other people's interests. In order to keep the analysis manageable, I again concentrate on the invented unit called a "contentious gathering": an occasion on which a number of people gather in the same place and visibly make claims that would, if realized, affect the interests of some other set of people. As a rule of thumb, a contentious gathering that enters my catalog must occur in a publicly accessible place and must have involved at least 10 people.

I have focused my attention on five regions: Anjou, Burgundy, Flanders, Île-de-France, and Languedoc. For these five regions (and for the period from 1600 to 1975), I have gone through major relevant collections of documents in national, departmental, and—less frequently—municipal archives, as well as attempting to enumerate contentious gatherings reported in some national periodicals and in the historical literature concerning the five regions. Even in the five regions, however, the enumeration is both incomplete and strongly biased. The incompleteness and bias, furthermore, are greater for the seventeenth century than for later periods. The most I can hope for is a general picture of differences among the regions and of changes over the long run in all the regions. For present purposes, however, that general picture should serve well enough.

In order to give a sense of the evidence, Tables 5.1– 5.5 in the Appendix to this chapter include a provisional listing of major contentious gatherings in the five regions from 1630 to 1649. Those two decades brought repeated rebellions to France. These rebellions led to the Fronde. They witnessed the government's extraordinary effort to build and rebuild its armies. Thus they provide an opportunity to consider the relationship between warmaking and rebellion—whether peasant or not.

The Burden of Government

In his *Traité de l'économie politique*, published in 1615, Antoine Montchrestien reflected on the cost of war. "It is impossible," he mused, "to make war without arms, to support men without pay, to pay them without tribute, to collect tribute without trade. Thus the exercise of trade, which makes up a large part of political action, has always been pursued by those people who flourished on glory and power, and these days more diligently than ever by those who seek strength and growth [1889 (1615): 142]." That money was the sinew of war was by then an old saw. But making the full line of connections—from war to troops to wages to taxes to cash and thence back to trade—was a special concern of seventeenth-century statemakers. Montchrestien and his contemporaries did not draw the obvious conclusion: that cutting off trade would be desirable since it would prevent war. The French conventional wisdom, instead, settled into something like these propositions:

1. In order to make war, the government had to raise taxes.
2. To make raising taxes easier, the government should promote taxable commerce.

A large part of what we call mercantilism flowed from these simple premises. Both the raising of taxes and the promoting of commerce, however,
attacked some people's established rights and interests; they therefore
produced determined resistance. Thus began a century of army building,
tax gathering, warmaking, rebellion, and repression.

Much of the royal domestic program consisted, in effect, of undoing
the Edict of Nantes. The 1598 edict had pacified the chief internal rivals of
the crown—the Catholic and Protestant lords who had established
nearly independent fiefdoms during the turmoil of the religious wars—
while Henry IV was bargaining for peace with a still-strong Spain. The
edict had granted the Huguenots the right to gather, to practice their
faith, and even to arm and to govern in a number of cities of France's
south and west. It also absolved those officials who had raised troops,
arms, taxes, and supplies in the name of one or another of the rebel
authorities (Wolfe 1972: 225 – 230). The Edict of Nantes had frozen in place
the structure of forces that prevailed in the France of 1598, while restor-
ing the ultimate powers—including the powers to raise troops, arms,
taxes, and supplies—to the crown. For a century subsequent kings and
ministers sought to unfreeze the structure, to dissolve the autonomous
centers of organized power that remained within the kingdom.

Protestants were by no means the only threat. Great Catholic lords also
caused trouble. As seen from the top down, seventeenth-century France
was a complex of patron—client chains. Every petty lord had his *gens*,
the retainers and dependents who owed their livelihood to this "good
will," to his "protection" against their "enemies" (to use three of the time's
key words). Some of the *gens* were always armed men who could swagger
in public on the lord's behalf, avenge the injuries he received, and protect
him from his own enemies. The country's great magnates played the
same games on a larger scale. They maintained huge clienteles, including
their own private armies. They held France's regional military governor-
ships and kept order with a combination of royal troops and their own.
Indeed, at the century's start France did not really have a national army,
in the later sense of the word. In time of war or rebellion the king fielded
his own personal troops. He also recruited the armies of the great lords
whom he could both trust and persuade to take the field on his behalf.

Great Catholic lords, including such members of the royal family as the
successive princes of Condé, tried repeatedly to strengthen their holds
on different pieces of the kingdom. In those insurrectionary years, gentlemen — conspirators had a reasonable hope that if they kept fishing in
troubled waters, people's grievances against royal taxes, troops, laws, and
officials would sooner or later coalesce into disciplined resistance. More
than anything else, the popular contention of the seventeenth century

swirled around the efforts of ordinary people to preserve or advance their interests in the face of a determined royal drive to build up the power of the state.

The France of 1598 was, then, a weakened country—weakened by internal strife, but also weakened by threats from outside. Three remarkable kings spent the next century reshaping the French state into an incomparable force within its own borders and a powerful presence in the world as a whole. Henry IV, Louis XIII, and Louis XIV made the transition from a leaky, creaking, wind-rocked vessel which alternated among mutiny, piracy, and open war, which had either too many hands on the wheel or practically no steering at all. They ended their work with a formidable, tight man-of-war.

The Prevalence of War

Remember how much war the seventeenth century brought. To take only the major foreign conflicts in which French kings engaged, there were:

1635 – 1659: War with Spain, ending with the Treaty of the Pyrenees
1636 – 1648: War with the Empire, ending with the Treaty of Westphalia
1664:   Expedition against the Turks at Saint Gotthard
1667 – 1668: War of Devolution, ending with the Treaty of Aachen
1672 – 1679: Dutch War, ending with the Treaty of Nimwegen
1688 – 1697: War of the League of Augsburg, ending with the Peace of Rijswijk
1702 – 1714: War of the Spanish Succession, ending with the Peace of Utrecht

If we included the minor flurries, the list would grow much longer. In 1627 and 1628, for example, the British temporarily occupied the Ile de Ré, on France's Atlantic coast, and sent a fleet to support besieged La Rochelle. In 1629 and 1630, while still battling domestic rebels, Louis XIII was sending expeditionary forces into Italy. In 1634 the king occupied and annexed Lorraine. War had long been one of the normal affairs of the state. Now it was becoming the normal state of affairs.

One of the century's ironies is that the two great guides in the early decades of French militarization were men of the church. Richelieu and Mazarin fashioned a policy of conquest. That policy required in its turn the recruiting, organizing, supplying, and paying of unprecedented armies. The effort brought to prominence such financiers as Nicholas

Fouquet, who was adept at the creation of *combinazioni*, or the quick mobilization of credit. It called forth such administrative virtuosos as Michel Le Tellier, indefatigable in the creation of armies and the large support structures essential to keep them going. The consequence was the reshaping of the state into an administrative apparatus oriented increasingly toward the production and use of armed force.

If the dominant process in seventeenth-century France was the militarization of the state, its paradoxical effect was a civilianization of royal administration. Increasingly the representatives of the crown with whom local people had to deal were full-time civilian administrators. The administrators owed their livelihood not to the "protection" of a great regional lord but to the support of a minister in Paris and the sustenance of the royal apparatus as a whole.

That happened in two ways. The first was the long drive to disarm every place, person, and group that was not under reliable royal control; the drive took the forms of bans on dueling, dismantling of fortresses, and dissolutions of civic militias, as well as the incorporation of private forces into the royal army. The second was the expansion of the numbers and powers of royal officials—most obviously, the intendants and their staffs—who were charged with raising the revenues, controlling the supplies, and securing the day-to-day compliance necessary to build and maintain a big military establishment. Over the century as a whole, the crown was successful in both regards: It greatly reduced the possibility of armed resistance within the kingdom, and it enormously increased the resources available for royal warmaking. Yet success came at the price of bloody rebellion, of brutal repression, and of expedients and compromises that committed the crown to an immense, exigent clientele of creditors and officials. These statemaking processes stimulated the large-scale contention of the seventeenth century.

War and the Means of Warmaking

Seventeenth-century statemakers who wished to expand their ability to make war had to do more than organize armies. They had to find the essential resources: men, food, horses, wagons, weapons, and the money to buy them. Although military commanders seized the matériel of war directly when they could, French armies acquired the bulk of their resources through purchase—not always from willing sellers, as we shall see, but purchase nonetheless. The government raised money for its military purchases in a variety of ways: through forced loans, through the sale of offices and privileges, through fines and confiscations, and a number of other devices to which officials increasingly applied their ingenuity as the seventeenth century wore on. But in the long run one form of taxation or another provided the great majority of the essential funds. The seventeenth century brought spectacular increases in the French fiscal burden, and the prime reason for those increases was the rising cost of waging war.

Figure 5.1 combines some information concerning France's seventeenth-century tax burden with some speculative computations concerning the impact of the tax burden. The curve for "gross tax revenue" traces J. J. Clamagéran's estimates of total receipts from regular taxes in selected years. Since the latter half of the seventeenth century became the great age of raising money by irregular expedients — borrowing, selling privileges, forcing contributions, and so on — the curve probably underestimates the increase for later years. For lack of a figure near the period of the Fronde (1648 – 1652), the curve also disguises the fact that taxes kept rising into the 1640s. Nevertheless, the graph displays the fierce increase in total taxation after the 1620s, the lull of the 1650s, and the new acceleration after Louis XIV's accession to full personal power in 1661.

The other curves suggest two different ways of thinking about the impact of rising taxes. Expressing taxes as the equivalent of a volume of wheat has the clearest meaning for those who actually had wheat to sell: large farmers, landlords, tithe collectors, and some rentiers. For them, the general trend of taxes ran upward, the year-to-year fluctuations in the impact of taxes were dramatic, yet years of high prices could actually be advantageous — just so long as their supplies did not decline as rapidly as the price rose. When it came to people who had to buy wheat or bread to survive, however, the years of high prices were never advantageous; in those years, their tax obligations rarely declined, but much higher proportions of their incomes went into the purchase of food. Unless the government remitted taxes, those became terrible years of squeeze for consumers. Our curves for hours of work disguise that year-to-year variation, since they depend on conventional wage figures for an idealized semiskilled worker. Nevertheless, they indicate that (a) on the average and over the long run, the rising national tax burden could easily have tripled the amount of work time that the taxpaying French household devoted to the government; and that (b) the reign of Louis XIII (effectively 1615 – 1643) brought a spectacular rise in the per capita tax burden.

The surges in taxation corresponded closely to quickening preparations for war. In the later 1620s and 1630s they register the effects of Richelieu's shift from the quelling of domestic enemies to the challenging of Spain and the Empire. In the 1640s, Mazarin continued to drive for

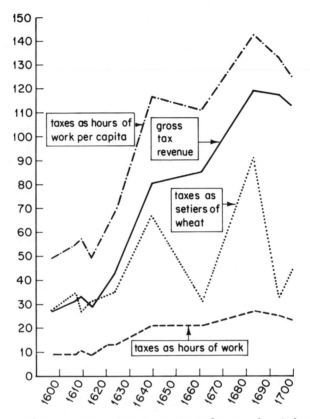

FIGURE 5.1. France's gross tax revenues, 1597 – 1699: raw figures and equivalents. Gross tax revenue: "impôts: revenu brut," in millions of livres, as reported by Clamagéran 1867 – 1876. Taxes as *setiers* of wheat: gross tax revenue expressed as the number of units of 100,000 *setiers* of first-quality wheat it would buy at Paris prices, as reported by Baulant 1968; divide by 10 to get millions of *setiers* of wheat. Taxes as hours of work: gross tax revenue expressed as a multiple of the hourly wage of a semiskilled provincial worker (*manoeuvre de province*), as reported by Fourastié 1969: 44 – 49. The wage figure is an interpolation of a general estimate and therefore tells us nothing about year-to-year fluctuations. Shown in hundreds of millions of work hours. Taxes as hours of work per capita: taxes as hours of work, divided by an interpolated figure for total population, as estimated by Reinhard, Armengaud, and Dupâquier 1968. The figure shown estimates hours of work per year per capita.

more taxes and bigger armies. In the later 1660s and the 1670s rising taxes signal the start of Louis XIV's great wars. Taxes were, indeed, the sinews of war.

Given the formidable growth of state power and the decreasing support of popular movements by great lords, the persistence of rebellion and resistance through the seventeenth century offers a measure of the

interests at stake. That ordinary people should have the urge to resist is
itself perfectly understandable. Warmaking and statemaking proceeded
at their expense. Warmaking and statemaking placed demands on land,
labor, capital, and commodities that were already committed: grain ear-
marked for the local poor or next year's seed, manpower required for a
farm's operation, savings promised for a dowry. The commitments were
not merely fond hopes or pious intentions but matters of right and obligation; not to meet those commitments, or to impede their fulfillment,
was to violate established rights of real people.

In addition to local and customary rights, raising new resources often
meant abridging or rescinding privileges the state itself had ratified.
Exemptions from taxation, rights to name local officers, established
means of consent, and bargaining over financial support to the crown—
all gave way as statemakers made the claims of the government supplant
the rights of individuals and communities. Popular indignation was the
greater because of a standard seventeenth-century tactic: offering privileges and profits to the tax farmer, venal officeholder, or other entre-
preneur who was prepared to give the crown ready cash in exchange for
the opportunity to draw future revenues from the local population. It was
bad enough that a rich man should profit from other people's sacrifices.
But when his privilege actually increased the local burden (as regularly
happened when a newly exempted official stopped paying his share of
the local tax quota, or when the office in question involved new or expanded fees), the rich man's neighbors were commonly outraged.

Not that the middlemen were the only objects of popular resistance.
Ordinary people often felt the military effort quite directly. Soldiers and
officials wrested from them the wherewithal of war: food, lodging, draft
animals, unwilling recruits. People hid those resources when they could
and defended them against seizure when they dared. On the whole,
however, the military got what they wanted.

The direct seizure of the means of war from the people lagged a distant
second behind the extraction of money. In a relatively uncommercialized
economy, demands for cash contributions were often more painful than
demands for goods. They required people either to dig into the small
stores of coin they had saved for great occasions or to market goods and
labor they would ordinarily have used at home. The less commercialized
the local economy, the more difficult the marketing. Taxes, forced loans,
the sale of offices, and other means of raising money for the state and its
armies all multiplied during the seventeenth century. Directly or indirectly, all of them forced poor people to convert short resources into cash
and then to surrender that cash to the state.

When rights were at issue and the force available to the state was not overwhelming, ordinary people resisted the new exactions as best they could. Tax rebellions, attacks on new officeholders, and similar forms of resistance filled the seventeenth century. Nevertheless, French state-makers managed to override rights and resistance alike; they succeeded in increasing enormously the financial burden borne by the population as a whole.

How did the statemakers succeed? By dividing their opposition, by using force, by routinizing the collection of revenues, by multiplying the specialists devoted to the extraction of those revenues, and by expanding the number of people and groups who had a financial interest in the state's survival. The definitive settling of the intendants in the provinces, accomplished after the Fronde had forced the temporary withdrawal of the intendants from the land, was no doubt the single most important strategem. The intendants of Richelieu and Mazarin were still serving, by and large, as temporary troubleshooters; after the Fronde, however, Mazarin, and then Colbert, expanded and regularized their service. The intendants supervised the collection of revenues, applied coercion when necessary and feasible, kept watch over the local expenditure of state funds, and stayed alert for new opportunities to tax, to sell offices, to preempt local revenues, and to borrow, borrow, and then borrow again.

Although the borrowing eventually increased the share of state revenues that went to service debts, it also expanded the number of people who had financial interests in the state's survival. It created a large class of officials who served their own advantage by helping to pay the expenses of the state. The tax farmer advanced cash to the crown in return for the right to collect taxes at a profit. The purchaser of a new office made a substantial payment to the crown in return for an annuity, for the right to collect the office's revenues, and, frequently, for some form of exemption from taxation. A gild paid over a sum of money—usually borrowed from its members and from local financiers—and received a royal guarantee of its monopolies and privileges. That became the standard royal expedient: In order to raise current revenue, the king's agents found someone with capital, then induced or coerced him to advance money now in return for a claim on future income and the assurance of governmental support in collecting that income. Such a routine deflected the indignation of ordinary people from the statemakers to the tax farmers, officeholders, and other profiteers who fattened themselves at the people's expense.

In order to reduce the political risks of this fiscal strategy, however, the crown had to tame and supplant its internal rivals. Otherwise, each new round of popular resistance would provide an opportunity for some set of magnates to offer themselves as champions of the people's rights. In parallel with its external warmaking and its internal fund raising, the crown undertook a massive effort of cooptation, neutralization, and suppression. After the failure of the Fronde, the great princes and their clienteles fell into line. With some important exceptions, the major blocks of Protestant autonomy gave way under the continuous grinding and blasting of Louis XIII and Louis XIV. The parlements, the other "sovereign courts," the provincial estates, the gilds, and municipalities all finally lost significant shares of their ability to resist royal demands and to ally themselves with ordinary people against the crown, as the intendants used a combination of force, fragmentation, and fiscal advantage to bring them into acquiescence. Thus the intendants and other royal officials became freer to use their growing repressive power when ordinary people dared to resist governmental demands directly. These changes had predictable effects on the character of popular contention: a decline in the involvement of major powerholders in big rebellions, an increasing focus of popular resistance on the exactions of tax farmers and officeholders, a decreasing readiness of royal officials to negotiate with groups protesting the violations of their rights.

Routines of Seventeenth-Century Contention

Anyone who digs into the materials of seventeenth-century contention notices some recurrent traits. There is the importance of the exactions of troops, the demand for taxes, and (toward the end of the century) the failure of local officials to apply proper controls over the food supply in times of shortage—all as objects of contention. There are the standard sequences in which existing communities respond to violations of their rights and privileges by assembling, electing leaders and spokesmen, issuing protests and demands, then (if not satisfied) retaliating against their enemies. There is the frequent collective appeal to an influential patron, a power judicial authority, or, preferably, both at once. There is the use of established festivals and ceremonies as occasions for communicating approbation or reprobation of public officials. There is the mutual modeling of crowds and officials, with the crowd sometimes borrowing the execution in effigy from the official treatment of absentee felons, and with officials sometimes borrowing the selection of a single spokesperson to state the crowd's grievances. There are the elementary forms of collective action: the sacking of private houses and tollgates; the expulsion of miscreants, including tax collectors, from the community; the deliberate blocking of the gates or the streets; the seizure of a disputed commodity, especially grain or salt; the staging of ritual mockery;

much more rarely, the mustering of armed men for an attack. There are the sustained rebellions that resulted from coalitions between aggrieved groups of ordinary people and disaffected or ambitious clusters of the privileged. There is the visible rupture of this pattern of coalition with the royal victory over the Fronde and the Frondeurs. All these features appear clearly in the seventeenth-century contention of Anjou, Flanders, Burgundy, Languedoc, and Île-de-France.

Some patterns of contention were common to many regions because the same sweeping processes were affecting the interests of ordinary people throughout France. Warfare, statemaking, and the development of capitalism dominated the seventeenth-century patterns. Through the century as a whole, war and preparation for war set the master rhythms.

War is a form of contention which creates new forms of contention. We might array the different ways in which ordinary seventeenth-century people acted together by increasing distance of the various sorts of action from the fact of war itself. Thinking only of those occasions on which people actually gathered together and made claims of one kind or another, we might prepare this rough scale:

1. Direct participation of civilians in combats among armies
2. Battles between regular armies and armed civilians
3. Resistance to direct exactions by the military: impressment and the commandeering of meat, wine, bread, sex, and lodging
4. Resistance to official efforts to raise the means of support for armies: especially taxation, but also the commandeering of corvée labor, wagons, horses, food, and housing
5. Resistance to efforts, official or unofficial, to divert resources — especially food — to armies
6. Conflicts emerging as by-products of the presence of troops: soldier — civilian brawls, clashes over military smuggling, and poaching
7. Resistance to attempts of officeholders to exact new or larger returns from their privileges and official duties
8. Local and private vengeance against violators of everyday morality, including established rules for the marketing of commodities
9. Conflicts between followers of different religious creeds

These were the major occasions for contention on anything larger than an entirely local scale. Most items on the list had a substantial, recurrent connection to warmaking. Resistance to officeholders' exactions, for instance, was linked to war: The offices in question were commonly created, or preempted, by the crown, as part of the drive to raise military revenues. Indeed, of the larger recurrent forms of contention in seventeenth-century France, only the struggles between Protestants and

Catholics, and some of the conflicts over food, were not obviously related to the creation, maintenance, and maneuvering of armed forces. Even food riots and religious conflicts, as we shall see later, had their links to war.

CIVILIANS IN COMBAT

Let us go down the list. If we include the forces of princes and great lords, then all five of our regions experienced army-to-army combat at various points in the seventeenth century. In battles of French forces against French forces (I speak of their current allegiances, not of their origins; the forces of the prince of Condé and other grandees were often Swiss, Croatian, or something else), Languedoc was no doubt the champion. As early as 1621, the duc de Rohan, using the Cévennes as his base, had Protestant armies in the field against the royal forces in Languedoc. The king's pacification of Languedoc in 1622 was only the first of many royal pacifications in that rebellious province. In Languedoc peace came unstuck easily.

When it came to clashes between French forces and those of foreign crowns, on the other hand, Burgundy and Flanders had much more experience of seventeenth-century war than did Anjou, Languedoc, or Île-de-France. Especially Flanders. After all, most of the region began the century as Spanish territory and came to the French crown only as the result of conquest, reconquest, and military occupation. In 1641, we find the civic militia of Lille (still a Spanish possession) turning back the French troops who arrived to besiege the city (Liagre 1934: 113). In the village of Rumégies, near Valenciennes,

> In 1660–1661, it was necessary to whitewash the church, "the walls having been blackened and damaged by the wars, since both inhabitants and soldiers fired their guns there, on account of which the whole church—roof, glass and paint—was run down." In 1667, toward Ascension (16 May), the curé, fearing the approach of the armies of Louis XIV, sent the church's ornaments and his parish register to Tournai. Part of the population evacuated the village. The rest stayed there and, in order to protect themselves, fortified the cemetery and dug a trench all round: a means of defense by which the inhabitants had profited "many times during previous wars" [Platelle 1964: 504].

Rumégies's people did, in fact, take a reluctant part in war after war. They dug their trench of 1667, however, on the eve of a crucial change. With the end of the War of Devolution in 1668, the province of Tournai, and thus Rumégies, became French territory. From that point on, the marauders and occupiers most to be feared were the village's former masters, the

Spaniards. The nearby frontier did not become relatively secure until the Peace of Utrecht, 45 years later.

ARMIES VERSUS CIVILIANS

Some of Rumégies's wartime ravaging may have resulted from battles between regular army units and armed civilians. Most of the time, however, armies chased each other through the village; the villagers defended themselves and their property as best they could. For a clearer case of civilian involvement in combat, we may turn to Burgundy in April 1637. That was the second year of France's direct participation in what later became known as the Thirty Years' War. According to the *Gazette de France*,

> The peasants from around St. Jean de Lône, Auxonne and Bellegarde, to avenge themselves for the burning that the garrisons of Autrey and Grey were doing along our frontier, recruited a few soldiers to lead them and, on the 21st and 22nd of this month, threw themselves into three big enemy villages, including 400-household Joux. After they had killed everything, they reduced the villages to ashes. They are determined to deal with all the other villages in the same manner, so long as the enemy gives them the example [1637: 263].

Even this tale, to be sure, does not show us armed civilians confronting enemy units. Except when householders defended themselves against invading troops, such encounters were rare or nonexistent.

RESISTANCE TO MILITARY EXACTIONS

The most frequent struggles between soldiers and civilians did not arise from military actions, as such, but from the attempts of military men to seize precious resources from the civilian population. The agents of Louis XIII and Louis XIV created armies much faster than they created the means to satisfy those armies' wants. They nationalized the troops at the same time, transforming them from private retainers of great lords to public employees of the national state. But only toward the end of Louis XIV's reign did something like a national structure for supplying, paying, and containing the growing armed forces begin to take shape. By that time, the armies were in almost perpetual motion—at least for the two-thirds of the year that the roads could support the artillery the seventeenth-century military had started to drag around with them.

The consequences were predictable. Pay usually came late and sometimes never. Commanders often lagged a year or more in paying their troops. Food supplies frequently ran low. Military housing was practically nil. Few young men willingly became soldiers; impressment and emptying of jails became common devices for recruitment. Mutiny and desertion were rarely far away. Commanders who wanted to keep their regiments intact threatened and coerced when they could, but only survived by promising or arranging rewards. They regularly promised booty from a captured city, sometimes at the same moment that they took ransoms paid by the city fathers in order to avoid pillage. In theory, they were supposed to pay the populace for the labor, food, lodging, and supplies their armies required. In practice, they tolerated or even encouraged their soldiers' commandeering of food, drink, lodging, services, goods, money, and sexual experience. Many generals and supply officers had it both ways: They pocketed the royal funds and let the troops forage. Only when the rapine threatened to call forth popular rebellion, or retaliation from military superiors and royal officials, did the commanders commonly call a halt.

The soldiers involved in snatching what they could get from the population thought the commandeered sex, meat, wine, bread, labor, and lodging was no more than their due. The victims, however, disagreed. Hence an unending series of local conflicts in which demanding soldiers faced indignant householders. One of the rare successes of the householders occurred during the 1632 rebellion of the duc de Montmorency in Languedoc:

> The sieur d'Alsaux, who during the rebellion seized a place called Montreal, between Carcassonne and Toulouse, had gone out to forage; the residents chased out the soldiers he left behind; at his return, they locked the gates and fired many musket rounds at him. Peasants of the region around Carcassonne knocked a number of his foreign troops off their mounts; and the 25th of September, when some of his Croats were passing close to a little village four leagues from the same city, the villagers went out and killed twenty-six of them, took all their baggage and treated the rest of them in such a way that they are not likely to feel the urge to return to France for a long time [*Gazette de France* 3 October 1632: 410−411].

More often, however, the reports that survive from the century run like the laconic note of March 1678 concerning the intendant of Burgundy: "M. Bouchu took care of the complaints he received from many localities about violence committed on the occasion of, and under the pretext of, the recruitment of soldiers [A.N. (Archives Nationales, Paris) G⁷ 156]." On the whole, "taking care" of such complaints meant hushing them up.

RESISTANCE TO OFFICIAL EFFORTS

The intendants faced a sharper dilemma when it came to popular resistance stimulated by official efforts to raise the means of support for armies. When ordinary people fought back against the demands of troops, troops were there to put them down. But when ordinary people rose against civilian demands for taxes, corvées, and supplies to support the army, the troops were often far away. The *maréchaussée* (the state police, one might say loosely) could deal with an individual or two but was usually helpless in the grip of a determined crowd. The *gardes des gabelles* ('salt-tax guards') and other armed forces in the service of the tax farmers acquired plenty of experience in small-scale-crowd control but likewise fell apart in the face of substantial risings; in any case, they generally confined their work to the particular purposes of the tax farmers. Municipal constables and militias, where they existed, tended to limit their efforts to their home bases and to be unreliable allies for royal officials.

What was the intendant, faced with determined opposition, to do? He could try to face it down with moral authority, threats, and the thinly armed force at his disposal. Or he could call on the military governors of provinces and regional capitals to send in royal troops to back him up; in that case, he not only confessed visibly to his inability to keep order on his own but also acquired obligations to a significant rival within his own bailiwick. Small wonder, then, that the intendants' reports to Paris often swing between utter silence about a resistance movement and detailed reports, appeals for aid, and cries of vengeance. Small wonder that the intendants often explained popular resistance as the result of plots, treason, and barbarism.

The very process of establishing French administration after conquest was full of the risk of resistance. In the part of Hainaut recently taken from the Spanish, the intendant Faultrier was busy organizing the collection of taxes in 1686. That meant negotiation and coercion, village by village. The village of Estrun, near Cambrai, had put up more than the usual resistance to the elimination of the privileges it had enjoyed under Spanish dominion. In the process of bringing the villagers into line, the intendant had exiled their curé and put one of their notables in jail. By January 1686, however, Faultrier thought his decisive action and his threats of more jailings had sufficiently intimidated the people of Estrun (letter of 3 January 1686, A.N. G^7 286). The tax farmer and the villagers came to a compromise agreement. Yet on 7 July the intendant was writing,

> They have since presented a declaration to the farmer's agent which I find very insolent; when people are only insolent on paper, it isn't hard for an intendant to punish them. I therefore didn't give their action much weight, but they went much farther. For when the agent tried to collect his taxes, they sounded the tocsin on him and the men he had brought to help him. The women began with stones, and their husbands finished with clubs. All

of them said that until they saw an order signed by the King they would not pay, and that my signature was not enough for a matter that important.

At that point, predictably, the intendant requested the dispatch of troops to enforce the royal prerogative (A.N. G^7 286). Over the seventeenth century as a whole, some version of this encounter between tax collectors and citizens was no doubt the most frequent occasion for concerted resistance to royal authority. That was true not only in Hainaut and Flanders but also in the rest of France.

RESISTANCE TO THE DIVERSION OF RESOURCES

As the century wore on, nevertheless, the locus of conflict moved increasingly to the market. The reasons for the shift are simple and strong: Royal officials turned increasingly toward the promotion of taxable trade and the use of the market to supply the needs of their growing state. The army, in particular, moved away from direct commandeering of its supplies (with the exception of troops, for the free-labor market never supplied enough soldiers) and relied increasingly on *munitionnaires* to buy up its necessaries. The new strategy regularized governmental demands somewhat and thus probably made them easier to sustain. It diverted indignation from intendants to merchants and *munitionnaires*. But it created new grievances.

The grievances, for the most part, concerned food. The other resources (always excepting manpower) required by the armed forces were sufficiently commercialized and abundant for the market to supply them without great stress most of the time. The simultaneous growth of cities, bureaucracies, armies, and a landless proletariat, on the other hand, placed great strains on the French food supply. In times of shortages and high prices, the new strategy led intendants, merchants, and local officials to challenge the established ways of assuring that local communities would have prior access to their means of survival. It challenged the inventories, exclusive marketing, price controls, and other tight regulations that had long been standard responses to shortages. Ordinary people responded to the challenge by substituting themselves for the delinquent authorities. They seized, inventoried, marketed, controlled, and punished on their own. The closer the authorities were to the local population, the more they hesitated either to suspend the old controls or to punish those who attempted to reinstate them. Hence there were many "disorders" involving the "complicity" of local authorities.

The conflicts rose to national visibility with the subsistence crises of 1693–1694, 1698–1699, and 1709–1710. The feeding of the army was but one of several factors in these crises, but it was an important one. Probably more so than it had to be, because the army contractors had lush opportunities to speculate with the stocks they bought up by royal authority. In Buxy, Burgundy, at the beginning of September 1693, local people seized the grain that had been purchased by Burgundy's *munitionnaire*. The intendant accused a judge, a royal prosecutor, and other officials of having encouraged the populace. Yet the root cause of the conflict, he reported, was that the *munitionnaire* was stockpiling old grains and buying new ones. "Allow me to tell you," he wrote to the *contrôleur general*,

> that we've never before seen in Burgundy what we're seeing now. It isn't usual for a *munitionnaire* to spend the whole year here getting his supplies, and even less so to employ a thousand persons who commit all sorts of irregularities in their purchases and in commandeering transportation, without our being quite able to speak openly about it for fear of slowing up the supply service (letter of 13 September 1693, A.N. G⁷ 158; cf. G⁷ 1630].

In short, the intendant had a strong presumption that the contractor in question was not only exceeding his authority but also profiteering in the grain trade.

Rarely was the impact of military procurement on conflicts over food supply so unmixed and visible; it is the market's genius to mix motives and diffuse responsibilities. In a more general way, nevertheless, the recurrent patterns of conflict reveal the sore points in the system. High prices, shortages, and hunger as such did not usually call up popular action; serious conflicts normally began with official inaction, with the withholding of stored food from the local market, with obvious profiteering, and, especially, with the effort to remove sorely needed grain from the locality. The latter was the case, for example, at Vernon in 1699, when the citizens roughed up the merchants who came to the local market to buy grain for Paris (Boislisle 1874–1897: I, 512). During that crisis, as well as those of 1693–1694 and 1709–1710, military demand was only one of several attractions drawing grain away from local consumption with the sanction of the state. In all five of our regions, the three crises brought out popular resistance to the diversion of food from local markets.

BY-PRODUCTS OF THE MILITARY PRESENCE

At one time or another, all five of our regions also produced conflicts that were essentially by-products of the presence of troops: soldier—civilian brawls, clashes over military smuggling or poaching, and the like. In the seventeenth century, whoever said "soldier" also said "trouble." In times of open war, foraging and conflicts over booty made the trouble worse than ever. An incident on the Flemish frontier in 1693 gives the flavor. The Sieur de Beauregard, acting captain of the free company of the governor of the city of Condé, was sent out on his own on 24 June; he had 70 men and a warrant to bring back booty. His force met a loaded wagon on the road from Brussels to Mons. Etienne Gorant, the driver, showed a passport covering far fewer goods than were in his wagonload. Beauregard seized the wagon and the driver; he sent them off to Condé with 20 men and a sergeant. "But that sergeant," he reported, "was pursued by a military detachment from Mons which, being larger, took away the loaded wagon without listening to his objections. The violent manner of the chief of the Mons detachment made it clear that he was in league with the merchants. Your petitioner has been to Mons, but has been unable to obtain justice [letter of 7 July 1693, A.N. G⁷ 287]."

Military commanders remained ambivalent about the struggle for booty. It could distract soldiers from conquest or defense and stir up the civilian population inconveniently. But in an age in which piracy, privateering, and regular naval warfare overlapped considerably, land forces did not make neat distinctions between legal and illegal acquisition of property either. When the pay of soldiers was meager, irregular, and a tempting source of income for greedy commanders, military chiefs often found it expedient to let the troops supplement their pay with pillage.

Another tactic was to wink at smuggling. Now the civilian population did not necessarily suffer—if soldiers could bring salt or coffee into the region duty free, they could easily sell it below the official price and still profit. But the tax farmer, always sensitive to attacks on his pocketbook, felt the pinch at once. Thus on 8 January 1633, as so often before and after, the king issued an edict against military salt smuggling. Its preamble stated the remonstrance of Philippe Harnel, the general contractor for France's salt tax:

> That soldiers garrisoned for his Majesty's service in the kingdom's frontier cities smuggle salt publicly every day, & go about in bands of twenty, thirty, forty or fifty soldiers armed with muskets and other offensive weapons, recruiting civilian salt-smugglers & many others whom they lead and escort to the borders of foreign lands & lead them back to their hiding-places with their wagons, carts and horses loaded with said illegal salt [Archives Historiques de l'Armée, Vincennes, A¹ 14].

Since those same soldiers were the chief force the crown had at its disposal for the tracking down of smugglers, royal edicts tended to be ignored, and salt farmers developed a strong interest in organizing their own paramilitary forces.

In the frontier areas of Burgundy, for example, both civilians and soldiers made money by bringing in contraband salt. An interesting cycle developed. Civilians who were agile enough to speed salt across the border were also attractive prospects for military service. If the salt-tax guards caught civilian smugglers with the goods, the tax farmer sought to have the smugglers convicted with fanfare and shipped off for long terms in the galleys, far from Burgundy. While the smugglers were being held in jail pending the royal ratification of their sentences, however, Burgundy's military commanders, as short of recruits as ever, frequently pled for the convicts to be given the choice between enlistment and the galleys. The military commanders often prevailed over the remonstrances of the tax farmers. The local army units then gained recruits who were of dubious reliability as men of war, but who certainly knew how to smuggle salt.

RESISTANCE TO OFFICEHOLDERS' EXACTIONS

Our next step out from war concerns resistance to attempts of officeholders to exact new or larger returns from their privileges and official duties. Its connection with war is indirect but real; most of the new offices and privileges in question came into being as part of the crown's effort to raise more money for warmaking. In May 1691, the intendant of Languedoc announced a schedule of fees for the newly established administrators of public sales. (They were the *jurés – crieurs publics*, parallel to the registrars of burials, whose establishment in Dijon about the same time caused a great deal of trouble.) Instead of merely collecting fees at public sales, the agent of the officeholders tried to set up a tollgate at the entrance to Nîmes and to collect the fees on all goods entering the city. The intendant stopped him but neglected to forbid him to do the same thing elsewhere. The agent tried the same game in Toulouse. The clerks, "who came from the dregs of the common people," reported the intendant, "asked 10 sous at the city gate for each wagonload of wood that came in, and a certain sum for each basket of peas, salads and fruits." Several women beat up a clerk. The intendant decided to punish both the women and the agent. In the case of the women, he said, "it seems important to me to get people out of the habit of making justice for themselves in such cases." As for the agent, his offense was a "genuine swindle" that could not be tolerated in such difficult times (letter of 2 June 1691, A.N. G⁷ 300). Yet the intendant faced a dilemma: People bought the new offices for their financial return and expected the government to guarantee the perquisites of office. If the offices were not attractive, they would not sell—and the government would lack the ready cash it needed for its incessant wars.

As a result, the intendants usually took the side of the officeholders. When the "young people" of Toulouse attacked the city's "clerk for marriage banns" in January 1698 and gave sword wounds to the clerk and his would-be rescuer, the same intendant of Languedoc despaired of getting action through the local courts. He proposed a royal prosecution "so that the people of Toulouse will understand that it is a major crime to attack and insult without reason those who are responsible for royal business [letter of 5 January 1698, A.N. G[7] 303]." The business of venal officeholders readily became "royal business."

VENGEANCE AGAINST VIOLATORS OF EVERYDAY MORALITY

The title is portentous, the contents are heterogeneous. Let us include here all those conflicts in which the rights and obligations at issue had a shadowy basis in law, but a strong grounding in popular belief. Some of the forms of contention examined under previous headings qualify here as well. The food riot is a notable example; one of the chief reasons for its rise at the end of the seventeenth century was, precisely, the declining legal support for the old system of local controls over food, in a time when popular beliefs in the priority of local needs continued strong. But there were others we have not yet encountered in descending the scale of proximity to war: the *rixe*, or local brawl, which pitted two groups of artisans or the young men of neighboring communities against each other in a struggle over honor and precedence; popular retribution against an actor, an executioner, or another public performer who failed to meet the public's standards; the charivari — serenade; the rescue of prisoners from their captors.

In the Dijon of 1625, for example, the executioner set up to decapitate Mlle Gillet, who had been convicted of infanticide. When the nervous hangman failed to kill the young woman with two sword blows, his wife took her turn and likewise botched the job. At that, the spectators stoned the executioner and his wife (A. M. (Archives Municipales) Dijon I 116). In the Nîmes of 1645, the friends of imprisoned paper cutter Cabiac snatched him out of jail. One of the two rival intendants of Languedoc,[1] Baltazar, treated the jailbreak as a sedition. The other intendant, Bousquet, pooh-poohed his colleague's alarm:

> At bottom, whether the son of Cabiac is guilty or innocent, we know that what's at issue is the revenge of a certain Cassague, collector of the paper-cutters' fees, on said Cabiac's family. In this case, justice is really serving to hide the guilty parties, and as a pretext for revenge of one side's private wrongs [Liublinskaya 1966: 133; letter of 1 May 1645].

[1] This was, of course, before the administrative regularization of the later seventeenth century. For information on the rivalry of Baltazar and Bousquet, although not on this particular conflict, see Beik 1974.

If it had not been for the irritating presence of rival Baltazar, intendant Bousquet would probably have handled the affair on his own, without divulging the details to the *contrôleur general* in Paris. Except when they grew too big for the local forces of order, these jailbreaks, brawls, feuds, charivaris, and similar events were contained and settled by the officials on the spot.

RELIGIOUS CONFLICTS

That was not true, however, of most religious conflicts. The balance of power between Protestants and Catholics remained an affair of state throughout the seventeenth century. Whether the initiative for a conflict came from local religious groups or from actions of the government, royal officials had to pay close attention to its outcome.

Often, members of one religious group attacked individuals belonging to the other. In 1611, in Paris,

> the Protestants went to bury a small child in their Trinity Cemetery, near the rue Saint-Denis; they went in the evening, but before sunset. Two members of the watch officially led the procession. A vinegar-maker's helper began to throw stones at them, and was imitated by his master and by several others. One of the watchmen was wounded. The *lieutenant criminel* of the Châtelet had them arrested and, on the first of July, the helper was whipped outside of Trinity Cemetery. But on Sunday the 21st of August, Protestants coming back from Charenton were insulted [Mousnier 1978: 75; Charenton was the location of the one church the Protestants of Paris were then allowed].

In Paris, the Sunday trips of the Protestants to Charenton were frequent occasions for abuse from Catholics, and sometime occasions for violence. When the news of the death of the (Catholic) duc de la Mayenne at the 1621 siege of (Protestant) Montauban arrived in the city, crowds attacked the carriages of the Protestants, battled with the watchmen stationed at the Saint Antoine Gate to protect them, and rushed out to burn down the church. Later,

> the other clerics and common people who had busied themselves with setting the fire and burning the Temple and drinking 8 or 10 kegs of wine that were in the concierge's cellar, and eating the provisions, after making a flag of a white sheet, came back to Paris through the St. Antoine Gate, 400 strong, shouting *Vive le Roy* [*Mercure françois* 1621: 854].

That "Vive le Roy" should remind us of the connection between popular hostility and official policy. In this instance the sanctioning of armed guards to prevent an attack on the Protestants makes it dubious that royal officials directly instigated the violence. Yet from early in his reign

Louis XIII sought to cow the Protestants, to demilitarize them, and to circumscribe their activities.

Local groups of Protestants and Catholics also fought intermittently. Where the Protestants were relatively strong, as in Nîmes, Montpellier, and much of urban Languedoc, we find a series of struggles over control of public offices. In the mainly Protestant city of Pamiers, the consuls sought to exclude all Catholics from the consulate. In March 1623, the Catholics demanded representation; they persuaded the parlement to decree equal representation of the two religious groups. The consuls closed the city gates to the parlement's emissary, and then to the emissary who carried confirmation of the decree by the king's council. Only when the king sent troops did the consuls give in (*Mercure françois* 1624: 381 – 385). Later the same year, the emboldened Catholics complained against the stay in the planned destruction of local Protestant churches and demanded a division of the city keys—two per gate—between Protestants and Catholics. By that time, Pamiers actually had three competing factions: the Protestants, the Catholics who had stayed in town during the Protestant– Catholic wars of Languedoc in the previous years, and the bishop, priests, and (presumably wealthier) Catholics who had fled Pamiers when the wars came too close (*Mercure françois* 1624: 871– 877). In 1625, the Pamiers Protestants joined those of a number of other cities of Languedoc in a new rebellion against the crown. In this case, as in most, the national conflict and the local one reinforced each other. Louis XIV continued the effort. Then, in the 1680s, the began the drive to rid France entirely of the Huguenot scourge.

The striving of kings and intendants to weaken the Protestants produced the most extensive religious conflicts of the seventeenth century. We have already seen Louis XIII marching out his armies to besiege La Rochelle, Montauban, Nîmes, and other Protestant strongholds. Those campaigns against the Protestants were veritable civil wars. They continued through the 1620s. By the time France reentered the world of international war after 1630, the autonomous military strength of the Protestants had cracked. Even during the Fronde, Protestants did not appear as a distinct national bloc, or as a major threat to the monarchy.

From the 1630s to the 1680s, the government ground away at the "so-called Reformed Religion" intermittently and without drama. Local battles continued. A case in point occurred in the Protestant stronghold of Le Mas d'Azil, near Pamiers, in October 1671. A day laborer who had recently converted to Catholicism

> was attacked in the middle of the fair by François and David Cave, former Huguenots . . . and many others armed with swords and staves. They wounded him so badly that he was left for dead. . . . The Brother Prior and

the Benedictine monk who happened by complained to them . . . and they
shouted against [the day laborer], *Get the Rebel, Get the Rebel, for taking a
religion that is worthless to its supporters* and other words forbidden by law
on pain of death [Wemyss 1961: 36, quoting interrogations of witnesses].

But no sustained, large-scale conflict developed at le Mas d'Azil or elsewhere until after 1680, when the government of Louis XIV began the
campaign to squeeze out the Protestants. In le Mas d'Azil the campaign
started in earnest with the decree of 29 April 1680, which forbade Protestants to sit on a city council, which they had previously divided equally
with the Catholic minority. In 1685, after the revocation of the Edict of
Nantes, local people went through the mechanics of conversion to
Catholicism en masse and without open resistance. A trickle of emigration began. The "new converts" of Le Mas d'Azil survived by strategem
and subterfuge. The first serious confrontations there began after the
Peace of Rijswijk (1697), when word spread that royal policy toward Protestantism was going to relax. The local Protestants—not nearly so converted as it had seemed—began holding secret "assemblies," or church
services, in the countryside. Royal prosecution drove Protestant religious
practice back underground very quickly that time. But whenever the
royal authorities and the Catholic clergy turned their attention elsewhere, the hidden organization of the local Protestants started to
reemerge (Wemyss 1961: 96–107).

Elsewhere in Languedoc the struggle between Protestants and royal
authorities turned to open rebellion, to civil war. The cockpits were the
mountain regions of the Vivarais and the Cévennes. As early as 1653 "a
band of seven or eight thousand Protestants tried to establish by force of
arms the right to hold services at Vals in the Vivarais [Bonney 1978: 398]."
That became the standard pattern: Protestants assembled to hold forbidden services in the countryside, royal officials sent troops to stop them,
the "assemblies in the desert" evolved into armed rebellions. By August
1683, the intendant of Languedoc was reporting that the Huguenots of the
Vivarais

are continuing not only to preach in forbidden places, but also to prepare for
war. It is true that they have no leaders, not even some moderately-qualified
gentry, as a result of the effort we have made to take away all those who
came into view or whom we suspected. Nonetheless those who remain have
set up a sort of encampment. They are organized by companies under
designated leaders. They have taken various castles, have dug in, have am-
munition and weapons and, in a word, show every sign of intending to resist
the king's troops, aroused as they are by ministers who preach nothing but
sedition and rebellion [undated letter (August 1693), A.N. G⁷ 296].

Within 2 years, the intendant was sending armies into the hills to search out and exterminate the Protestant guerrilla forces, who eventually became known as the Camisards. The outlawing of Protestantism in 1685 started a brutal civil war. With many interruptions and changes of fortune, the War of the Camisards lasted 25 years.

War and the Rhythm and Geography of Contention

Our scale of distance from war, it seems, bends back on itself. As we move away from the forms of contention that occurred as the most immediate consequences of royal warmaking, we approach another sort of war. No contradiction there: Early in the seventeenth century the distinction between international war and domestic rebellion barely existed. Later, every new surge of warmaking stimulated popular rebellion, and every popular rebellion posed a threat to the state's ability to wage war. In a state so strongly oriented to war, it could hardly have gone otherwise.

A new wave of conflicts followed each acceleration of French warmaking. The seventeenth century's most impressive examples were the dozen years of war against Spain and the Empire beginning in the late 1630s and ending in the Fronde, and the 1690s, dominated by the War of the League of Augsburg. In 1643, for example, the child—king Louis XIV and his mother, Anne of Austria, took power after the death of Louis XIII, Cardinal Mazarin took over the prime ministry from the lately deceased Richelieu, the resourceful Particelli d'Emery became finance minister, the war with the Hapsburgs continued, and the new team squeezed the country for revenues as never before. Conflicts and rebellions multiplied. Here is a partial list of 1643's larger affairs:

Multiple armed rebellions against the *taille* in Guienne and Rouergue
An uprising against the *taille* in Alençon
Armed rebellions against the *taille* in Tours and its region
Multiple local revolts against the *taille* in Gascony
Armed resistance to the collection of the *taille* in villages around Clermont
Attacks on tax collectors in the Elections of Conches and Bernay
"Seditious" crowds complaining about the lack of cheap bread in Bordeaux
Attacks on tax collectors in Caen, Bayeux, Vire, Mortagne, and elsewhere in Normandy

Insurrections in Tours and vicinity, beginning with the mobbing of
wine-tax collectors
Rebellious assemblies of notables in Saintonge and Angoumois

In Anjou, 1643 brought an unauthorized assembly of Angers's parishes
against the military-inspired *subsistances*. In Languedoc, the people of
Valence chased out the tax collectors with the declaration that the
parlement of Toulouse had forbidden the payment of the *taille*, while in
Toulouse itself a crowd killed a tax collector. At the edge of Île-de-France,
an assembly of "five or six hundred peasants" attacked the company of
soldiers sent to enforce the collection of taxes. Most of these conflicts
centered on the royal effort to raise money for the war.

The catalog of contentious gatherings in our five regions from 1630 to
1649, displayed in the tables in the Appendix, simply extends the same
pattern to two full decades. The tables show the relatively urban concentration of large-scale conflicts—or at least of those that have left
traces in the archives and historical literature. They show the bunching
of events in years and places in which local people were already organized and mobilized around their interests. And they show the repeated importance of taxation and other efforts to raise the wherewithal
of war. The timing of major conflicts varied from one province to another,
but it varied as a function of that province's relationship to a growing,
grasping national state.

A full analysis of seventeenth-century rebellion would include a presentation of the century's major risings: the several rebellions of the
Croquants (southwestern France, 1636 and after), the Nu-Pieds (Normandy, 1639), the Tardanizats (Guienne; 1655–1656), the Sabotiers (Sol-
ogne, 1658), the Lustucru rebellion (Boulonnais, 1662), the revolt of Audijos (Gascony, 1663), that of Roure (Vivarais, 1670), the Bonnets Rouges
(also known as the Torrében; Brittany, 1675), and the Camisards (from
1685 onward). Many others could easily find their way onto the list. All of
these risings involved significant numbers of peasants, or at least of rural
people. Their frequency, and the relative unimportance of land and landlords as direct objects of peasant contention within them, require some
rethinking of peasant rebellion. The universal orientation of these rebellions to agents of the state, and their nearly universal inception with
reactions to the efforts of authorities to assemble the means of warmaking, underscore the impact of statemaking on the interests of peasants.
Not that landlords and capitalists had no impact on the fate of the
peasantry; that was to come, with a vengeance. But in the seventeenth
century the dominant influences driving French peasants into revolt
were the efforts of authorities to seize peasant labor, commodities, and

capital. Those efforts violated peasant rights, jeopardized the interests of other parties in peasant production; and threatened the ability of the peasants to survive as peasants. Behind those incessant efforts lay the attempt of the national government to build a giant warmaking machine.

From the perspective of peasant rebellion in general; did the peasants of seventeenth-century France behave oddly? At the start of this chapter, I pretended as much. After a review of the evidence, the impression remains: Those peasants took part in rebellions, but their rebellions did not conform to widely held sociological models of peasant rebellion. Perhaps, however, we should blame the models rather than the peasants. To the extent that models of peasant rebellion concentrate on struggles between peasants and landlords for control of the land, they neglect crucial features of the situations of seventeenth-century French peasants, and of peasants in most times and places: (a) the delicate, risky balance they have typically worked out with *all* factors of production—labor, land, and capital—and not just the land; (b) the presence of multiple claimants—kinsmen, heirs, other community members, religious officials, merchants, and various governmental authorities, as well as landlords—to all factors of production; (c) the tendency of increased pressure from any of the claimants to threaten the interests of the other claimants, to incite peasant resistance, and, where successful, to force a reallocation of wealth, income, and social commitments—for example, by requiring the increased marketing of crops previously relied upon for subsistence; and (d) that in predominantly peasant countries the bulk of the alienable resources are embedded in peasant enterprises, and therefore that any large effort to increase governmental resources in such countries almost inevitably attacks peasant interests, and the interests of others who have claims on peasant enterprises. Where peasant communities have a measure of solidarity and some means of collective defense, where new or increased claims clearly violate publicly known agreements or principles, where some visible person or group that is close at hand stands to gain by the new demands on the peasants, and where effective coalition partners are available to the peasants, collective resistance becomes likely. When that resistance is sustained and involves organized attacks on the enemy, we have peasant rebellion. In a mainly peasant world, both statemaking and the expansion of capitalism promote most of these conditions at one moment or another. When the conditions combine, the resulting rebellion need not lock peasants and landlords in a struggle for control of land. It will sometimes produce a coalition of landlords and peasants against state officials, or capitalists, or both at once. Thus the experience of seventeenth-century French peasants moves from being a troubling exception to serving as a standard instance of rural rebellion.

Appendix: Contentious Gatherings in Anjou, Burgundy, Flanders, Île-de-France, and Languedoc, 1630 – 1649

A "contentious gathering," for the purposes of the compilation in Tables 5.1 – 5.5, is an occasion on which 10 or more people gather in a

TABLE 5.1

Contentious Gatherings in Anjou, 1630 – 1649

Year	Place	Event	Sources
1630	Angers	Uprising against official suspected of tax profiteering	AMA (Archives Municipales, Angers) BB 72
1630	Angers	"Emotion" at rumor of mayor's assassination	AMA BB 73
1630	Angers	Attack on bakers	AMA BB 73
1630	Angers	Sacking of royal official's house; murder of tax collectors	AMA BB 73; Louvet 1854 – 1856; II, 167 – 170; Lebrun 1966: 123 – 126
1641	Angers	Attack on tax collectors	Mousnier 1964: I, 487, 490; Porchnev 1963: 614
1643	Angers	Concerted refusal to pay taxes	Mousnier 1964: I, 592 – 593; Porchnev 1963: 619 – 620; Lebrun 1966: 129 – 130
1643	Doué	Attempt to expel tax collector	Mousnier 1969: I, 502 – 503
1647	Angers	Attack on tax collectors	AMA BB 81; Débidour 1877: 39 – 41
1648	Angers	Church congregation protects bailiff who protests billeting	Jousselin 1861: 432 – 433
1648	Angers	Citizens lock troops out of city	Débidour 1877: 75
1649	Angers	Militia forms	AMA BB 81; Débidour 1877: 86; Jousselin 1861: 434 – 435
1649	Angers	Militia and citizens erect barricades	Débidour 1877: 374; Jousselin 1861: 434
1649	Angers	Attack on tax collector	Débidour 1877: 89; Jousselin 1861: 436
1649	Angers	Attack on castle and on homes of soldiers	Débidour 1877: 104; Jousselin 1861: 437
1649	Epluchard	Attack on tax collector	AMA BB 82; Jousselin 1861: 439 – 440
1649	La Pointe	Freeing of prisoners; seizure of salt	Jousselin 1861: 437
1649	Angers	Reception of new bishop	Gazette de France 1649: 270
1649	Angers	Reception of new governor	Gazette de France 1649: 283
1649	Angers	Fight between soldiers and citizens	Jousselin 1861: 445 – 446

TABLE 5.2
Contentious Gatherings in Burgundy, 1630– 1649

Year	Place	Event	Sources
1630	Dijon	Insurrection of Lanturelu	AMD (Archives Municipales, Dijon) B 267; AMD I 117, 118; Patouillet 1971; Porchnev 1963: 135– 143; *Mercure françois* 1630: 148ff.
1632	Dijon	Citizens refuse entry to army of prince of Condé	*Gazette de France* 1632: 242
1632	Dijon	Citizens refuse entry to army of Monsieur	*Gazette de France* 1632: 260
1636	Dijon and vicinity	Concerted resistance to troops and tax collectors	Mousnier 1964: I, 349– 352
1637	Saint-Jean-de-Lône, Auxonne, Bellegarde	Attacks on enemy villages by local peasants	*Gazette de France* 1637: 263
1639	Voitout	Violent resistance to tax collector	*Gazette de France* 1639: 132
1641	Troyes	Butchers' attacks on tax collectors	Bonney 1978: 328– 329
1642	Troyes	Butchers' attacks on tax collectors	Bonney 1978: 328– 329

publicly accessible place and visibly make claims that would, if realized, affect the interests of some other set of persons. (The appendix of Tilly 1978a gives more details on the application of the definition to the study of nineteenth-century Great Britain.) I have used that definition, reinforced by a series of rules of thumb, in cataloging events reported in (a) some major national series; notably G^7, for the Generalities of Burgundy, Flandre Flamingante, Flandre Maritime, Hainaut, Île-de-France, Languedoc, and Tours, in the Archives Nationales, Paris; (b) some seventeenth-century periodicals, notably the *Mercure françois* and the *Gazette de France;* (c) major police series and proceedings of the munici-

TABLE 5.3
Contentious Gatherings in Flanders, 1630– 1649

Year	Place	Event	Sources
1636	Rocroi	Peasants resist foraging of troops	*Gazette de France* 1636: 323
1637	Bicques	Cities of Douai, Lille, and Orchis send delegation to cardinal requesting tax exemption	*Gazette de France* 1637: 200
1641	Near Lille	Urban militia battles French troops	Liagre 1934: 113

TABLE 5.4

Contentious Gatherings in Île-de-France, 1630–1649

Year	Place	Event	Sources
1632	Paris	Procession of poor through streets	*Gazette de France* 1632: 348
1633	Near Paris	Disorderly assemblies of young people	*Gazette de France* 1633: 348
1636	Paris	Disorderly gatherings	*Gazette de France* 1636: 244
1638	Chartres	Violence and pillage by troops	*Gazette de France* 1638: 176
1641	Cheroy, Nemours, Aigneville	Attacks on tax collectors	Bonney 1978: 329
1642	Chartres	Attack on tax collectors	Bonney 1978: 329
1642	Paris	Disorderly assemblies of young people	*Gazette de France* 1642: 148
1643	Saint-Germain près Montargis	Peasants resist exactions of troops	Mousnier 1964: I, 534–536
1644	Paris	Masons and other workers gather and commit "outrages"	*Gazette de France* 1644: 538
1644	Argenteuil	"Emotion" against tax collectors	BN Fr (Bibliothèque Nationale, Paris, Manuscrits Français) 18432
1645	Paris: faubourg Saint Denis	Resistance to salt-tax officers	BN Fr 18432
1648	Paris	Citizens throw up barricades versus arrest of judge	Mousnier 1978: 258–272
1648	Paris area	Peasants surround duc d'Orleans	Mousnier 1978: 258
1649	Charenton	Battle at bridge between royal party and opposition	*Gazette de France* 1649: 126
1649	Brie-Comte-Robert	Battle between royal convoy and enemy	*Gazette de France* 1649: 136–138
1649	Paris	Confrontations between troops and citizens	BN Fr 6881
1649	Melun	Confrontations between troops and citizens	*Gazette de France* 1649: 1199–1200

pal council in some communal archives, notably those of Angers, Dijon, and Lille; (d) scattered series, notably A^1, in the Archives Historiques de l'Armée, Vincennes; and (e) a wide variety of historical works, both general and specialized. The compilation is not finished, much less "complete," whatever that might mean. On the average, it contains one or two contentious gatherings per province per year, whereas in nineteenth-century Great Britain the application of a similar definition to much more

TABLE 5.5

Contentious Gatherings in Languedoc, 1630– 1649

Year	Place	Event	Sources
1630	Carcassonne	"Rioting"	Bonney 1978: 321
1632	Province as whole	Duc de Montmorency raises rebel force and battles royal troops	Porchnev 1963: 155– 156 etc.
1632	Beaucaire	Rebellion of troops at castle against crown	*Mercure français* 1632: 542, 741ff.
1632	Montréal	Citizens expel occupying troops	*Gazette de France* 1632: 410– 411
1633	Vivarais	Rebellion	Liublinskaya 1966: 21
1633	Toulouse	Brawl between troops and citizens	BN Fr 17367
1633	Carcassonne	"Rioting"	Bonney 1978: 321
1639	Montpellier	"Riot"	Bonney 1978: 327
1640	Gimon	"Seditious assembly"	*Gazette de France* 1640: 630
1643	Valence	Forcible resistance to tax collector	Liublinskaya 1966: 36– 38
1643	Toulouse	Attack on tax collector	Mousnier 1964: I, 589
1643	Ribaute	Protestant assembly	Liublinskaya 1966: 40– 47
1644	Nîmes	Dissident municipal assembly	Liublinskaya 1966: 77– 82
1644	Montpellier	Resistance to edicts of intendant	Porchnev 1963: 639– 640
1644	Montpellier	Dissident Protestant assembly	Liublinskaya 1966: 100– 104
1645	Montpellier and elsewhere	Uprising against taxes	Porchnev 1963: 242– 260, 643– 644; BN Fr 18432; Mousnier 1964: II, 737– 738, 763– 772
1645	Nîmes	Forcible freeing of prisoner	Liublinskaya 1966: 133– 137
1645	Aubenas	Illicit Protestant assembly	Liublinskaya 1966: 140– 141
1645	Carcassonne	Protests against bishop	Porchnev 1963: 654
1646	Gevaudan	Antitax rebellion	Liublinskaya 1966: 189– 190
1646	Béziers	Resistance to reestablishment of police authority	Mousnier 1964: II, 789– 790, Porchnev 1963: 655– 656
1646	Cities on Rhone	Attacks on fishermen who blocked river	Liublinskaya 1966: 184– 186
1648	Toulouse	Seizure of salt from salt-tax collectors	Mousnier 1964: II, 828

comprehensive material identifies over 1000 contentious gatherings in the average year. The compilation is unquestionably biased toward larger events, those to which authorities attributed national significance, and those that occurred in urban areas. The contentious gatherings enumerated for 1630 – 1649 include a smaller proportion drawn from archival material, and a larger proportion drawn from periodicals, than for those identified for later in the century. The material from seventeenth-century "Flanders" is very thin, because most of the area lay under Spanish domination most of the century, and I have not worked in the Belgian and Spanish archives that contain much of the day-to-day correspondence concerning Spanish administration. With all these qualifications, the catalog is still useful: it serves both to put information from different provinces on a roughly comparable basis and to place major conflicts in the context of less extensive contention.

6

How (And, to Some Extent, Why) to Study British Contention

Introduction

"Historians of modern Britain," writes John Stevenson,

> have always had some interest in questions of popular protest and public order if only for their bearing on the topic of the *revolution manquée,* why and how Britain in the eighteenth and nineteenth centuries escaped a revolutionary upheaval similar to those experienced on the continent. Riots, rebellions and industrial conflict have frequently been viewed—explicitly or implicitly—as a barometer of social and political stability [1979: 1].

British historians have commonly scanned the stream of conflicts, small and large, for evidence concerning the state of the polity.

The conflicts of the 1820s and 1830s have inevitably attracted attention. The campaign for Catholic Emancipation, the rural uprisings of 1830, the drive for Reform, the repeated struggles between workers and masters, the early strivings of the Chartists, the apparent march toward a great confrontation of the classes have a drama of their own. Their patterns and connections cry out for analysis. That for several reasons:

1. The sheer variety and intensity of contention in the period make it a privileged field of observation.
2. The visible forms of action—parades, brawls, electoral rallies, meetings, demonstrations, and so on—were undergoing rapid and decisive change; in a sense, the "repertoire" of British con-

tention that had prevailed during the eighteenth century was fast giving way to the repertoire that has prevailed into our own time.

3. The continuous interplay among contenders and authorities provides an exceptional opportunity to watch processes of repression, facilitation, coalition, cooptation, and mediation at work, and on their way to altering the national structure of power.

4. The outcomes of the conflicts in the era of Reform seem to have been pivotal for the politics of nineteenth-century Britain and for the fate of the British working classes.

The period from the late 1820s into the early 1830s deserves close study for its own sake, for the sake of its place in the long-run transformation of British political life, and for the sake of our understanding of mobilization and contention in general.

The mobilization and contention of the period took place in the context of profound economic and political change. Britain was urbanizing rapidly; industrial production was expanding, increasing in scale and moving cityward; a coal-and-iron economy was visibly taking shape. Handloom weavers, only lately flourishing, were beginning their long and painful decline. In agriculture, the proletarianization of the labor force proceeded apace. While London continued its rapid expansion, Manchester, Liverpool, and other manufacturing cities became the very emblems of the Industrial Revolution. At the same time, national political institutions were altering fast:

> During the decade 1825−35 the nature of parliamentary government was being transformed. The older notions that the business of government was essentially executive, and that whatever general measures of social policy were needed were properly the concern of parliament as a whole, and should normally be introduced not by the government but by private members, were dying. . . . The modern speech from the throne, the lengthening of sessions, the drastic reduction of private members' time and the constant increase in government's all date from these few years [MacDonagh 1977: 5].

In that process, the government took to making large inquiries into the state of the nation and legislating national reforms: not only the Reform Act of 1832 but also Catholic Emancipation (1829), the Factory Act of 1833, the Poor Law of 1834, among others. These were, for their time, momentous measures.

The decade after 1825, then, brought Britain extraordinary turbulence and change: on the one hand, swelling conflicts at the local and the national scale; on the other, startling transformations of the country's political and economic organization. What was going on? Could we, for example, reasonably think of the period as bringing Britain the equivalent

of a revolution? If not that, was it a close brush with revolution? Many
historians have thought one or the other.

In his grand review of *The Age of Revolution*, E. J. Hobsbawm places
three revolutionary waves in the period from 1815 to 1848: those of
1820 – 1824, 1829 – 1834, and 1848. Although the wave of 1848 was larger
and more visible, the revolutionary changes of 1829 – 1834 were in some
regards more definitive. "In effect," writes Hobsbawm,

> it marks the definitive defeat of aristocratic by bourgeois power in Western
> Europe. The ruling class of the next fifty years was to be the "grande
> bourgeoisie" of bankers, big industrialists and sometimes top civil servants,
> accepted by an aristocracy which effaced itself or agreed to promote primar-
> ily bourgeois policies, unchallenged as yet by universal suffrage, though
> harassed from outside by the agitations of the lesser or unsatisfied
> businessmen, the petty-bourgeoisie and the early labour movements. . . .
> 1830 marks an even more radical innovation in politics: the emergence of the
> working-class as an independent and self-conscious force in politics in Bri-
> tain and France, and of nationalist movements in a great many European
> countries [1962: 111].

If no revolution, in any strong sense of the word, occurred in the Britain
of 1830, the revolutionary wave nevertheless splashed over the British
Isles:

> Even Britain was affected, thanks in part of the threatened eruption of its
> local volcano, Ireland, which secured Catholic Emancipation (1829) and the
> re-opening of the reform agitation. The Reform Act of 1832 corresponds to
> the July Revolution of 1830 in France, and had indeed been powerfully
> stimulated by the news from Paris. This period is probably the only one in
> modern history when political events in Britain ran parallel with those on
> the continent, to the point where something not unlike a revolutionary
> situation might have developed in 1831 – 2 but for the restraint of both Whig
> and Tory parties. It is the only period in the nineteenth century when the
> analysis of British politics in such terms is not wholly artificial [Hobsbawm
> 1962: 110 – 111].

Similarly, Michael Vester places the "decisive rise of the workers' movement" in the years from 1826 to 1832. The development of cooperation
among trades and across regions in major strikes played its part. "Even
more influential," declares Vester, "was the movement for Reform, revived
in 1830, which in 1832 brought only the property-owning bourgeoisie
into Parliament. This outcome tore away the remaining sympathy of
workers for the middle classes. By means of their growing economic,
political and publishing institutions, workers developed solidarity at a
national level [1970: 27]." At that point, according to Vester, the English

working class became conscious of its position and fate at a national scale.

E. P. Thompson goes one step further than Hobsbawm and Vester. He claims that "England was without any doubt passing through a crisis in these twelve months [from spring 1831 to the next year] in which revolution was possible [1964: 808]." Thompson places the fullest maturity of the old English working class at just that point. Indeed, he considers Reform itself to have grown from the demands of an increasingly conscious and determined working class, and to have been snatched from the working class by a frightened bourgeoisie. How close Britain came to revolution in the 1830s is, and was, a matter of strenuous debate. But almost all historians agree that the British conflicts of the time were intense, and their effects, far-reaching.

British contention of the period matters not only for the historical record but also for comparative politics. Over and over again, Britain of the Reform era appears as an exemplary case. Of what Britain is an example—of failed revolution, of peaceful conflict resolution, of the cooptation of the petty bourgeoisie, of the creation of national electoral politics—is, again, a matter of debate. For Gabriel Almond, the Reform Act "is generally viewed as the exemplar of incremental democratization, a largely peaceful adaptation of a political system to basic changes in economy and social structure [1973: 23]." Almond sees the further effects as far-reaching:

> In the short run, antisystem pressure is reduced, but in the longer run the introduction of electoral reform triggers demands for further extensions of the suffrage to enfranchise the working class, and for welfare legislation. Public policy in the next decade or two alternates between welfare measures intended to alleviate working conditions, the lowering of food prices by eliminating agricultural protection, and repressive measures [1973: 33].

Then, through further political "linkages," much of the apparatus of British government is supposed to have altered through the chain reaction started by Reform. "The changes that the Reform Act have [sic] triggered," says Almond, "take some thirty years to settle down into a more or less stable system of interaction, with the party, cabinet, and modern bureaucratic system emerging during the second half of the nineteenth century [1973: 34]." Thus, in one view, the British "political system" solved a major problem with Reform, but the full ramifications of the solution took decades to work themselves out.

In another variant of a fundamentally optimistic view, Reinhard Bendix accords "the system" rather less importance and the demands of workers rather more:

In England, lower-class protests appear to aim at establishing the citizen-ship of the workers. Those who contribute to the wealth and welfare of their country have a right to be heard in its national councils and are entitled to a status that commands respect. In England, these demands never reach the revolutionary pitch that develops rather frequently on the Continent, al-though occasionally violent outbursts disrupt English society as well. If the political modernization of England for all its conflicts occurred in a relatively continuous and peaceful manner, then one reason is perhaps that through-out much of the nineteenth century England was the leader in industrializa-tion and overseas expansion. English workers could claim their rightful place in the political community of the leading nation of the world [1964: 67].

Workers' demands for fair representation, according to Bendix, ultimately prevailed because they were compatible in principle with the mainte-nance of the polity, because British powerholders displayed an excep-tional capacity for accommodation, and, no doubt, because British pros-perity provided payoffs for all political participants.

One can also insist on the distinctiveness of the British experience and stress the importance of the 1830s, without adopting so Whiggish an outlook as Bendix's. Keith Thomas declares,

The years 1831–1832, when the Reform Bills were at stake, can be plausibly regarded as a revolutionary crisis, held in check by the "constitutional" element among the reformers and averted in the nick of time by the surren-der of the king and lords to extraparliamentary pressure. . . . The crisis was resolved by the passage of the first Reform Act, which conciliated the middle classes but left the proletariat unenfranchised [1978: 70; the omitted material contains the inevitable quotation from Francis Place].

"The peaceful extension of participation was often as much a matter of luck as of judgment. The 1832 Act was intended by many of its supporters as a purification of the old electoral system rather than the beginning of a new one; it might never have got through if it had been recognized as the thin edge of the wedge [Thomas 1978: 71]." Muddling through, it seems, sometimes produced the equivalent of revolutionary change.

One can be still more skeptical of the ruling class's good intentions and yet consider the era of Reform an important transition. Barrington Moore argues that

to concentrate on the strength of their position in the formal and even the informal apparatus of politics would give a misleading impression of the power of the gentry and the nobility. Even if the Reform Bill of 1832, which gave the industrial capitalists the vote, disappointed the hopes of its more ardent advocates and belied the fears of its more ardent opponents, its passage mean [sic] that the bourgeoisie had shown its teeth [1966: 33].

That has, in general, been the Marxist interpretation of the struggles around Reform: They marked and facilitated the accession of industrial capital to a full place in the British structure of power. In these varied guises and more, Britain of the 1820s and 1830s serves as a reference point for comparisons with other countries that somehow staggered into the politics of a capitalist age via other routes.

Studying Contention in Great Britain

Someone who takes the conflicts and transitions of the 1820s and 1830s seriously has the choice of at least two approaches: head on and from behind. Head on, one can review the arguments of Stevenson, Hobsbawm, Thompson, and others, argue out the conditions under which a revolution could have occurred, and assess the available evidence concerning both the chances of revolution and the effects of Reform. From behind, one can examine a wide range of conflict, collective action, and change in Britain, place the 1820s and 1830s in comparative perspective, treat the particular struggles which took place around Reform as variants of collective action and conflict in general, and only then attempt to trace the ways in which those struggles were extraordinary. Both are, I think, essential. Here I describe a from-behind approach, in which analysis of the context and consequences of Reform is but one of several objectives. The description presents work in progress rather than firm results. It dwells on research procedures, strategies, and materials — partly because the work is still in progress, partly because the details strongly affect the quality and character of the results.

My collaborators and I are studying British contention in the late 1820s and 1830s. We have undertaken a large, systematic analysis of a wide range of conflicts, partly out of interest in the period for its own sake, partly out of concern for the comparison between Britain and other countries, but mainly in order to improve our understanding of three big, sticky problems in the dynamics of collective action: (a) how interactions with authorities impinge on ordinary people's collective action—most obviously, how the authorities' strategies of repression and facilitation with respect to different groups and types of action affect the ways that ordinary people work together for their shared interests; (b) how and why the repertoires of collective action—especially those forms that people use to press their interests against those of other people—vary and change from group to group, setting to setting, time to time; and (c) how the character of shared interests affects the kinds of organization ordinary people create or adopt, and how the interests and organization interact to shape the forms of collective action in which they engage. The main themes, then, are *interaction with authorities, repertoires of contention,* and the interplay of *interests, organization, and action.*

The three themes have strong connections. They all assume that the people whom authorities call "rioters," "protesters," "insurgents," and similar epithets are pursuing shared interests—in fact, are choosing more or less deliberately among different possible ways of pursuing their shared interests, with some sense of the likely outcomes and the probable reactions of competitors, enemies, authorities, and other powerful people. They also assume that people learn by doing, and by other people's doing. The image they convey runs something like this: Sets of people who have common interests sometimes build social organization around those interests. As threats or opportunities impinge on those interests, they sometimes mobilize for action, and sometimes act collectively on behalf of their interests. When they act collectively, they ordinarily have a limited number of forms of action—a repertoire—at their disposal. Repertoires of collective action vary from one group to another, but in general they are limited and change rather slowly. Repertoires change as a function of the group's organization and experience, but they also change as a function of the constraints imposed by other groups, including authorities. Authorities and other powerful people monitor other people's collective action as continuously as they can; they employ bargaining, repression, coalition, cooptation, and facilitation to protect and advance their own interests in the outcomes of ordinary people's collective action. The actions of authorities and other powerful people have strong impacts on the outcomes of collective action; they therefore help shape and reshape the prevailing repertoire.

This sketch is crude and abstract: a caricature. Like a caricature, it calls attention to the salient traits of one particular approach to the study of collective action. The line of thought parades under different names: resource mobilization, political process, rational action, and so on. Whatever we call it, the line of thought presents collective action as problem-solving behavior. The problem solving is rarely easy; it is often inefficient or ineffective. With the arrogance of retrospect, we will often look back at it and imagine a different, better solution to the problem. Collective action is problem-solving behavior nonetheless.

Following this line of thought, my collaborators and I are examining a large number of "contentious gatherings" which occurred in Great Britain during the years 1828–1834. The contentious gathering, as defined, eliminates a wide range of collective action. It aims our attention at those special moments in which people stand together publicly and seek to make their collective will prevail.

The set of contentious gatherings we are examining consists of every event meeting our criteria we have encountered in a thorough reading of seven periodicals from the beginning of 1828 to the middle of 1835. (We read 6 months beyond the 1834 cutoff in order to capture late reports.) The publications are the London *Times*, the *Morning Chronicle*, *Hansard's Parliamentary Debates*, *Mirror of Parliament*, Parliament's *Votes and Proceedings*, the *Annual Register*, and the *Gentleman's Magazine*. The set is likely to maximize our national coverage at the expense of a certain bias toward events in London as well as toward events involving Parliament and national politics. Once we have identified a qualifying contentious gathering, we seek further information concerning the event in a variety of other sources: the correspondence of the Home Office in the archives of the Public Record Office, additional periodicals, such as Cobbett's *Political Register*, historians' works on the 1820s and 1830s, and others. In going through the sources, we use a generous definition of possible contentious gatherings—for example, noting every announcement of meetings of private bodies, whether or not the announcement indicates the likelihood that members of the body will make contentious claims. The roughly 5000 issues of the various periodicals we have examined have yielded around 150,000 mentions of possible contentious gatherings.

When the process of filtering out the mentions of events that actually qualify and collating multiple mentions of the same events is finished, we expect to have 50,000 or 60,000 accounts describing 12,000 – 15,000 contentious gatherings. The remaining 90,000 – 100,000 accounts will serve as useful background material on the gatherings and issues of 1828 – 1834. The numbers, to be sure, exaggerate the richness of the evidence; the majority of the mentions run a sentence or two. For one type of event—the meeting whose participants sent a petition to Parliament—we have hundreds of instances but precious few details. Nevertheless, taken as a whole, the set of events provides an exceptionally comprehensive picture of contention in one important period of the nineteenth century.

After a long process of sorting and ordering, we eventually create a standardized machine-readable description of each event. I have given a picture of the machine-readable record in Chapter 2, "Computing History." In essence, the description consists of answers (sometimes numerical, but usually in words and short phrases drawn from the accounts of the events) to a flexible questionnaire: Where did the contentious gathering take place? Who took part? What did they do? What happened then? What was the outcome? And so on through many questions, reiterated for each group and place involved. The form of the record makes it easy to search the file for various combinations of issues, groups, locales, and actions. (For more detail on materials and procedures, see Schweitzer 1978, 1979; Schweitzer, Tilly, and Boyd 1980; Schweitzer and Simmons 1978; Tilly and Schweitzer 1980.)

Additional Collections of Evidence

Some further tasks follow almost automatically from the work I have just described. The main categories are these:

1. Further documentation of contentious gatherings
2. Reading and comparing supplementary sources
3. Collection of data on areas and groups

Let me take up each one briefly.

The *further documentation* of contentious gatherings goes beyond the seven basic periodicals to a search of our microfilm and photocopy collections of documents from the Home Office papers, to a limited number of other archival sources, to the *Political Register*, the *Poor Man's Guardian*, the *Scotsman*, and several other contemporary periodicals, and to a selection of published works by historians. This further documentation presents knotty problems: whether to incorporate the new information directly into the basic machine-readable file or hold it separate while treating the basic file as a transcription of accounts in our seven standard periodicals; what to do when the new information disagrees substantially with the account we have drawn from the seven basic periodicals; how to keep the selective availability of additional information from introducing new and risky biases into our analyses; at what point to cease the search for supplementary information. We have not yet resolved any of these problems.

The *reading and comparing* of supplementary sources overlaps with the work of further documentation, but only incompletely. They differ because the reading and comparing has other objectives: (a) to help estimate the completeness and bias of the enumeration of contentious gatherings drawn from the seven standard periodicals; (b) to help gauge to what extent, and in what regards, the character of the source at hand affects the quality of the descriptions of contentious gatherings we construct from the source. For both purposes, we must produce independent enumerations and descriptions of contentious gatherings — including gatherings not mentioned in our seven standard periodicals — from supplementary sources. Then we must compare the enumerations and descriptions with our basic sample. It is delightful when a work as concentrated and comprehensive as E. J. Hobsbawm and George Rudé's *Captain Swing* comes along for comparison with our accounts of 1830's agrarian conflicts. The Home Office papers are rich enough in contentious gatherings to make a sustained comparison feasible, if enormously time-consuming. Such publications as Cobbett's *Political Register* yield many fewer events than our basic sources, but comparisons with them provide some sense of the political orientations of our sources. Beyond that, the work of validating our sample and checking the biases of our descriptions becomes more and more difficult.

The *collection of data* on areas and groups involved in contentious gatherings could last forever. The task has a megalomaniac version, an ambitious version, and a modest version. The megalomaniac version is to assemble comparable information on every single group and locality *at risk* to be involved in contentious gatherings—in short, every group and locality in Great Britain. In principle, that would be desirable, for the comparison of similar groups that did and did not act tells us a good deal about the conditions favoring collective action. In practice, such a program would be foolish, guaranteed to collapse under its own weight.

The ambitious version is to seek a standard set of information for each group and each locality involved in any of the 15,000 contentious gatherings. Likely items in such a standard set would be size, political status, leadership, and involvement in other forms of collective action not captured by the enumeration of contentious gatherings. With a small set of items and reasonable rules for abandoning the search when information is no longer readily available, the ambitious version might well take 5 or 10 person-years of effort. That is more effort than we can currently afford to commit.

The modest version is enough to strain our resources. Its elements are (a) for large areas such as counties and major cities, assemble information on size, general population composition, industrial activity, and other readily available characteristics; (b) cumulate information from all contentious-gathering accounts concerning a particular group or area to characterize the group or area at the point of an individual contentious gathering—starting with such simple matters as how many previous contentious gatherings the group or area has been involved in; and (c) commission special studies of groups and areas that appear repeatedly in accounts of contentious gatherings. In any case, only as we get into the major analyses described below do we see clearly which items of information not contained in the accounts are so important that they deserve the effort to search them out elsewhere.

The further documentation of events, the reading and comparing of supplementary sources, and the collection of data on areas and groups follow almost automatically from our basic research design. Beyond these obvious next steps, however, we face choices. The choices entail further choices. Let me review the three major problems—interaction with authorities, repertoires of contention, and interests/organization/action—on which we are concentrating and describe a concrete program of research under each of the three headings.

Interaction with Authorities

How do interactions with authorities impinge on ordinary people's collective action? In a radical simplification, we can think of the relevant actions of authorities as falling into a single range from repression to facilitation. Toward one end of the range, authorities are making collective action costly for some sets of people; at the extreme, authorities not only penalize people for acting collectively but also hinder their mobilization, attack their organization, their resources, and their persons—that is repression. Toward the other end of the range, authorities are lowering the cost of collective action for some sets of people; at the extreme, authorities are operating the government as a means to the ends of that group's collective action—that is facilitation. Authorities vary their repression—facilitation as a function of the political position of the group involved, the kind of action they are taking, and the claims they are making.

The first question that arises, however, is this: How *much* do authorities vary their response from one set of groups, actions, and claims to another? It appears, for example, that magistrates were more likely to send in constables or call in the militia against workers than against middle-class reformers. Will that impression hold up to close examination? If it does, how much of the difference is attributable to the groups involved, how much to the sorts of actions they take, how much to the kinds of claim they make, how much to the interaction among all three? The contentious gatherings of 1828—1834 are sufficiently abundant to allow telling comparisons: between middle-class and working-class electoral rallies, between workers supporting Reform and workers resisting wage cuts, and so on.

The repression and facilitation of different forms of action likewise pose interesting problems. On the one hand, a form of action such as the public meeting or Rough Music acquired a legitimacy from toleration and use; the authorities' infringement on anyone's use of that form threatened, however distantly, the rights of other people who commonly used that form of action to pursue their ends. On that ground, we might reasonably expect the forms of action used by powerful people to be available to many of the powerless. On the other hand, authorities and powerful people gave rather different readings to similar actions by disparate groups; whether a currently peaceful assembly constituted a riot, for example, depended on the magistrate's judgment as to whether the participants were likely to commit a crime if left unimpeded. A magistrate was, I think, generally readier to conclude that assembled day laborers harbored some criminal intent than he was to make the same judgment about assembled merchants. Did the right to assemble afford the day laborers any substantial protection? Again, controlled comparisons of similar actions by different groups promise to shed light on a vexing issue.

Similarly, the period from 1828 to 1834 offers several opportunities to watch changes in the ways authorities dealt with a given pattern of collective action. Let me mention only two examples. The national organization, widespread assessment of dues, and sustained agitation of the Catholic Association in Ireland played a significant part in the passage of Catholic Emancipation in 1829. Parliament acknowledged that part by abolishing the Catholic Association in the same legislative bundle that gave Catholics the right to serve in its ranks. Soon, proponents of parliamentary reform were adopting similar organizational tactics to advance their own cause—and the authorities seem to have found their ability to counter those tactics compromised by the legitimating precedent of Catholic Emancipation. During the Swing rebellion of 1830, in contrast, the government's initial passivity and the magistrate's initial leniency soon altered as the vision of a general insurrection spread. These cases, and others like them, challenge us to trace and explain the changing approaches of authorities to repression and facilitation.

Given some understanding of the authorities' response, we still need to interpret the impact of that response on people's collective action. In the short run, how does the intervention of authorities in well-established sequences of action affect those sequences and their outcomes? Is it true, for example, that people were much more likely to be hurt in the course of a demonstration, meeting, or rally if police forces intervened than if the gathering ran its course? In the medium run, did the way the authorities responded to one attempt at collective action visibly affect the behavior of the same or similar people on the next occasion? Did a magistrate's stepping in to conciliate a strike, for instance, increase the likelihood that other workers in the vicinity would strike? In the long run, did well-defined approaches to the repression and facilitation of particular actions, claims, and groups produce durable changes in the pattern of collective action? In the case of major waves of repression, such as the one that followed the Swing rebellion, for example, can we detect significant differences in the character of rural conflicts before, during, and after the rebellion? Did a change in the power position of some substantial group—for example, the arrival of the bourgeoisie in the policy at Reform—change the acceptability of the forms of action employed by them and their working-class allies? These are challenging questions. Fortunately, they lead quite directly to analyses of British contentious gatherings: short-run analyses comparing the internal sequences of actions in similar events; medium-run analyses comparing successive rounds of collective action; long-run analyses examining the before, during, and after stages of major crises, governmental actions, and alterations of power.

So far I have simplified the problem of interaction with authorities by (a) taking the action of various contenders as a given and proposing to examine the responses of authorities to that action; or (b) taking the action of authorities as a given and proposing to study its impact on collective action by ordinary people. The simplification is useful, but artificial. Ultimately, we must analyze the *inter*action of ordinary people with authorities and of various contenders with one another: the parry, thrust, advance, retreat, and bluff which go on continuously. Our evidence concerning contentious gatherings offers four valuable opportunities for the treatment of interaction: (a) the analysis of internal sequences; (b) the interplay between local and national struggles; (c) links within series of contentious gatherings; and (d) variations among authorities.

The first is the analysis of *internal sequences*. We break the participants in a contentious gathering into "formations," then break the actions of the formations into "action phases." In order to qualify as a contentious gathering, an event must include at least one articulation of a claim by some set of 10 or more people. (In general, a claim is any stated expectation that would, if realized, require another actor to expend valued resources: labor power, information, money, and so on.) The first set of 10 or more people to make a claim enters the record as formation 01. The object of that claim, whether present or not, becomes formation 02. Subsequent formations (03, 04, etc.) enter the account because they include at least one of the following characteristics:

1. They are identified in the account as being a distinctly different person, or body of people, from the first two formations, and they make a distinctly different claim from other formations.
2. As a subset of an existing formation, they start or stop making a claim at a distinctly different point in time from the others; for

example, persons who are arrested during an event cease to act collectively with the rest of their formation and become a separate formation.

3. As a subset of one formation, they start or stop being the object of a claim at a distinctly different point in time from the others.
4. However similar to other formations, they are geographically separated from the others.
5. They are the object of another formation's claim.

Having divided all participants (including absent persons who are objects of claims made during the contentious gathering) into formations, we break the actions of formations into phases. A new action phase begins whenever any formation:

1. Begins to make a claim
2. Begins a new response to a claim
3. Visibly ceases a response to a claim
4. Visibly ceases to make a claim
5. Changes location
6. Changes personnel

The action phases may include actions that occurred before the contentious gathering, as such, began; when a meeting that became a contentious gathering was announced in advance, for example, we record the advance announcement as the first action phase. Action phases may also include actions that occurred after the gathering ended; when Parliament heard a petition formulated at a contentious gathering, for example, we record the hearing of the petition as a final action phase.

As a result of all this detail, it is possible to follow the twists and turns of the entire contentious gathering—at least in those cases where the record itself documents the sequence of action. Although more complex strategies of analysis have their own seductions, the obvious way to discipline the analysis of sequences is to work with a series of dichotomies: events in which aggrieved parties are relatively successful versus events in which they gain little or nothing; violent versus nonviolent events; events that escalate versus others; events in which authorities intervene versus others, and so on.

The second opportunity to analyze interaction takes us to the *interplay between local and national struggles*. In 1828 and 1829 (the sole years for which detailed observations are fully available at this writing), there is an obvious correspondence between the rise and fall of issues such as repeal of the Test and Corporation Acts, Catholic Emancipation, or Friendly Society legislation within Parliament and the ebb and flow of contentious gatherings in Britain as a whole. The correspondence is not coincidental: Many of the events in question consist, precisely, of assemblies that demonstrate some group's concern about one or another of these issues. It is likely that our search procedure exaggerates the correspondence. After all, Parliament's *Votes and Proceedings* bring hundreds of events into our view solely because the people present sent petitions to Parliament. With due allowance for that effect, however, it looks as though each parliamentary crisis did activate meetings, demonstrations, rallies, and other sorts of contentious gatherings throughout Britain. If so, we have evidence of a remarkable national orientation for contention. We have the chance to see which sorts of groups, regions, actions, and issues displayed the greatest coordination between local and national events. And we have the opportunity to explore more subtle forms of interaction: between the content of parliamentary discussion and the demands or complaints uttered by participants in contentious gatherings; between cabinet maneuvering and the tactics of popular contention; between the formation of political coalitions outside the government and the realignment of collective action.

The third opportunity to deal with interaction concerns *links within series of contentious gatherings:* the many meetings for and against Catholic Emancipation in 1828 and 1829; the multiple industrial conflicts of 1829 and 1830; the hundreds of attacks on farmers, hayricks, and threshing machines constituting the Swing rebellion of 1830; the mobilization for Reform from 1830 through 1832, and so on. We need to identify the patterns of communication and collaboration by which similar actions spread from one locality or group to another. How much signaling and modeling went on? For example, how often did people in one locality adopt tactics that had lately been successful in similar circumstances elsewhere? How did the information flow? Where it is possible, the identification of tendencies for disparate actors to act together, or in response to one another, would tell us a great deal about the political texture of the time.

The fourth, and final, opportunity to analyze interaction takes up *variation among authorities.* In a close examination of repression and collective action in Lancashire from 1750 to 1830, Frank Munger (1977) has shown that regular constables were gradually replacing the justices of the peace in the control of smaller gatherings, that troops were being used increasingly against the workers in large industrial conflicts, and that the repressive activities of magistrates varied considerably with the economic organization of the locality. (In the major industrial centers, for example, the magistrates were significantly more inclined to call in, or send in, repressive forces against the participants in contentious gatherings than were their counterparts in the rest of the county.) Those differences, furthermore, made a difference. Deaths and injuries, for instance, occurred much more frequently in the course of contentious gatherings in which ground troops intervened.

Munger's findings raise questions about the Britain of 1828 – 1834. Do the same regularities hold for all of Britain? What of the places of other authorities: the lords lieutenant, the mayors, the home secretary, employers, churchmen? Our evidence concerning contentious gatherings does not tell us all we need to know. Much of the authorities' maneuvering took place behind the scenes. But to the extent that different authorities appeared visibly in the course of contentious gatherings, or became the objects of their claims, we have the opportunity to trace the correlates and effects of their involvement.

In sum, how interactions with authorities impinge on ordinary people's collective action raises a challenging series of problems:

1. Responses of authorities to different combinations of actions, groups, and claims
2. The impact of authorities' actions on collective action
   a. short run: intervention in sequences of action, and so on
   b. medium run: how response to one round of action affects the next round
   c. long run: the effects of major crises, political events, and responses to series of collective actions
3. The interaction among contenders and authorities
   a. internal sequences
   b. relations between local conflicts and national politics
   c. links within series of events
   d. variation among authorities

Our collection of evidence on contentious gatherings makes possible a significant start on each of these problems.

Variations and Changes in Repertoires

In examining hundreds of contentious gatherings, one quickly develops a sense of *déjà lu:* not only with respect to recurrent actors and long-lived issues but also with respect to the forms of actions themselves. One meeting fades into the next, one march up the street resembles another, even attacks on looms and poaching affrays take certain limited, repeated forms. We can conveniently capture that sense of limited repetition in a theatrical metaphor: Any group who has a common interest in collective action also acquires a shared *repertoire* of routines among which it makes a choice when the occasion for pursuing an interest or a grievance arises. The metaphor calls attention to the limited number of performances available to any particular group at a given time, to the learned character of those performances, to the possibility of innovation and improvisation within the limits set by the existing means, to the likelihood that not only the actors but also the objects of their action are aware of the character of the drama that is unfolding, and, finally, to the element of collective choice that enters into the events which outsiders call riots, disorders, disturbances, and protests.

The Britain of 1830 was in the midst of a major, and relatively rapid, shift from one sort of repertoire to another. Let us think of them, crudely but conveniently, as the repertoires of the eighteenth century and of the nineteenth century. In the eighteenth-century repertoire, the antitax rebellion, the food riot, and the concerted invasion of fields or forests were the most distinctive forms of revolt. But a great deal of relatively peaceful collective action went on, first, through deliberate (although sometimes unauthorized) assemblies of corporate groups that eventuated in declarations, demands, petitions, or lawsuits, or, second, via authorized festivals and ceremonies in the course of which ordinary people symbolized their grievances.

As compared with other repertoires, this eighteenth-century array of performances had some special characteristics worth noticing:

- A tendency for aggrieved people to converge on the residences of wrongdoers and on the sites of wrongdoing rather then on the seats of power (sometimes, of course, the two coincided)
- The extensive use of authorized public ceremonies and celebrations for the acting out of complaints and demands
- The rare appearance of people organized voluntarily around a special interest, as compared with whole communities and constituted corporate groups
- The recurrent use of street theater, visual imagery, effigies, symbolic objects, and other dramatic devices to state the participants' claims and complaints
- The frequent borrowing—in parody or in earnest—of the authorities' normal forms of action; the borrowing often amounted to the crowd's almost literally taking the law into its own hands

The newer repertoire that was becoming dominant in the Britain of 1830 was essentially the one with which we work today: featuring special-purpose associations, directed especially at the seats of power, frequently involving the explicit announcement of programs and organizational affiliations, relying relatively little on routine public gatherings, festivities, and ceremonies. The strike, the demonstration, the electoral rally, and the formal meeting are obvious examples. Employed in the service of a sustained challenge to the existing structure or use of power and in the name of some defined interest, this array of actions constitutes what we have known since the nineteenth century as a social movement. The point of calling these well-known changes alterations of *repertoires* is to stress that the available means of action were (and are) learned, historically specific, rooted in the existing social structure, and seriously constraining. The theoretical advantage of doing so is to focus explanations of collective action on group choices among limited sets of slowly changing alternatives.

To get a quick sense of the contrast between the "eighteenth-century" and "nineteenth-century" repertoires, we might reflect on two contentious gatherings from 1829. On 23 February 1829,

> a large body of journeyman weavers assembled yesterday afternoon in the open space opposite the Duke of Bedford Public-House, Seabright-Street, Bethnal-Green-Road, to hear a letter from the Duke of Wellington, in answer to a memorial presented to His Grace by the journeymen on the 3d instant. The memorialists ascribed the dreadfully distressed condition in which they have been for some time past to the repeal of the laws prohibiting the importation of foreign wrought silks, and the answer of His Grace, expressing in plain terms his opinions on that subject, may be considered an important document [*Times* (London), 24 February 1829: 4].

Wellington replied that smuggling, rather than legal imports, was the problem and promised his efforts for both temporary and permanent relief of their suffering. The meeting passed resolutions of thanks (very likely ironic) to the duke for his consideration but reiterated the demand for prohibition and empowered a committee to work toward that end.

A few days later, on 6 March, "a number of boys and disorderly lads" gathered at the Castle Hill of Inverness

> for the purpose of burning a sort of effigy expressive of their hatred of Popery. They afterwards adjourned to the High-street, and encamped in front of the Exchange, directly before the Police-office. Here they continued for some time, shouting and huzzaing, till one of their number procured another effigy, or scarecrow, which he hoisted up, and immediately the whole party set off *en masse* down Church-street. They turned up New-street, and, we regret to state, broke the door and windows of the Catholic chapel. On return to their former position, their number had greatly increased, and the authorities began to be alarmed. With a view to intimidation, a boy, who was rendering himself conspicuous in the affairs, was suddenly seized and clapped into the Police-office. This, however, operated

but as a signal to the mob, and in a few minutes the windows of the Police-office were demolished, the door broken, several of the watchmen hurt with stones, and the culprit liberated [*Times*, 17 March 1829: 3].

The crowd milled for a while, then dispersed. The magistrates, continued the account, "have offered a reward for the discovery of the persons who broke the windows of the Chapel and Police-office, and have very properly issued an address to the inhabitants, requesting that heads of families, masters, and employers, may look diligently to those under their charge."

The contrast between the two events is instructive: The weavers meet, elect a chairman, form a committee, and pass resolutions. The lads of Inverness meet, burn an effigy, march up the street, smash windows, and kick in doors. Their actions spring from two different repertoires: the Inverness youngsters, from a repertoire that had been prevalent in the eighteenth century and was now, in 1829, on its way out; the Spitalfields weavers, from a repertoire some of whose elements have eighteenth-century precedents but that was on its way to dominating the collective action of the nineteenth century—not to mention the twentieth. The new repertoire gave a large place to self-selected special interests and formal associations, maintained a strong connection with electoral politics, and tended to produce, on the average, larger and more highly coordinated actions.

Pressed into service, the metaphor of repertoire seems useful. But is it more than a convenient evocation, something besides a name for the fact that groups differ in the ways in which they act together? In order to bear much analytic weight, the notion of repertoire must represent a detectable tendency for existing groups to rely repeatedly on a limited number of well-defined forms of collective action. We ought to find groups modifying and replacing those forms incrementally in the light of success and failure in achieving their ends. Abrupt shifts and sudden inventions should be rare. Those repertoires, furthermore, should not be perfectly uniform for all groups in Great Britain, but they should vary somewhat with the interests, organization, and particular experience in collective action of the group in question. The agenda for the study of repertoires therefore consists, first, of determining whether repertoires, in some strong sense of the word, actually exist and, second, of examining how and why the particular forms of collective action vary and change.

What opportunities do we have to work at these broad tasks? We have the opportunities (a) to look closely at the histories of particular forms of collective action; (b) to examine variation in the collective-action repertoires of particular localities, groups, and movements; (c) to decompose the major types of action into their elements; and (d) to assemble continuous information on forms of conflict and collective action that do not necessarily constitute "contentious gatherings," as our definitions identify them.

The histories of particular forms of collective action take us to questions such as these:

1. Did donkeying, and other forms of Rough Music, decline notably as a form of action during the period from 1828 to 1834? Which groups and regions retained it?
2. Did the extension of the electorate with the Reform Bill of 1832 promote a wider use of the electoral rally, and other actions resembling the electoral rally, as a vehicle for the stating of grievances and demands that were not strictly electoral?
3. Can we detect the adoption by non-Catholic groups in Britain of the Catholic Association's successful tactics? Did it happen before leaders of Reform more or less self-consciously borrowed the model of Catholic Emancipation?
4. Did the sorts of assemblies that demanded tribute, wage changes, and the destruction of threshing machines during the Swing rebellion of 1830 tend to disappear from the laborers' repertoire after the dramatic repression of the rebellion?
5. Did the demonstration, as a distinctive form of action, somehow crystallize in Britain during the mobilization for Reform?

These and similar questions require a broad familiarity with the evidence and a supple use of the sources. The analysis of the patterns that show up in our machine-readable descriptions of these particular types of action should, nevertheless, provide a good sense of the main trends and a useful specification of just what has to be explained.

Study of the repertoires of particular localities, groups, and movements is likewise challenging. On the one hand, the idea of a repertoire of collective action, as I have formulated it, should apply most clearly and effectively to particular localities, groups, and movements rather than to Britain as a whole: A determinate set of people does the learning, remembering, and choosing. On the other hand, the effectiveness of any repertoire depends on relationships *among* groups: A demonstration, for example, accomplishes political work because several parties recognize that the ability to bring people into the streets to display their numbers and determination on behalf of a specific set of claims helps to place the group and its claims on the regular political agenda. The entry of the demonstration into the British repertoire involved magistrates, mayors, and home secretaries, as well as the demonstrators themselves. In that sense, a repertoire could easily be lodged in the political structure of a national state—or some other political unit—rather than in the collective memory of a particular interest group.

In either case, fortunately, the same empirical procedures recommend themselves. At the level of the contentious gathering, we must follow particular sets of people from one event to the next in order to trace the range of actions in which they engage. Where we have evidence about their deliberations on the way to action, we must scan the deliberations for indications of the alternative actions among which they were choosing. Having thus established the repertoires of particular sets of people as best we can, we must then look at the variation in those repertoires: To what extent do they vary by trade, by locality, by political orientation, and by the nature of the claims and the character of the authorities involved?

These questions become especially interesting when we are dealing with a *movement* of some kind: a sustained challenge to the existing structure of power whose leaders speak in the name of a broad interest. In the years from 1828 through 1834, the Reform movement is the dominant example, but such movements as those for Catholic Emancipation and factory reform also deserve close attention. To some extent, large movements seem to develop their own repertoires, which spread across the diverse groups and localities that take part in them. Whose repertoires prevail? How does the movement repertoire form and spread? The cataloging of specific forms of action according to actor and situation is essential.

That cataloging leads directly to the third procedure in the analysis of repertoires: the decomposition of major types of action into their elements. We begin, reasonably enough, with events bounded and labeled more or less as contemporaries bounded and labeled them: This set of actions is a food riot, that one, an attack on machinery, and so on. This first approach borrows the observations and interpretations of the time; it thereby promises to identify the coherent alternative forms of action that were built into the existing social structure.

Yet it is possible, in principle, that repertoires and conventional categories did not coincide. We might discover, for example, that the event called a "food riot" consisted of varying combinations of well-learned actions:

- The public complaint against profiteers
- The articulated demand that local authorities assure and control the food supply
- The inventorying of food in private hands
- The blockage of shipments
- The public sale of seized food at below the market price

All of these occurred sometimes in "food riots," yet it was rare for all to occur in the same event. Perhaps the individual actions, rather than the events into which they compounded, constituted the repertoire.

In any case, it is likely that different kinds of events had coherent elements in common. The open-air protest meeting and the demonstration, for example, both commonly featured a march through public space in which people carried symbols both of their identity and of the cause they supported. Perhaps the evolution of the forms of contention occurs mainly through the creation, combination, and alteration of such elements while other elements stay more or less constant. If so, the analysis of repertoires will take a new turn. We will concentrate on the decomposition of the major types of action, as seen by contemporaries or historians, into their elements.

Our machine-readable descriptions of contentious gatherings provide some of the necessary material. The items we describe include (a) the *event* as a whole; (b) each *place* in which some action occurred; (c) each *formation*, or set of people acting together, taking part in the contentious gathering; (d) each *action phase* —each visible change in the behavior of any formation in the course of the event; (e) each *source* from which we have drawn evidence for the description; and (f) further *comments* on the description of individual items or of the event as a whole. To illustrate how the transcription works, let us look at two events from 1830's agrarian uprisings. The first took place in Kent on 28 October 1830; as the second event recorded for that day, it acquired the name 830 10 28 02. The *places* involved, as recorded in machine-readable form, were:

KENT	HOLLINGBOURNE	MR. RICHARD THOMAS'S FARM
KENT	HOLLINGBOURNE	MR. THOMAS SAMWAY'S HOUSE
KENT	HOLLINGBOURNE	MR. JOSEPH OLIVER'S HOUSE
KENT	HOLLINGBOURNE	MR. WILLIAM HORTON'S HOUSE

The *formations* were:

01 LABOURERS	(other names: body of men, agricultural labourers, mob)
02 THOMAS, RICHARD	
03 SAMWAY, THOMAS	(other names: farmer)
04 OLIVER, JOSEPH	(other names: farmer and tanner, witness; gentleman)
05 HORTON, WILLIAM	(other names: farmer)
06 ROPER, BATCHELOR	(other names: farmer)
07 SOMEONE	

08 MOB, PART OF   (other names: prisoners; labourers;
                          Edward Chapman, Mathew Walter,
                          William Robinson)
09 JUDGE   (other names: learned judge)

The formations 01 (LABOURERS), 07 (SOMEONE), and 09 (JUDGE) entered
the event because they made claims—07 having arrested 08 (PART OF
MOB)—whereas the other formations qualified as objects of claims. Most
of the claims were wage demands. The action phases ran as follows:

Sequence number	Acting formation(s)	Object of action	Action verb	Action
0101	01		assemble	On Thursday, the 28th of October last . . . a body of men from 80 to 100 . . . assembled
0201	01	02	*demand[a]	They said they assembled to have their wages raised, and . . . wished every married man to receive half-a-crown a day and every single man 2s.
0301	02		*agree	. . . regular rate of wages . . . conform to . . .
0401	02		go away	. . . gave a cheer and went away
0501	01	03	come to	They . . . came to my house [Thomas Samway]
0601	01	03	demand	They . . . demanded an increase of wages . . .
0701	03	01	*answer	I said I was willing to pay what the others did . . .
0801	01		go away	. . . they said that was no answer, and went away
0901	01	04	come to	The mob came to my house [Joseph Oliver]
1001	01	04	demand	The witness here stated the demand which the prisoners and their companions had made to other witnesses.
1101	01		go away	. . . they went away . . .
1201	01		*go to	[go to]
1301	01	05	demand	They demanded higher wages, and asked [William Horton] for money
1401	01		go away	After beating the door with sticks they went away

(continued)

Sequence number	Acting formation(s)	Object of action	Action verb	Action
1501	01	06	*demand	Mr. Batchelor Roper, another farmer, deposed to the same facts
1601	01		*end	[end]
1701	07	08	*arrest	[arrest]
1801	09	08	*try	[three names above] . . . indicted . . . guilty

a Starred action verbs represent our inferences from the text, as do bracketed descriptions of the action. The *source* for the one account that we have of this event is the trial report in the London *Times*, 23 December 1830. More material from the account is in our machine record, but the truncated summary in this table gives the main elements of the record.

Let us look at a second event, which took place in Sussex about 10 days later, on 8 November 1830. The one place involved was the parish of Guestling. Formations were:

01 LABOURERS   (other names: paupers)
02 HEADS OF PARISH (other names: Mr. Parsons)
03 LATE MASTERS   (other names: employers)
04 MR. PARSONS

Action phases were:

0101 01 02 notify   . . . gave notice to the heads of the parish that their company was requested to meet them at 10 o'clock Monday . . .
0201 01   assemble   . . . about 130 labourers were assembled
0301 01 03 resolve   They soon informed their late masters . . . they had resolved on receiving higher wages
0401 01 04 demand   . . . we demand that you do immediately give up 500. a year to our employers
0501 04 01 agree   The parson very readily agreed to do so . . .
0601 01 04 cheer   . . . the men gave three cheers . . .
0701 01   go to   . . . every one went to his . . . home . . .

The action phases provide an abbreviated but comprehensible narrative of the event. In the one case, the local agricultural laborers assemble to proceed from farm to farm. In the other, they assemble to address the heads of the parish. (In the second case, according to material I have omitted, the laborers asked for wages of two shillings threepence in winter and two shillings sixpence in summer, proposing that the parson—whose name was, indeed, Mr. Parsons—remit the necessary

500 pounds from his local tithe.) In both cases, they demanded higher wages and got them. Since in both cases we record WAGE DEMANDS as the "major issue," that, too, is readily apparent from the machine record. The action-phase transcriptions make it possible, then, to follow the various sequences by which the hundreds of similar events unfolded in the fall of 1830.

The general mix of action verbs for an area, population, or period tells us something about the character of the action. In all events for the year 1829, for example, the verbs that appeared 20 times or more are listed here. (An asterisk indicates that we have inferred the verb from the text; in all other cases, the word is the one employed in our source.)

meet (303)	resolve (90)	cheer (111)
enter (47)	destroy (20)	attack (29)
assemble (121)	arrive (35)	separate (35)
petition (265)	parade (21)	applaud (27)
*oppose (112)	*end (452)	*arrive (23)
adjourn (40)	disperse (39)	address (26)
proceed (48)	thank (114)	requisition (25)
collect (25)	*meet (114)	*cheer (22)
refuse (21)	*gather (33)	follow (24)
*arrest (34)	stone (31)	beg (27)
*support (24)	*hear petition (211)	*address (25)

The list makes it clear that many of 1829's contentious gatherings were meetings: assemble, address, resolve, cheer, petition, and so on. Not all, however; destroy, parade, attack, stone, and arrest also find their places on the list. A simple approach to decomposing types of action into their elements, then, consists of identifying the recurrent sequences, two or three verbs at a time, of these and less frequent action verbs. If we can then match particular sets of those sequences with contemporary definitions of major types—the recurrent sets of action verbs which together identify an event as a food riot or an electoral rally, for example—so much the better. If we can do that, we have some chance of using the action verbs to pin down similarities and dissimilarities among different types of collective action.

The action verbs provide the most promising start for the decomposition of types of action, but not the only one. Our action-phase descriptions also include identifications of all formations that joined in a particular action, identifications of all formations that were objects of a given action, and concise narratives of the action at each phase. The identifications make it feasible to join actors with their characteristic forms of action, and even to sort out implicit coalitions among groups that commonly act together. The concise narratives make it feasible—at a considerable effort—to place the spare action verbs in a richer context of interaction.

Under the heading of repertoires, our final opportunity is to assemble continuous information on forms of conflict and collective action that do not necessarily constitute "contentious gatherings," as our definitions identify them. The evidence already collected provides a start on that task. Our first broad reading of the periodicals brings back thousands of mentions of three forms of action: strikes, meetings, and petitions. The great majority of these actions fail to meet our exacting standards for contentious gatherings. (In some cases, we are undoubtedly ruling out valid events because our evidence is insufficient, but in the majority of the cases, it seems unlikely that 10 or more people gathered in a publicly accessible place and made visible claims of the sort we require.) The accounts of strikes and meetings provide an ample, if biased, portrait of the way those crucial sorts of events worked in the Britain of the 1820s and 1830s. The enumerations of petitions to Parliament are comprehensive, although they provide little information on the way most petitions came into being. Beyond the basic sources of our enumeration, the voluminous papers of the Home Office likewise contain thousands of accounts of strikes and meetings. They also offer scattered information on the genesis of petitions. For these three types of action, at least, our sources make possible general sketches of variations over time, space, and social setting. Those sketches will be invaluable bases for the interpretation of the ebb and flow of contentious gatherings.

In summary, the study of repertoires involves:

1. Close examination of the histories of particular forms of collective action that show up within contentious gatherings
2. Study of variation in the collective-action repertoires of localities, groups, and movements
3. Decomposition of the major types of action into their elements
4. Tracing forms of conflict and collective action that do not necessarily constitute contentious gatherings, as we define them

Together, these efforts should help us decide whether the learning, choice, and adaptation implied by the metaphor *repertoire* were actually guiding popular collective action in the 1820s and 1830s.

Interests, Organization, and Action

These varied analyses of collective action rest on a strong, simple cornerstone: the idea that collective action springs from shared interests, as mediated by the social organization of the sets of people who share those interests. The thought is old, but not self-evident. Many sociologists and historians have, in fact, imagined that shared beliefs or common exposure to the stresses of social change were the essential grounding of collective action. To emphasize interests and organization as the foundations of collective action is to propose a relatively rationalistic account of that collective action.

But which interests? In general, the interests that count for collective action are rooted in the organization of production. Britain of the 1820s and 1830s was a capitalist world in the making, increasingly divided between a small number of capitalists and a growing mass of workers who were either already proletarian or facing proletarianization. (I mean proletarian, not in the extreme form of working in large manufacturing establishments under strict time discipline, but in the classic sense of working for wages using expropriated means of production; agricultural laborers and small-shop employees qualify.) A full class analysis will go from that general observation to a careful delineation of exceptions and variations: the continuing power of great landlords, the survival of master artisans, the partial (if precarious) independence of handloom weavers, the multiple varieties of agricultural tenure. The class analysis becomes the basis for the attribution of interests.

We arrive at one of those pulse-quickening choice points: a point combining high risk with high opportunity. The risk is evident enough. Any attribution of interests is risky, and in this case our main body of evidence bears only indirectly on those interests. We must work with some combination of hypothesis, indirect inference, and outside evidence. Yet the opportunity is also great, for the observations on thousands of contentious gatherings, down to everyday affairs, show us ordinary people articulating their interests time after time, in a wide variety of circumstances. At least these three possibilities for fresh inquiry arise: (a) analyses of the way collective-action repertoires vary as a function of combinations of interest and organization; (b) the pitting of imputed against articulated interests; and (c) examination of changes in groups' power positions as determinants of their forms of action.

Given an analysis of class interests as defined by the relations of production, Britain of the 1820s and 1830s offers the spectacle of wide variation in the organization based on those interests: informal craft structures, friendly societies, trade unions, clubs, communities, and sometimes no substantial organization at all. Although the forms of organization correlated roughly with the relations of production, and although the forms of organization themselves shaped the interests of one group of another, to some extent one can separate the two. That presents the first challenge: to see how collective-action repertoires vary as a

function of different combinations of interest and commitments. Fastidi-
ous comparisons promise the greatest intellectual return: among the
groups of workers in different industrial cities studied by Asa Briggs,
John Foster, and others; between London's Spitalfields silk weavers and
other artisans; among the small merchants of the industrial north, the
commercial south, and the agricultural midlands.

Brian Brown's analysis of the Lancashire mass strike in 1842 gives an
idea of the possibilities of such comparisons. Building on the ideas,
definitions, and procedures of our study of 1828–1834, Brown drew accounts of contentious gatherings from the *Northern Star* (Manchester) to
make detailed comparisons among parishes. He found, among other
things:

1. Negative relationships between the frequency of Chartist contention
   and the recent pace of industrialization and urban growth
2. No relationship between the frequency of Chartist contention and
   the urban proportion of the population
3. A strong positive relationship between the frequency of Chartist
   contention and the proportion of textile factory workers in the labor
   force
4. A strong relationship between Chartist and non-Chartist contention
5. Powerful effects of changing repression on the frequency and success of strike activity

Brown's analysis starts us on the way to detailed examination of the
day-to-day organization and collective action of Lancashire's textile
workers during the time of Chartism (Brown 1979). Parallels in the period
from 1828 to 1834 spring to mind at once. The next task—for Brown and
for us—is to specify and document the social relations and social processes that connect the industrial workers' collective action with their
interests (as defined by their position in the structure of production) and
with their day-to-day organization.

The *pitting of imputed against articulated interests* addresses an ancient problem of political analysis: the degree to which people's "real"
interests, as determined by an external standard, govern their behavior.
Do people commonly act on misapprehensions of their interest, on mistaken beliefs, on the basis of false consciousness? Does interest, instead,
somehow override mistaken belief? Or—on the model of a class in itself
becoming a class *for* itself—does interest channel belief? I am more inclined to the third view: that interest, at least in the long run, channels
belief. Whether that view is correct or not, however, we need evidence.
The evidence should permit us to compare the interests people actually

articulate in the course of collective action with those we impute to them on the basis of their general social position.

The machine-readable transcriptions of contentious gatherings lend themselves to a crude version of the comparison. Both the summaries of major issues and the descriptions of action phases permit the matching, in the general way, of different kinds of formations with the sorts of demands, complaints, and other claims they made. We can, for example, determine whether handloom weavers who acted defined themselves publicly as members of a trade facing misery, further proletarianization, and extinction. We cannot plumb their psyches; but we can catch some of their words.

The words suggest a more refined analysis which is thinkable with the materials at hand, although not with the part we have made machine-readable. The more refined analysis follows the lead of E. P. Thompson and others who have used a close reading of working-class texts to establish the programs, grievances, and world views of workers. It is possible to go through our accounts of contentious gatherings, sort out the reported utterances of different groups of participants, then examine those texts for characteristic ways of defining the group, distinguishing it from other groups, and stating analyses and grievances. It is then possible to compare the language of those utterances with the language of other standard texts: radical tracts, the popular press, the literature of friendly societies, and so forth. Which ones match best? Which ones, if any, display class-conscious separation from other classes? In which ones do we find similar analyses, categories, and vocabularies? The comparison of texts can range from a broad, thoughtful reading to a precise count of key words; we must strike a balance between richness and reliability. So long as it is done intelligently, the comparison of the language of the crowd with the language of alternative analyses and programs that are available to the crowd should allow us to situate the crowd and its interests more confidently.

A related possibility. Why not undertake a parallel reading of the texts of the crowd's allies, antagonists, and objects? We might be able to achieve two valuable results. The first is to determine whether the analyses, categories, and vocabularies of these other groups somehow articulate with those of the groups whose collective action we are analyzing—articulate by negation, by complementarity, or by partial agreement. The pattern of agreement and disagreement should give us a means, fragile but useful, of understanding the interests at work in the coalitions and oppositions of the time. The second attainable result is a rough mapping of the political positions of different parties to collective action. In principle, for example, we ought to be able to use the language of parliamentary debate to place formations that appear repeatedly in our contentious gatherings within broad categories: clearly, members of powerful groups that have their own spokesmen in Parliament; members of groups that do not have their own people in Parliament but on whose behalf members commonly speak; groups whose right to act politically the members recognize implicitly or explicitly but on whose behalf no one speaks; and groups whose right to exist or to act politically (such words as *mob* and *rabble* come to mind) the members tend to deny. Mixed cases—notably those in which well-defined parliamentary factions differ in their placement of the groups in question—are doubly interesting. Given the strong relationships we are discovering between the rhythms and contents of parliamentary debate, on the one hand, and those of contentious gatherings, on the other, I will not be surprised to discover (a) that most formations which appear frequently in contentious gatherings also came up repeatedly in parliamentary discussion; (b) that the parliamentary discussion arrays them with relative precision from major powerholders to outcasts; and (c) that the parliamentary placement of the groups involved is a reliable index of their current national political position.

The final opportunity to study interests, organization, and action consists of *examining changes in groups' power positions as determinants of their forms of action*. The phrase is a mouthful, but it refers to a well-known phenomenon. In general, we know that powerful groups use different means to work their wills than do the powerless. In fact, we commonly use the different means as a gauge of power: Anyone who can go straight to a cabinet member for a solution to a problem looks powerful. People who break windows to emphasize their grievances probably have little power. So far as I know, no one has worked out that relationship in detail.

Our study of British contention provides some intriguing opportunities for research on the question. The most inviting is, again, Reform: With enfranchisement, did the collective-action repertoires of master artisans, shopkeepers; and other petty bourgeois change? We have some indications that they did. The Birmingham Political Union, for example, marched at the front of the Reform campaign and stood as a model of unity across classes. Yet the class coalition sundered immediately after the passage of the Reform Bill:

> Most of the five hundred mercantile and professional men who had joined the union now left it, and some of them, including Parkes and Green, went so far as to advertise their resignations. To these seceders, the council once more became the much-riddled "Brummagem legislature" elected by "Attwood's scum," an absurd body which supposed that their public-house talk about issues had serious consequences for the nation. Perhaps their

departure was to be expected. What was unanticipated was the defection of the shopkeepers from the activities of the union. Almost at once the council had to recognize the altered status of the shopkeepers: the council's declaration of the "middle classes" on distress included "the tradesmen" for the first time with the manufacturers and merchants, a move made necessary, McDonnell observed, because the shopkeepers no longer identified with the workers on the question of distress [Flick 1978: 101].

A sharper statement of class realignment would be hard to find. In Birmingham and elsewhere, the enfranchised petty bourgeois seem to have abandoned the collective-action repertoire of Reform as travelers flee the plague. Our evidence concerning contentious gatherings before, during, and after the agitation for Reform permits a first reading of that shift: How generally, how visibly, and how did the victors of Reform abandon their erstwhile working-class allies?

Other "natural experiments" come immediately to mind: the changing power position of Dissenters with Test and Corporation repeal, of Catholics with Emancipation, of the local poor with the 1834 Poor Law. Nor need we limit our attention to major legislation. If some form of the indexing of power position via parliamentary debate I proposed earlier yields reliable results, then *changes* in that indexed position for one group or another give us a warrant to look for changes in their forms of collective action, insofar as their participation in contentious gatherings reveals those changes. The analysis need not, for that matter, take place at the national level. For many purposes, it will be more illuminating to search out power shifts within a city or a region and then to examine repertoire changes associated with those power shifts. Here we encounter an advantage of the broad approach to Britain and to collective action we have taken: If we had concentrated from the start on Reform struggles, we would have no opportunity (a) to consider the extent to which Reform's political context, process, and consequences were unique, that is, distinct from those associated with the other major political struggles of the period; (b) to examine the impact of each struggle on the next, such as to determine whether the organizational forms of the Catholic Emancipation campaign served as models for mobilization during the struggles of Reform; or (c) to follow the shifting coalitions and division of power that showed up during Reform across a series of conflicts and mobilizations.

In summary, examining the interplay of interests, organization, and action takes us toward three main kinds of investigation:

1. Analyses of the ways in which collective-action repertoires vary as a function of combinations of interest and organization; for the most

part, controlled comparisons of periods, places, and groups will serve best

2. The pitting of imputed against articulated interests for particular groups, periods, and places
3. Examination of changes in groups' power positions as determinants of their forms of action

These are general questions indeed. They sum up a pressing and coherent agenda for the study of collective action in many times and places. They also apply precisely to the momentous struggles occurring in the Britain of 1828–1834 and suggest a valuable series of inquiries into the "contentious gatherings" of the time. Our return to such large questions provides me with some justification for dragging readers through the tawdry technical problems the serious student of popular collective action confronts.

Conclusions

Some historians of nineteenth-century Great Britain, to be sure, will find this way of posing historical questions eccentric and the procedures I have proposed for their resolution ponderous. In fact, quite a few historians will feel that the careful study of contentious gatherings dignifies trivial events and ignores the genuine springs of politics. Speaking of the Hobsbawm–Rudé analysis of the Swing rebellion, S. G. Checkland and E. O. A. Checkland declare,

> This approach maximizes the oppressive nature of the regime in dealing with protest, arguing that politicians, officialdom and the military were more prone to violence than were the workers. This kind of thinking rests upon the attitude that protest, because it occurs, is a symptom of tension meaningful for society as a whole, that the 'crowd' which carries it out is rational and controlled, free of any tendency to pass into a 'mob', and that the authorities in dealing with the situation should have taken this into account.
>
> The opposing view is that the protests, though frightening to contemporaries, were not all that formidable or concerted, but were a discrete set of incidents, spasmodically related to the worst times and the most adversely affected groups, and encapsulated within particular regions. The question might well be asked by those who take this view: if the labourers had developed a serious consciousness of oppression, and of their role and their solidarity, why then did not the envisaged link-up take place? . . . By extension this approach argues that regrettable though the need for public discipline may have been, protest was on a modest scale, not comparable to what has occurred in other societies. [From the *Introduction* by S. G. and E.O.A.

Needless to say, the Checklands subscribe to the latter view. Almost needless to say, I subscribe to the former. The study of contentious gatherings stands straight in the line occupied by Hobsbawm and Rudé: arguing that everyday conflicts result from, and reveal, durable social divisions; claiming that, on the whole, contention is problem-solving behavior; thinking that the grievances and demands ordinary people stated sprang from experience and reflection; and suggesting that participants in widely separated events pooled their knowledge and responded to one another's successes and failures. Despite our heavy reliance on coding, classification, and computers, our basic procedures simply extend and standardize methods long since developed by Hobsbawm, Rudé, and other pioneers in the historical study of popular collective action.

Note, furthermore, that the research program attends to the very questions the Checklands raise in objection to Hobsbawm and Rudé. Why, indeed, did the "envisaged link-up" not take place? In fact, our preliminary evidence on the Swing rebellion shows signs of direct communication, and intense mutual observation, among agricultural laborers in different localities. The belated but vigorous repression applied to Swing broke a movement that was still growing and coalescing—or, at least, so the early rounds of evidence suggest. If that first impression holds up, it will lead us to doubt Hobsbawm's and Rudé's argument that repression was too late and too ineffectual to affect significantly the course of the rebellion. In any case, the fine-grained enumeration of individual events makes possible a good, hard look at the question. By the same token, the cataloging of contentious gatherings allows us to rethink the Checklands' assertion that "protest was on a modest scale," if not to make the full comparison with "other societies" that their criticism calls for.

Will these research procedures dispose of the question with which we began: whether Britain brushed revolution in the 1830s? Not by themselves. If we were sure of the necessary and sufficient conditions for revolution, and if those conditions had to do chiefly with the visible forms of collective struggle, then the research program I have sketched would address the question squarely. We have, however, competing definitions and contradictory theories of revolution, in some of which popular attitudes, maneuvers among the powerful, or chance play crucial parts. My research program yields little reliable information on popular attitudes, maneuvers among the powerful, or chance. But no other research program yields much information on these elusive matters. To the extent that our usual inferences concerning popular attitudes, maneuvers among the power, and chance come from the historical materials left by collective action and the authorities' response to it, my studies of Britain in the 1820s and 1830s provide a systematic base for those inferences.

We need not leave the question of revolution entirely moot, however. Consider the one extreme: If revolution requires a unified class oriented to a coherent program for the seizure of power and the transformation of social structure, revolution had no chance in the Britain of 1832. Our evidence shows the variety and intensity of popular resistance to British authorities, but it shows nothing like a disciplined program on the march. Yet consider the other extreme: If revolution grows from the convergence of sustained and serious challenges to the existing structure of power—whether or not each individual challenger has joined with others in a self-consciously revolutionary program—then Britain surely approached revolution in the 1830s. At a minimum, the accumulating catalog of thousands of contentious gatherings shows the breadth of popular involvement in challenges to the exercise of power by local and national authorities.

The contentious gatherings of 1828–1834, then, were not only meaningful in their own terms. They help us understand the political changes that were going on in Britain as a whole in ways that parliamentary speeches and the correspondence of leaders cannot. Not that the worlds of Parliament and of popular contention existed on opposite sides of an unbridgeable chasm. On the contrary, they interacted continuously. But in the contentious gatherings of the time we see the interests, organization, and accumulated tactical experience of ordinary people in action and in confrontation with the national structure of power.

Exploration

7

Proletarianization: Theory and Research

What and Where Is Proletarianization?

My argument is as simple as a needle . . . and, I hope, as sharp. Like a needle in a thicket, however, the argument easily gets lost in details, elaborations, and qualifications. So let me start with a bald statement, then elaborate.

Proletarianization is the set of processes that increases the number of people who lack control over the means of production and who survive by selling their labor power. From the perspective of ordinary people's lives, proletarianization is the single most far-reaching social change that has occurred in the Western world over the past few hundred years and that is going on in the world as a whole today. Sociologists have provided no coherent account of proletarianization's causes, forms, and consequences. In fact, sociologists have given little attention to this dominant social process. The models of large-scale change prevailing in North American sociology, with their stress on differentiation and integration, are utterly inadequate to deal with proletarianization. The problem does not lie in poor data or inappropriate methods, although both are obstacles to our understanding. The problem resides in bad theory. Outside of sociology—and notably in history—historically grounded Marxist theory has so far shown the greatest promise of dealing adequately with proletarianization. Get some good theory; data and methods will fall into place.

Plenty of sociology consists of crystallizing folk beliefs and then organizing the evidence for and against them. That is not all to the bad. Folk beliefs, after all, accumulate experience in the same way that stumps accumulate lichens: The lichens eventually change the contours of the stumps.

Yet reliance on crystallized folk beliefs, decorated as science, brings the risk that we accept the ideas as much for their comfortable familiarity as for their intrinsic merits. Witness this passage from a 10-year-old standard text on the sociology of economic development:

> What we are witnessing is the increasing differentiation of functions, which constitutes the basic process of social change associated with economic development. It is quite true that agriculturalists in a backward economy perform a wide range of functions, but this is also one of the reasons that their labor is so low in productivity. Increases in human productivity appear to require an increasing division of labor and specialization of function. And this is a process that is quite pervasive in a society, not simply a matter of work alone. At the higher levels of human productivity, then, we find societies in which individuals carry out a limited number of more specialized tasks. This makes them more dependent upon one another and requires that they be brought more into contact with one another through a wide range of social mechanisms. This also means that they will be interacting with one another in quite limited aspects of their broader lives as individuals [Ness 1970: 11].

The passage crystallizes Western folk wisdom, and contemporary sociological theory, concerning the historical association between prosperity and changes in the organization of work. Differentiation causes increasing productivity, which causes prosperity. Differentiation, runs the account, also causes changes in the structure and quality of routine social life. What causes differentiation is less clear; it may be an inevitable consequence of increasing social scale, a standard response to pressing social problems, or a deliberate invention adopted with an eye to stepping up production.

In that summary, our author does exactly what the author of a text on the sociology of economic development should do: He states the view prevailing among specialists in the field. He also remains faithful to the field in one other regard: He ignores the process of proletarianization.

Proletarianization? The word has three concentric circles of meaning. In the narrowest circle, *proletarians* are people who receive wages from capitalists for relatively unskilled work performed in large establishments under intense discipline. Proletarianization therefore consists of the degradation, fragmentation, and intensification of labor. In this sense of the word, proletarians are essentially creatures of the last century or so of capitalist industrialization. This narrow meaning has taken over.

But we have other, broader choices. In *Das Kapital*, after all, Marx's analysis of the growth of the English proletariat stresses agricultural labor and the influence of enclosing landlords, not manufacturing and factory owners. A larger circle, then, designates as proletarian everyone who sells labor power to capitalists and produces via means of production controlled by capitalists. In that case, proletarianization has two components: workers' increasing dependence for survival on sale of their labor power, capitalists' increasing control over the means of production. By this definition—just so long as we are moderately generous in our use of the words *capitalist* and *control*—proletarianization goes back to the origins of European capitalism.

The broadest circle of proletarians includes everyone who sells labor power, regardless of the modalities of that sale. For that broad circle, proletarianization occurs with an increase in the number of workers who receive wages, a decrease in the number of workers who exert substantial direct control over the means of production. In this third, very broad, sense of the term, the phrases "socialist proletarian" and "proletarian Ph.D." imply no contradiction. People in socialist countries commonly work for wages at means of production over which they have little or no control, and so do highly trained professionals, in socialist and capitalist countries alike.

If the first circle, despite its currency, is excessively narrow for historical analysis, the third reaches so far as to obliterate the specific historical traits of the last few hundred years. Let us settle on the second: proletarianization as an increase in the number of workers dependent for survival on the sale of their labor power to capitalists (broadly defined) who control the means of production. By this standard, the current worldwide process of proletarianization has been proceeding for five centuries or so—beginning mainly in western Europe, accompanying the advance of capitalism into other domains, taking place chiefly in small towns and rural areas over most of its history, transforming agriculture and small-scale manufacturing long before the era of factory and mill. In terms of impact on the quality of everyday life, proletarianization is—and was—the most powerful process in the complex of changes that we vaguely and variously call industrialization, economic development, or the growth of capitalism.

The Importance of Proletarianization

Proletarianization is and was a powerful process in two regards: quantitative and qualitative. In quantitative terms, the last few hundred years have brought an extraordinary proletarianization of our world. In 1700, according to Paul Bairoch's estimates, the world's labor force included

about 270 million people. By 1970, the number was just under 1.5
billion—a sextupling since the start of the eighteenth century (Bairoch
1971: 965). As of 1700, it would be surprising to discover that more than
10% of the world's labor force consisted of people who survived by selling
their labor power. As of 1970, depending on the tightness of the definitions employed for the words *capitalist* and *control*, we can reasonably
guess that nearly a majority of the world's labor force was proletarian. To
illustrate that possibility, let us crank back to 1960. Table 7.1 presents Paul
Bairoch's rough estimates of the world's labor force in "developing" and
"developed" countries. That at least half the world's labor force was then
in agriculture and that we often use the loose term *peasant* for workers in
relatively uncapitalized, labor-intensive agriculture should not divert our
attention from the large proportion of Third World agriculturalists who
are essentially wage laborers without effective control over the land and
the large share of all Third World landlords who are actually capitalists of
one stripe or another. Suppose we estimate conservatively that 80% of the
"developed" labor force of 1960 consisted of people working for wages
under capitalist control, that in the "developing" world the proportions
were 20% for agriculture, forestry, hunting, and fishing, 25% for all other
industries. The conservative estimates produce a world total of 465 million proletarians: 37% of the total. The figures are, of course, speculations;
they are not fantasies. From 1700 to 1970, the world's proletariat most
likely multiplied 30 or 40 times as the labor force sextupled. (The following chapter offers more precise, although still speculative, estimates of

TABLE 7.1
Paul Bairoch's Estimates of the World Labor Force, 1960
(millions of workers, by type of country)

Industrial category	Type of country		
	"Developing"	"Developed"	World total
Agricultural, forestry, hunting, fishing	357	136	734
Mining and quarrying	3	7	12
Manufacturing	45	114	181
Construction	10	28	48
Commerce	30	52	92
Transport, storage, communication	11	26	49
Services	49	83	148
Total labor force	505	446	1263
Total population	1320	986	3040

Source: Bairoch and Limbor 1968, tables 2, 3, 5.

the growth of the European proletariat from 1500 to 1900.) In recent decades, the increase in Third World agricultural wageworkers has no doubt constituted the largest single contribution to the world's proletarianization. Over the whole history of capitalism, indeed, agriculture and rural industry have provided the main sites for proletarianization. Cities and large-scale manufacturing have, despite their proletarian reputations, only intermittently served as the chief loci for the production of proletarians.

Qualitatively, the creation of a proletariat has transformed all arenas of social life: reducing the likelihood that children would take over the economic enterprises of their parents; snapping the links among marriage, inheritance, and reproduction; swelling the numbers of people who must buy most of their food and are therefore vulnerable to swings in food prices; altering the character and pacing of work itself. The paths, paces, and penalties of these changes have varied greatly from one time and place to another, depending on the existing systems of production and reproduction, as well as on the kind of production involved. It is a long way from the creation of an eighteenth-century textile industry in Swiss highland villages to the rise of export-oriented rice production in twentieth-century Vietnam. But both were active sites of proletarianization.

Eighteenth-century Switzerland and twentieth-century Vietnam had in common a two-sided situation: concentration of capital and/or land on one side, expropriation of workers from the means of production on the other. (That the villagers in both places should often have participated actively in their own collective proletarianization by snatching at chances for wage labor, by competing for the available land, or by having many children, only emphasizes the power and generality of the process.) Concentration of capital and/or land does not necessarily entail expropriation of workers. The remarkable increase in the importance of family farms in the world grain market over the past century demonstrates the possible coincidence of concentration and deproletarianization (see Friedman 1978). Nevertheless, historically speaking, proletarianization has linked itself closely to the concentration of land and capital. It is precisely the contingency of that strong link that lays down a challenge to theory and research.

To be sure, we often attribute the changes for which I am making proletarianization responsible to "industrialism" or "modernism" in general. Our folk beliefs certainly run in that direction. "Industrialism," however, hardly seems a good name—much less a good explanation—for transformations that occur so regularly in the agrarian sector. As for "modernism" or "modernization," the idea is so vague and global as to lack theoretical bite. For my part, I see a historically specific relationship between the changes in the quantity and quality of social life reviewed earlier and the development of capitalism. But, for the moment, that connection is not essential to the argument. All we need agree is that, whatever else was happening, the proximate process that brought the changes about was the increase in the number of workers dependent on the sale of their labor power for survival. It was proletarianization. Yet our standard texts ignore the process.

What Sociologists Say, and What They Ignore

The texts represent the state of our field. If we look to Gerhard Lenski, as he constructs a general account of the links between systems of stratification and modes of production, we find no discussion of proletarianization, and an implicit reliance on the standard view of differentiation. The growth in the scale of economic organization, reports Lenski, "has facilitated another development, intensive specialization. According to the Department of Labor, there are currently more than twenty thousand different kinds of jobs in this country, most of them extremely specialized in nature [1966: 301]." Later he tells us that the problem most workers face is that their jobs are not only specialized but also relatively easy to learn; as a result, workers are easy to replace (Lenski 1966: 377). But of the alienation of labor power, we hear not a word.

If we open one of the innumerable symposia on industrialization from the mid-1960s, all with interchangeable names—"Industrialization and Society," "Society and Industrialization," and so on—we will encounter the ubiquitous Wilbert Moore. One of his many summary statements avoids asking how an industrial labor force comes into being in the first place: It presents an ideal sketch of full-scale industrial organization and then discusses the fit between that structure and the character of "newly developing areas." "The worker is," runs the passage closest to our subject, "in addition to his relations to the machine and to fellow-workers, related to the productive organization in other ways. He has a financial relation, through the payment of his wage or salary. He is likely to be the object of various staff services. Above all, he is subject to a structure of authority [W. Moore 1966: 306]." The process by which these social arrangements come into being simply disappears.

In *Wirtschaft und Gesellschaft*, Max Weber titled a discussion "Expropriation der Arbeiter von der Beschaffungsmitteln," expropriation of workers from the means of production—ostensibly, right on the mark (1972

[1921]: 77 – 80). When we turn to that discussion, however, we discover an enumeration of the technical rationales for producing by means of expropriated labor, rather than an analysis of how and why the expropriation occurs. At its very best, in short, the literature of sociology mentions proletarianization and then rushes on to deal with other problems.

The analysis of proletarianization, to be sure, stands at the very heart of Karl Marx's historical work. The first volume of *Das Kapital*, especially in its sections on primitive accumulation, returns again and again to the means by which English landlords, merchants, and manufacturers expropriated their workers and substituted alienated labor power for production by smallholders, artisans, and others who exercised some substantial control over the means of production. Marxist historians and economists have continued to pay serious attention to these changes and their successors—not only to the initial creation of a proletariat but also to the subsequent standardization, segmentation, and surveillance of work. Marxist interest in proletarianization has not, however, seeped into sociology's mainstream. At least not until recently. For most of the discipline's history, sociologists have shown little interest in one of the dominant processes going on in their own world.

Could that be because the answers are obvious? I think not. Let us narrow our attention to European proletarianization, since that is the process I know best, and since it often serves, implicitly or explicitly, as a model for the analysis of proletarianization elsewhere. One of the crispest and most telling questions we can ask about the European experience is the standard components-of-growth question: How much of the net increase in the European proletariat in one century or another was due to migration into and out of Europe? How much to natural increase? How much to reclassifications—to changes in status that occurred in people's own working lives? More concrete questions follow immediately from the big components-of-growth questions. How often, for example, and under what circumstances did the children of artisans or peasants spend their own working lives as proletarians? Did the fertility and mortality patterns of nineteenth-century wageworkers mean that they more than reproduced themselves? Did those patterns, and their consequences for recruitment into the proletariat, change significantly from the eighteenth to the twentieth centuries? In the various rural "emancipations" of the nineteenth century, what proportion of the formerly servile workers actually ended up in control of enough land for a household's survival? Do proletarianization and rapid population growth ordinarily go together? If so, is it possible that proletarianization is not merely a result of "population pressure" but also a cause of rapid natural increase?

Important further issues hang in the balance: A proletariat that swells its numbers mainly through its own relatively high fertility, for instance, is a more plausible bearer of continuous working-class culture than one which draws all its increase from skidding artisans and peasants. But that self-augmenting proletariat would presumably have little exposure to an experience that commonly fosters class-conscious militancy: the threat of losing control over one's land, craft, tools, or other means of production. Such theoretical choices matter both for their own sake and because they have become the hidden pivots of important historical debates. E. P. Thompson's magnificent study of the making of the English working class, for example, demonstrated the need for a good deal of continuity, of cumulative experience, on the part of the members of that class. The counterinterpretation of Luddism or Chartism as relatively incoherent responses to rapid industrialization, on the other hand, points toward much greater discontinuity. At present, we have many fragments of answers to the components-of-growth questions and their derivatives, but we have no clear indications as to which way the general answers will run.

Many other features of European proletarianization remain problematic. We cannot yet say, for example, to what extent the factory was the dominant site of proletarianization, since we know for certain that many people entered the proletarian world via agricultural wage labor, cottage industry, inflation of the apprentice system, or urban service work. We sometimes suppose, but do not really know, that school, church, and police colluded to train the sorts of docile, prudent, time-conscious workers that capitalists prefer. We cannot now be sure that the sort of "family economy" analyzed by Frederic Le Play, A. V. Chayanov, and Carle Zimmerman disintegrated as proletarianization advanced. All these are pressing questions. They are sociological questions. Yet the literature concerning them comes almost entirely from historians. Moreover, most recent work on the question follows a broadly Marxist approach—at least to the extent of taking for granted that changing relations of production profoundly influence other aspects of social life.

Why historians should plunge into the study of proletarianization and its consequences while sociologists avert their eyes is an interesting question. The answer no doubt lies partly in the bad political odor of Marxism in the world that has nurtured sociology and partly in the greater comfort of sociologists with ideas that crystallize folk beliefs. But if those are the fundamental explanations, then it is all the more puzzling that historians should have concerned themselves so freely, and so well, with proletarianization. Surely historians are not, on the average, excessively cordial to Marxism or notably hostile to folk theories. We have to consider at least one other possibility: that sociology is not the fact-grubbing field it seems to be. Perhaps something about its fundamental theories limits sociology's ability to deal with such processes as proletarianization.

Can Sociology Comprehend Proletarianization?

How easily can the standard theories and methods of contemporary sociology deal with proletarianization? Not very easily. The basic problem is theoretical. The chief theories available to sociologists who wish to analyze large-scale processes of change come from a tradition we can conveniently trace back through Emile Durkheim. Durkheimian theories build on a conception of a vague social unit called a society. That society responds to internal problems and external pressures through sequences of differentiation and integration. In most versions of the theory, including Durkheim's, the differentiation produces stress, strain, malintegration, and deviance, to which the society responds with some combination of social control and further differentiation. In most versions of the theory, as applied to recent social change, occupational differentiation is absolutely central. In one of Talcott Parson's later formulations, he asserted,

> The critical development was the differentiation of labor (or, more technically, of services) from the diffuse matrix in which it had been embedded. This differentiation involved distinguishing the work-role complex from the family household and also increased the "mobility of labor"—the readiness of households to respond to employment opportunities by changing residences or learning new skills. . . . These processes established what sociologists call the *occupational role*, specifically contingent upon status in an employing organization structurally distinct from the household.*Usually the employing organization has only one member in common with the household; it also has premises, disciplines, authority systems, and property distinct from those of the household. Typically the employed person receives (according to his employment status and role performance) a money income that is the main source of his household's access to the market for consumer goods. The employing organization markets its product and pays the employee wages or a salary, whereas the typical peasant or artisan sold his own products. The organization thus comes between the worker and the consumer market [1971: 77].
>
> * Neil J. Smelser, *Social Change in the Industrial Revolution* (Chicago: University of Chicago Press, 1959).

Let us forget about criticizing Parsons's analysis in its own terms, as useful as that task would be. Note how the argument runs. First, it hides the effective human actors and depersonalizes the process by which the change occurs. Second, Parsons adopts the same retrospective device we saw Wilbert Moore employing earlier: He describes the social arrangements that eventually emerged and attempts to identify the essential prerequisites and concomitants of those arrangements. Third, his account strips the hypothetical process of differentiation from its historical context, making no concession to the possibility that where and when the process occurred significantly affected its character or outcome. Finally, Parsons assumes the classic Durkheimian model of structural differentiation.

Placed together, the four planks become a nearly impermeable barrier to an effective analysis of proletarianization, for in that process real people—landlords, rich peasants, master artisans, manufacturers, merchants, capitalists—seize control of the means of production and exclude others from that control. A valid analysis of proletarianization has to lay out the alternative ways in which the seizure of control and the exclusion take place. A valid *explanation* of proletarianization specifies the causes of the seizure and the exclusion. In all this, differentiation is a red herring: Although, on the average, the firm and the household became more distinct from one another, much of the actual historical experience in question consisted of *de*-differentiation. In the case of Europe, the enormous growth of cottage industry and the homogenization of agricultural labor are obvious illustrations. Whatever the overall trend, the proximate conditions for the proletariat's growth were not differentiation but concentration and expropriation. I believe the same is true today. If so, what has to be explained is how capitalists and landlords increased their control over the means of production, how they dispossessed workers from that control, how they drew workers into full-time wage labor.

The data and methods to which sociologists studying large-scale social change commonly turn make it more difficult to grasp the actual workings of proletarianization. Administratively generated series concerning health, wealth, production, and income at the national level, one-time sample surveys, and even well-conducted censuses shed only the most indirect light on processes of concentration and expropriation. Vital records and enumerations of the labor force sometimes come closer, but only on condition that their analysis be integrated with information on local conditions of production and consumption. The frequent, nefarious practice of substituting the comparing of different social units at the same point in time for the tracing of change in the same units over time virtually guarantees ignorance about concentration and expropriation—not to mention that arraying the units as if they were at different positions along the same evolutionary track assumes precisely what must be proven. The retrospective case study in which evidence is thick for the present and thin for the past provides little better purchase on such processes as proletarianization. Glossing standard historical works on industrialization, economic growth, and the development of capitalism is not a bad way to start thinking about proletarianization, but it is a poor way to do the requisite research. In short, the standard tools fit the problem badly.

The chief difficulty, however, is not methodological. It is theoretical. Sociologists continue to use data and methods that fail to grasp the realities of proletarianization because sociologists' theories make no room for the process. Prevailing models of differentiation and integration systematically mislead us as to the loci and character of alterations in the organization of production. We need models that are historically grounded, both in the sense that they explicitly take into account the time and place in which a process occurs as an influence on its course and in the sense that they direct our attention to evidence concerning the ways in which concrete social experiences changed over considerable periods of time. We need models that feature power, exploitation, coercion, and struggle. That is why Marxist theory, for all its unresolved problems, has so far served as our most reliable guide to the historical study of proletarianization; Marxist models generally attend to history, at least to the extent of treating the development of a given mode of production, such as capitalism, as historically specific, and Marxist models always feature power, exploitation, coercion, and struggle.

When it comes time to reflect on sociological theory and research, the study of proletarianization offers a distressing object lesson and a stirring challenge. Proletarianization played a large part in bringing our own social world into being and continues to transform life throughout the globe. Sociology's contribution to the understanding of proletarianization has so far been largely negative: misleading theories, inadequate methods, massive avoidance of the problem. Bad theory, especially, stands in the way. What a shame . . . and what an opportunity!

8
States, Taxes, and Proletarians

Capitalism and Statemaking Today

These are heady moments for the study of European capitalism and statemaking. In the wakes of such general essays as Barrington Moore's, Perry Anderson's, and Immanuel Wallerstein's have arrived whole schools of criticism and inquiry. Jerome Blum has surveyed the end of the "old order" in rural Europe, Fernand Braudel has released the full three volumes of his *Civilisation matérielle, économie, et capitalisme,* and the second volume of Wallerstein's *Modern World System* has appeared in print. Another literary event has attracted little notice but deserves our attention here. That is the appearance of Catharina Lis and Hugo Soly's *Poverty and Capitalism in Pre-Industrial Europe.* Lis and Soly provide a rich, thoughtful survey of the whole period from the year 1000 to about 1850: the character and origins of the poor, the impact of capitalism on poverty, the attempts of ruling classes and governments to control poor people. Any effort to do all that in 200 pages has to be sketchy and is likely to lack systematic comparisons of one region, population, or process with another.

Lis and Soly's effort *is* sketchy; it does lack systematic comparisons. Still, it does an extraordinary job of digesting the abundant multilingual literature—documenting, for example, the crucial importance of rural industry in the growth of a European proletariat. And the book has a point of view: It rejects notions of poverty as a natural consequence of technological backwardness or of unrestrained population growth and insists that "poverty can be fully understood only as the consequence of an established structure of surplus-extractive relations [Lis and Soly 1979: 215]."

Accordingly, Lis and Soly emphasize the forms and mechanisms of inequality rather than the determinants of national income and per capita production. Confronted with the supposed crisis of the seventeenth century, for example, they challenge the standard Malthusian scenario: A rigid, inefficient agricultural system buckles under the stress of a growing population, as an expanding state absorbs whatever surplus previously existed. They point out how similar pressures produced different outcomes in France and England:

> Subsistence crises were unavoidable in France because the forms of surplus extraction in an absolutist state which was based on the small peasant proprietor excluded any possibility of increased production. The old mode of production was simply "sucked dry"; it was in no sense altered. In contrast, a nearly unique structure emerged in England, based on landlords, capitalist tenants, and wage labourers, which led to a radical transformation of agrarian production [Lis and Soly 1979: 100].

Consequences: general impoverishment, but little transformation, of the work force in France and increasing productivity, but massive proletarianization, in England. France's era of rapid proletarianization came later. In both countries, and in Europe as a whole, "the rise of capitalist means of production required the construction of public mechanisms of support, which not only kept the reserve army of the poor under control in order to guarantee political order but also offered the possibility of providing employers sufficiently cheap wage labour at every moment to reach their economic targets [Lis and Soly 1979: 220 – 221]." Thus, for Lis and Soly, the development of capitalism, the growth of the proletariat, and the creation of national means of controlling the poor were not distinct processes but different aspects of the same great change in the condition of ordinary Europeans.

I agree. One of the virtues of the Lis – Soly book is its presentation of materials for a connected account of capitalism, proletarianization, and state actions with respect to poor people. My purpose here is not to summarize the materials or to attempt the whole connected account, but to call attention to a few of the connections—including some that Lis and Soly themselves do not make. In particular, I want to stress the widespread, if implicit, collaboration of European capitalists and statemakers in the extensions of bourgeois property and the growth of wage labor. The fiscal strategies of European states played, I think, a significant part in linking statemaking and capitalism. Hence the subject: states, taxes, and proletarians.

In that subject, all the major themes of this book join. There they come: capitalism, statemaking, proletarianization, war, collective action . . . and the interaction of sociology with history. Although this chapter will slip past problems of research technique quickly, even those problems figure importantly in the study of states, taxes, and proletarians. For, as we shall see, the essential evidence is at once abundant, scattered, and slippery. One major aim of this chapter is to show why the evidence is worth collecting and handling with care.

Let us begin with a general set of ideas on states, taxes, and proletarians: A cluster of working hypotheses, we might call them. In the era of capitalism, any group who controlled a state had some interest—at least defensive—in warmaking. War was becoming increasingly expensive. It required the rapid mobilization of capital. In general, only capitalists held, or had access to, the requisite capital. Over the long run, however, the resources for warmaking and other governmental expenses were embedded in the labor and property of the rest of the population. One form of taxation or another extracted those resources from the rest of the population.

Increasing taxation, especially taxation in cash rather than kind, had several important effects. First, it diverted resources from peasants, landlords, and others. Second, it promoted the commercialization of production by forcing people to market commodities and labor in order to acquire the wherewithal for tax payments. Third, it incited resistance, especially when in addition to causing economic hardship it:

1. Enriched local powerholders at the expense of their neighbors;
2. Violated previous rights, charters, and treaties; and
3. Visibly reduced the ability of people to fulfill their moral and political obligations within household or community.

Statemakers commonly loaned political power, including access to the disposition of armed force, to those capitalists who advanced them funds for military activity. They also entailed future state revenues in favor of the capitalists and provided political guarantees that those revenues would continue to flow. Thus, on the average, the importance of capitalists in the creation of state credit augmented their political power and gave them an interest in the state's financial viability. Presumably these effects were stronger where and when the state was relatively weak, its expenditure was large, and the economy was not extensively commercialized. Presumably the effects were also stronger when merchants and other capitalists had independent bases of power.

Under these circumstances, two partly independent changes—the growth in capitalist political power and the commercialization incited by taxation—promoted the concentration of capital. The concentration of capital, plus the direct effects of taxation, accelerated the growth of the proletariat at the same time as it helped transform a small portion of the peasantry into capitalist farmers. In the process, capitalists and statemakers collaborated in the creation of bourgeois property: unified, disposable, and private. In place of fragmented, overlapping, multiple claims on the same land, labor or commodity there developed a situation in which, at the extreme, only two claimants remained: an individual owner and a taxing state.

Bourgeois land reforms, from the French reforms of 1791 onward, sometimes consolidated peasant property but generally gave the capitalists more leverage in squeezing out smallholders. Redistribution of church lands, *desamortización*, even the various abolitions of serfdom, all tended in that same direction. Land reforms were especially potent in proletarianizing poor farmers who lived without firm title to the land from which they drew their sustenance: squatters, customary tenants, people depending on common woods and fields. But capital concentration and commercialization also fostered the growth of the proletariat through the expansion of opportunities for wage labor, which in turn encouraged the natural increase of proletarian families. Presumably these effects were stronger where and when small landlords were already weak and few, where capitalists held extensive state power, and where markets were readily available.

This general account is, I remind you, a string of working hypotheses. It has its paradoxes and evasions. Despite Immanuel Wallerstein's declaration that the early modern Dutch and English states were strong (since they did their work of capitalist domination with relatively slight apparatus), most observers see something of an inverse correlation between capitalist power and the strength of the state: Prussia held its merchants in check, runs the standard account, whereas the Dutch state—when it existed at all—acted as a quintessential executive committee of the bourgeoisie. What is more, the political and economic geographies of Europe suggest a similar inverse correlation: The band of mercantile cities running from northern Italy, down the Rhine, and over into the Low Countries was the last to consolidate into large, strong states. Yet my account suggests mutual reinforcement of state power and capitalist power.

I am still puzzling with this paradox, and tiptoeing gingerly around the mine field of a question that lies beyond it: To what extent are states simply the instruments of their dominant classes? I suspect that the answers reside in the recognition that statemakers wielded some independent power in the short run, that they were constantly involved in forming or responding to class coalitions rather than single classes, and that a middle position between complete bourgeois hegemony and total subordination of the bourgeoisie favored a coalition that simultaneously strengthened capitalists and the state. In that case, my account should apply better to France and England than to Hungary or Holland.

So much for general approaches. In my own work, I am making no effort to assemble evidence for the whole risky interpretation. I have, however, cut into this set of connections at several different points. Perhaps we should focus on two of them: the process of proletarianization and the effects of taxation. Both have appeared in previous chapters; now it is time to join them. First, some observations on the growth of the European proletariat. Then, some ideas on taxation and its consequences. Finally, an attempt to link the two topics to each other and to the broad theme of states, taxes, and proletarianization.

Proletarianization

Let us adopt a broad conception of the proletariat. Instead of the popular image of unskilled manufacturing workers producing for wages in large establishments under intense time discipline, think of the middle category I proposed in the preceding chapter. It is essentially the class Marx described in *Capital:* all workers who survive by selling their labor power to capitalists (including capitalist landlords) who dispose of the means of production. Proletarianization, in that broad conception, results from two coordinate processes: (a) the substitution of wage labor for other forms of return to labor; and (b) the expropriation of the means of production from the producers themselves. Expropriation, in my view, is the fundamental process, and the extension of wage labor is primarily a means by which capitalists accomplish that expropriation. In any case, to the extent that work combines the two—expropriated means of production and wages—the workers are proletarians.

By that standard, proletarians have been around Europe for a long time. They were important in rural areas well before the era of the factory. In an ill-documented but much-repeated estimate, Alan Everitt has opined that at the start of the seventeenth century one-quarter to one-third of England's and Wales's rural population consisted of essentially landless laborers (1967: 398). As of 1688, in an estimate repeated just as often as Everitt's, Gregory King was claiming that 66% of all English families were headed by laborers of one kind or another (Mathias 1957: 45). By the time of the 1831 British census, 76% of the males in agriculture were wageworkers (Great Britain: xiii). If that were all we had to go on, we could plausibly conclude that Britain's rural population proletarianized early and extensively, and that the seventeenth century marked the major acceleration of the process.[1]

That much would fit, without too much effort, with the multiple local and regional studies revealing the seventeenth- and eighteenth-century growth of a rural proletariat: J. D. Chambers for the Vale of Trent, David Levine for Leicestershire villages, Keith Wrightson and David Levine for a village in Essex, and more. So far, so good. Unfortunately, other general estimates from the eighteenth and early nineteenth centuries, notably those of Joseph Massie and Patrick Colquhoun, smudge the time line by running lower than King's estimate (Mathias 1957: 45; Colquhoun 1806, 1815). We can tidy up the line again by means of judicious manipulations of the definitions involved. But, in fact, all we may conclude with any confidence is that well before the nineteenth century a majority of Britain's rural population consisted of landless laborers and that rural proletarianization continued to the mid-nineteenth century before starting an unsteady but substantial decline.

Given the great increase of the total British population after 1650 or so, the absolute increase in the rural proletariat must have been in the millions. The evidence at hand suggests two further conclusions: that until recently the rural labor force was more proletarian than the urban and that until some time in the nineteenth century the countryside, not the city, was the prime site of British proletarianization. Not only agricultural change, narrowly defined, but also the proliferation of cottage industry account for that rural predominance.

If that is the case, both landlords and merchants must have played significant parts in creating the opportunities which, in their turn, promoted the growth of the proletariat. Through consolidation and expansion of their holdings, landlords squeezed out the intermediate groups: customary tenants, smallholders, squatters. F. M. L. Thompson guesses that the "peasantry"—essentially those who worked the land with their own labor—had some sort of title to half of England's land in 1500 and that

---

[1] We could also, incidentally, note that from a peak of 80% at the middle of the nineteenth century, the agricultural population deproletarianized from then up to our own time. Landless laborers joined the rural exodus in disproportionate numbers, and family farms were left to dominate the countryside (Bellerby 1958: 3). Agricultural deproletarianization and the concomitant relative rise of the family farm employing little hired labor have occurred widely in the richer agricultural areas of Western countries during the twentieth century, especially where large-scale, mechanized grain production has taken over. In Britain and in the Western world as a whole, however, proletarianization was by the middle of the nineteenth century moving so fast in manufacturing and services that it overwhelmed the countertrend in agriculture. In the twentieth-century world at large, the agricultural labor force continues to proletarianize.

their share had sunk to less than 10% by the end of the eighteenth century. "They emphatically failed to establish," says Thompson,

> a position of outright ownership in any way commensurate with their late medieval position as occupiers and customary dual-owners, and in this their history is in marked contrast to that of other European countries. One reason was the Tawney reason, the inability in the face of the vagaries of manorial customs or the unscrupulous conduct of lords, to establish tenures as copyholds of inheritance with fixed terms as to rents and entry fines, but it was a factor of limited operation. While some sixteenth-century yeomen prospered, grew rich at the expense of their neighbours, became freeholders through the neglect or indifference of stewards of manors, and elevated themselves into the ranks of the gentry, others were reduced to the status of tenants-at-will or labourers by the financial pressure of the raising of rents and fines; nevertheless, many survived tenurially unaffected. . . . The condition of survival for the peasant was less the tenurial one, whether he happened to live on a manor with certain or uncertain fines, and more the economic one, whether he was capable of making a living under changing market and technical conditions, and whether he was willing to resist the temptation to sell out at attractive prices [1966: 514].

The neat escape into the passive "were reduced" and the convenient depersonalization of "market and technical conditions" shift the apparent responsibility to peasants who made bad bets on the future. Whether we put this benign gloss on the consolidation process or stress, with Marx, the role of forced enclosures (cf. Lazonick 1974, Cohen and Weitzman 1975), the key agents of the transformation remain the larger landlords and their managers. Great estates and capitalist farms, as F. M. L. Thompson says, came to dominate the English landscape.

We must not neglect the merchants who found the means to employ landless rural labor in the working of wood, metal, and, especially, cloth for distant markets. Examining rural conflict in western England from the 1580s to 1660, Buchanan Sharp discovers the "existence of a large rural industrial proletariat living on wages earned in various clothworking occupations and dependent on the market for food [1980: 3]." He points out their active involvement in the food riots and antienclosure risings of the period and remarks on the way in which the government's own resort to deforestation and enclosure as an alternative to parliamentary taxation—as a fiscal expedient—threatened the livelihood of the artisans and incited their resistance. What is more, Sharp makes a specific link between the creation of that proletariat and capital concentration:

> Capitalists had come to dominate the broadcloth industry and the new-drapery—products, aimed at an export market, which demanded considerable investment in raw materials and in the distribution of the finished

product. Similarly, in mining and ironmaking demand for increased output resulted in substantial capital investment in large units of production. In these sectors of the economy, the skilled man was a propertyless wage earner or pieceworker, depending for employment upon the clothier or ironmaster, and for his food, upon the market. The locations of such industries were among the most disorderly places in the kingdom, and the connection between landlessness, rural industrialism, and direct action can hardly have been accidental [Sharp 1980: 7].

How did the concentration of land and capital promote the growth of a proletariat? Mainly by narrowing the alternative employment opportunities for the local population, and secondarily by providing incentives for proletarian families to reproduce at a rapid pace. The chief competing explanation of rural proletarianization is population pressure resulting from autonomous declines in mortality (see Chambers and Mingay 1966 and Flinn 1970). That explanation cannot be expunged in the present state of the evidence, but it certainly does not provide much of an account of the geography or timing of proletarianization; activities of landlords and merchants do.

As the tangled estimates for Britain suggest, for the time being we are in no position to build up estimates of the magnitude and timing of European proletarianization, region by region. However, it *is* possible to get an idea of the quantities involved by extrapolating from the few well-delineated regional analyses we do have. After some exploration, I have used Karlheinz Blaschke's study of the kingdom of Saxony (1967) as a basis for thinking about the Continent as a whole. Saxony—the region of Leipzig, Dresden, and Chemnitz—was a major arena of German industrialization. Like many other industrial regions, Saxony experienced widespread growth of cottage industry well before the industrial concentration of the nineteenth century.

If the whole continent had behaved like Saxony, according to my estimates, Europe's nonproletarian population would have risen from about 39 million people in 1500 to 50 million in 1800 and 85 million in 1900. In that period, the urban proletariat would have risen from 1 million to 10 million to 75 million, the rural from 16 million to 90 million to 125 million. As in the case of Great Britain, the figures have some strong and mildly surprising implications: a massive, disproportionate increase in the proletarian sector of the population; a countryside that was long much more proletarian than the city; a process of proletarianization that took place mainly in rural areas before 1800; a contrast between the moderate numerical growth and substantial increase in the *proportion* proletarian before 1800 and the rapid *numerical* increase combined with moderate rises in proportions after 1800. Nor are these implications arbitrary consequences of basing estimates on the most industrial areas of Europe. A similar computation based on changes in rural Sweden yields estimates of a huge proletarianization of the whole population, due especially to the growth of a rural proletariat. Although the words *proletariat* and *proletarianization* have now taken on a big-industry air, this stress on rural proletarianization jibes nicely with Marx's own emphasis on expropriation in the countryside.

One question that Marx did not address at all effectively was the demographic side of proletarianization. Marx criticized Malthus vigorously for having generalized into universal laws the peculiar conditions of population growth under capitalism. But Marx's own alternative to Malthus was neither clear nor consistent. So far as I can make out, Marx usually assumed that whatever increase in the size of the proletariat occurred resulted directly from the expropriation of workers—especially, in the cases he discussed, agricultural workers—who began life with some control over the means of production. Proletarians who were already proletarians simply reproduced themselves. The natural increase of proletarians, in other words, was zero, and all growth of the proletariat was due to social mobility.

There are, of course, not two but three broad sources of growth or decline in a population: natural increase (the difference between fertility and mortality), social mobility (the difference between changes of status into and out of the population), and net migration (the difference between geographic moves into and out of the population). Thinking about the possible weights of those components of change in the European proletariat since 1500 or so leads to some interesting conclusions. Although migratory movements *within* Europe were complex and crucial, we can sum up the likely effects of intercontinental migration on the European proletariat simply: between 1500 and 1800, most likely a net loss on the order of 10 million proletarians and very few nonproletarians; during the nineteenth century, at net loss of some 50 million people, almost all of them from the European proletariat.

If we take those guesses as facts, we can place some logical limits on the contributions of natural increase and social mobility to the growth of the proletariat. Let's assume that my extrapolation from Saxony to the entire European population is accurate. In that case, any plausible assumptions about the relative natural increase of proletarians and nonproletarians lead to the conclusion that natural increase, not social mobility, played the major part in the growth of the proletariat since 1500 and, especially, after 1800. If, for example, we set nonproletarian natural increase for the nineteenth century equal to proletarian natural increase at about .8% per year, we arrive at the conclusion that proletarian gains through social mobility must have been on the order of .2% per year—and, in fact, it is quite unlikely that nonproletarian natural increase ran that high. A more plausible scenario would resemble this:

	Percentage per year	
	1500 – 1800	1800 – 1900
Nonproletarian natural increase	.25	.60
Proletarian natural increase	.50	.90
Proletarian gains through social mobility	.35	.10

Although the numbers merely sum up informed speculations, they sum up the speculations within limits set by the logic of population growth. Any reasonable reconstruction, I think, attributes the major role in the proletariat's growth to natural increase.

If that theoretical conclusion holds up, it has strong implications for the character of the proletarianization process. Consider this implication: Commonsense discussions of proletarianization portray it as an event that happens to individuals in their own lifetimes—they lose control of land, tools, or materials; they start working for someone else. If that is the predominant experience, we can readily understand themes of resistance and revolt in working-class life, but we should be puzzled by indications of continuity from one generation of workers to the next. To the extent that natural increase is the predominant source of proletarian growth, continuity is easier to understand, and we begin to resolve the apparent discrepancy between the frequency of dispossession and the rarity of overt resistance. That is only one of several important implications of the balance between social mobility and natural increase.

By now the documented historical literature on European migration, social mobility, and natural increase is vast. But it is also fragmented and disorderly. I have tried to draw order out of it elsewhere (e.g., Tilly 1978b, 1978c, 1979). I cannot undertake to review the evidence here. Let me rest with simple assertions. First, my strong emphasis on natural increase is defensible, but far from proven, in the light of the work that has accumulated so far. Second, the most controversial feature of my account of the population changes involved is not really the emphasis on natural increase, but either (a) the suggestion of considerable fertility control of one sort or another in poor, benighted populations; or (b) the small role attributed to externally generated population pressure as a cause of proletarianization. Third, regional and temporal variations were strong and correspond to variations in the local organization of production.

In order to understand the variation, we need to divide Europe into different productive settings: estate systems such as those of East Prussia; large-farm systems such as those of southern England; specialized farming areas of the type of coastal Flanders; peasant farming of a western French style; cottage industry such as that of Lancashire before steam-driven factories; urban craft production such as that of northern Italian cities; and the large-shop or factory production that has so shaped our current image of proletarianization. Each of these settings had its own characteristic pace, extent, and form of proletarianization; the mix among settings of these different types was probably the most important proximate determinant of the timing and character of a given country's proletarianization.

The place of markets, merchants, and landlords in the economic geography of proletarianization is no doubt obvious. Petty merchants held the whole system of cottage industry together, linking cheap village labor to distant markets. Now, petty merchants were not expropriators in the classic image: They spent relatively little effort on seizing other people's means of production; only relatively late in European industrialization did they often convert themselves into commanders of big shops and large, grouped, disciplined work forces. Their contribution to proletarianization was profound and subtle: They opened up the opportunities for wage labor to which rising natural increase was a standard response, and they expropriated indirectly by means of transfers of capital. As Jan de Vries, reflecting on Rudolph Braun's important work, puts it:

> The society being created in the Zurich uplands had its counterparts wherever rural industry spread. It was a society of great insecurity because employment depended on the putting-out merchant's circulating capital, which could be withdrawn quickly whenever the conditions of distant markets, currency uncertainties, or raw material supply problems encouraged the merchant to place his capital elsewhere. Almost inevitably such a society suffered from desperate poverty [1976: 110–111].

Merchants and landlords played different roles but likewise had strong effects on the paths of proletarianization, in each of the other productive settings.

Proletarianization and Statemaking

What does all this have to do with states and taxation? I see two important connections. First, a state's general fiscal strategy affected the relative viability of different forms of production. One standard comparison deals with the way in which taxation impinged on large landlords. In Brandenburg-Prussia after the Thirty Years' War, we find great landlords largely exempted from taxation and allowed enormous administrative, political, and military power within their own districts, whereas excise taxes aimed at merchants and commerce supported much of the growing state apparatus. In England, we find relatively light land taxes and few categorical exemptions, whereas customs revenues loomed large. In France, we find considerable reliance on land taxes, with the crown bartering widespread exemptions to old nobles in return for political acquiescence and military support and to new nobles in return for the mobilization of capital and the staffing of public offices.

The Prussian strategy promoted large, grain-exporting estates producing with coerced labor service. The English strategy promoted a general commercialization of agriculture, with landlords actively involved in stepping up production. The French strategy promoted the transformation of landlords and capitalists into rentiers. To be sure, such a summary simplifies excessively. Admittedly, the relationship ran both ways: The configuration of social classes in Prussia, England, and France shaped the fiscal strategy each state followed. Yet, with Gabriel Ardant, I believe that state fiscal strategies, once adopted, have durable effects on the economic options within states, as well as on the structures of those states as such.

The second connection with states and fiscal strategy is the likely impact of taxation on the commercialization of the factors of production. When rising taxes impinged especially on households that were little involved in production for the market, they tended to force those households to sell their labor power, commodities, and —*in extremis* —capital. Under some circumstances, that pressure might stimulate increases in productivity and might form barriers to proletarianization. On the whole, however, the pressure to commercialize probably promoted the growth of the proletariat via the differentiation that ordinarily occurred in prospering agricultural communities, via the effects of wage-earning opportunities on natural increase, and via the advantages achieved by local capitalists in a more extensively commercialized economy.

Taxes and Statemaking

Although these effects were indirect, they could be extensive. Think about the French experience with taxation. For purposes of illustration, in Figure 8.1 I express the total national tax burden from 1600 to 1966 in

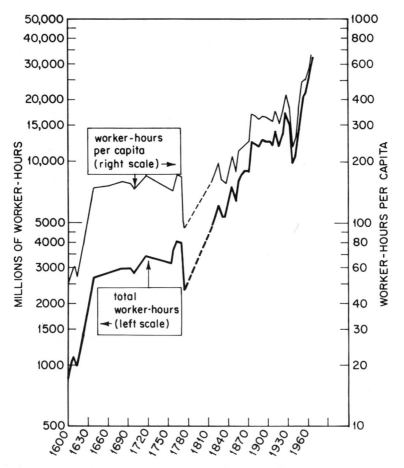

FIGURE 8.1. Total French taxes, 1597−1966, stated as worker hours of wages and worker hours per capita.

terms of hours of work per capita per year, using Jean Fourastié's long wage series for a semiskilled provincial worker as our reference point (Clamagéran 1867−1876; *Annuaire Statistique* 1966; Fourastié 1969: 44−49). These are conservative measures. Because real wages rose greatly in the long run, these measures greatly understate the increase in the state's purchasing power. On the other hand, by using personal work time as a standard, they give a sense of the state's rising impact on the daily life of the average citizen.

The statistic in question is gross receipts from regular taxes. As of 1600, they were equivalent to about 50 hours of work per person per year. By 1700, they had more than tripled, to 180 hours per capita. In 1800, the figure was back around 180, after great perturbations during the early French Revolution. By 1900, the number was 320 hours. And in 1966, after a spectacular rise from the early Depression, the figure had reached above 650 hours of work per person per year. From 50 in 1600 to 650 in 1966 represented a 13-fold increase in the amount of time a hypothetical average person spent working to generate revenue for the state.

The great increases arrived during the seventeenth century, especially before 1650, and during the twentieth century. Before the twentieth century, war and preparations for war had the major impact on rises in the tax burden. After 1900, war remained the most volatile major determinant of tax levels, but expenditures for administration and social services took over the majority position.

The dramatic seventeenth-century rise in taxation marks the age of Louis XIII and Louis XIV, of Richelieu, Mazarin, and Colbert. In order to subdue their domestic rivals and, later, their international competitors, these great statemakers attempted to recruit, equip, supply, and pay armies of an unprecedented scale and to do so without relying on the good will of princes and lords who controlled their own private armies. The essential resources for that effort were embedded in the countryside—in the daily routines, mutual obligations, and collective and private property of ordinary people. The statemakers' problem was to extract those resources without inciting uncontrollable rebellion and without destroying the people's capacity to pay again in the future. They often failed in the first regard and sometimes failed in the second.

France has known more than one age of rebellion, but the seventeenth century certainly belongs among them. How resounding the roll call of great revolts: the Croquants, the Nu-Pieds, the Tardanizats, the Sabotiers, the Lustucru, the revolt of Audijos, that of Roure, the Bonnets Rouges, the Camisards, and, of course, the mid-century Fronde. Most of these great events actually consisted of multiple local rebellions which federated or interacted, and which resembled the much more numerous isolated rebellions stretching from one end of the century to the other. Almost without exception the great revolts and the small began with resistance to some new or expanded form of taxation. They began, most often, with a violation of local rights, the deliberate overriding of a previous agreement, an official's visible profiteering by means of his fiscal powers, or an attack on a local institution which had served as a bulwark against royal demands. As the crown pressed every means possible to augment its revenues, the seventeenth century became the golden age of antitax rebellions.

Yet the armies grew, taxes rose, and the statemakers succeeded. In recent decades, historians have occupied themselves much with debunking Absolutism: contrasting the bold theory with the feeble practice, displaying the absolutist state's limits, compromises, and continuities with its predecessors. As J. S. Morrill has commented, that demonstration has been so successful that we now need a reminder, from time to time, of the power the French crown did acquire during the seventeenth century:

> In the course of the seventeenth century the monarchy extinguished all other patrimonies and ancient principalities within the bounds of the kingdom. Louis XIII and XIV ruled as kings of France, not as king here, duke there. Their writs, the same writs, ran everywhere. The Crown enunciated the doctrine "no land without seigneur," extinguished the *allodia* and declared the whole of France to be royal domain. The seventeenth century witnessed the creation of a common coinage throughout France and the sponsorship of linguistic unity and purity. The Crown's legislative autonomy was acknowledged. . . . The king asserted (though this was periodically challenged) complete freedom to choose his own ministers, advisers, judges, a freedom restricted in practice but not in theory by the spread of venality and the introduction of the *paulette*. The king's claim to be the source of all justice was greatly strengthened. His ability to tax at will, or at least within the limits of practical prudence, his ability to sustain a large standing army (and, as the century wore on, to monopolize coercive power) and his growing control of the Church in France, most obviously through the restoration of religious unity and the revocation of the edict of Nantes, more subtly through his rights within the Church, and sponsorship of the catholic reformation, are all extensions of inherent strengths of the monarchy [Morrill 1978: 962 – 963].

How could all that happen? The full answer to that question comprises France's seventeenth-century political history. But there were some recurrent elements. The great statemakers used military force. They made alliances which divided their enemies. They routinized the collection of revenues and created specialists in the extraction of those revenues. They gave more and more groups—purchasers of public offices, corporate bodies that received charters and privileges, great lords who were drawn into the circle of the court—a political and financial stake in the crown's survival. The definitive establishment of the intendants as provincial representatives of the crown cemented the new governmental structure.

More than anything else, the intendants served to accelerate the flow of resources to the central government. They did so by taxing, by borrowing, by selling offices, by commandeering, by a hundred other expedients. Recurrently, however, the critical routine looked like this: Locate some store of capital, persuade or coerce the holder of that capital to put it at the disposition of the crown, locate or create some future source of revenue that can be exploited by royal authority, give the persons who have advanced capital claims on the future revenue, and back the claims with the state's growing coercive power. Tax farming took exactly that form. So did forced loans, the sale of offices, and most other means by which the seventeenth-century crown raised the means to wage war. The system lumbered along to the Revolution and helped create the fiscal crisis behind the Revolution.

In addition to profound political implications, this system had significant economic consequences. First, it created a complex, ambivalent relationship between capitalists and statemakers. The statemakers both tracked and courted the mobilizers of capital, seeking on the one hand to capture them and on the other to assure their continuing activity. (The rules forbidding nobles to engage in many sorts of commerce, I believe, had less to do with maintaining the honor of a superior caste than with the statemakers' desire to make sure that rich men who bought ennobling and tax-exempting positions passed on their money-making activities to others who would continue to generate capital and pay taxes.) Willy-nilly, the state developed an interest in promoting and protecting the accumulation of capital.

Second, the drive to raise the means of warmaking promoted the commercialization of labor and of commodity production. Rising taxes forced ordinary people to sell commodities and labor power they had not previously supplied through the market. As a state, fattened with increasing revenue and strengthened with growing armed force, shifted from the direct commandeering of resources to their purchase via the market, merchants and producers gained new incentives to commercialize. Moreover, the statemakers knew it: When they surveyed the "prosperity" of various provinces in the seventeenth and eighteenthcenturies, intendants and other observers consistently emphasized production—actual or potential—for cash. Promoting the national market became something of a state religion, and resisting it, a civil sin. The expanding efforts of royal officials to ensure the supply of food to the national market marked the most visible aspect of an unrelenting campaign for commercialization. Shriller and shriller rose the condemnation of attempts to withhold food from the market, or to give priority to local subsistence needs.

Checking the Connections

We arrive at the junction between the two broad processes this chapter has traced: the rise of national taxation and the growth of the proletariat. Both the protection afforded capitalists and the commercialization of the economy facilitated proletarianization. They facilitated proletarianization by means of their effects on the concentration of capital, by means of

the political power they lent to expropriators, and by means of the
pressure to market labor power. To be sure, the linkage was anything but
simple, uniform, and automatic: The startling contrast between a Spain
(in which the vast landless labor force of the south seems to have formed
as a result of the grant of great estates to the military leaders of the
Reconquista) and a Holland (in which peasants seem to have collaborated
in their own destruction with little pressure from great landlords) in-
structs us to search for alternative paths to the proletariat. To be sure, I
have not come close to surveying the evidence for my hypothetical links
between taxes and proletarianization. That comes next.

If the general argument is correct, what should the historical record
show us? In general, it should turn out that when European powerholders rapidly expanded their capacity to make war, or simply made war
on a large scale, two consequences followed: First, they relied heavily on
capitalists as sources and instruments for the mobilization of the necessary funds and acquired commitments to the capitalists in the process;
second, the various forms of taxes they levied incresed significantly. The
prior capitalization of the economy should make a difference in both
regards. On the one hand, where capitalism was far advanced, we should
find capitalists setting the conditions under which the managers of states
could raise the resources of war. Within those important limits, on the
other hand, we should find that the advance of capitalism made it easier
to acquire those resources by means of straightforward increases in existing monetary taxes, rather than via extraordinary levies, forced tribute,
and payments in kind. For a given military effort—the *ceteris paribus* is
indispensable—we should find statemakers in little-capitalized economies employing more coercion, applying more of that coercion to domestic capitalists, and building a larger fiscal apparatus through a wider
variety of expedients. From the sixteenth to eighteenth centuries, on this
rough scale, Great Britain, the Netherlands, and Denmark stood near the
capitalist extreme, whereas Brandenburg-Prussia and most of eastern
Europe balanced them on the opposite side, with Spain and France in
between. Or so goes the argument.

What difference, then, should the fiscal pressure make? The less
capitalized the economy, according to my analysis, the more a given
demand for resources should have required alterations in the structure
of production, promoted commercialization of land and labor, and excited popular resistance. Obviously, the forms of production and the
structures of power made a difference in these regards: Prussian serfs
living on scattered estates under the military and economic control of
landlords who were simultaneously state officials, for example, had little
opportunity to rebel. We might speculate, indeed, that the more political

power landlords exercised, the more a given amount of fiscal pressure tended to transform cultivators into dependent landless laborers. We begin to discern at least three distinct routes into the proletariat: a first (we might call it "English") in which capitalist landlords drove peasants into landless wage labor; a second ("Dutch" is a possible name) in which a minority of peasants used the market to convert themselves into capitalists and most of their neighbors into wageworkers; a third (perhaps "Prussian" will do for it) in which landlords monopolized market production, produced by means of labor service forced from a dependent peasantry, and thereby delayed the day when those dependent producers would become full-fledged, formally free, wage laborers.

So far, this tissue of hypotheses includes no demographic change. Where capital concentration and commercialization had gone further, my argument implies, we should find that:

1. A higher proportion of all producers were proletarians.
2. Fertility, mortality, and nuptiality responded more directly and vigorously to fluctuations in the opportunities for wage labor, including wage levels.
3. In periods of economic expansion, natural increase was the dominant component of the proletariat's growth on the large scale, although migration played a crucial role in the short run and on the small scale; movement out of the world of peasants and artisans was never the dominant source of growth.

All these remain—need I insist?—*ceteris paribus* hypotheses. Genuine cash-crop farmers, prospering from the sale of their wine, wheat, or wool, did appear in some regions of Europe; those were, almost by definition, regions of intensive commercialization. Nevertheless, they seem to have been far off the main trend of European development.

The round of demographic hypotheses recalls the fundamental importance of an activity that my summary has neglected: small-scale manufacturing. After its dispersion into cheap-labor regions of the European countryside in the early phases of capitalism, manufacturing only regrouped in cities during the nineteenth and twentieth centuries. During the earlier centuries of capitalist development, cottage industry and similar forms of production transformed many rural areas. That flourishing of dispersed, small-scale manufacturing both complicates and clarifies matters: complicates them by introducing another alternate response to pressure and opportunity; clarifies them by helping explain how the rural poor survived and even multiplied, for daily, seasonal, or lifetime alternation between agriculture and industry gave land-poor cultivators a means of bare subsistence, their landless children a chance to form their own impoverished families, and petty capitalists a source of cheap labor whose full costs of reproduction they did not have to pay. So far as I can tell, regions of intensive rural industry (such as the kingdom of Saxony, which served as a base for the estimates of European proletarianization hazarded earlier) provided Europe's prime sites for rapid natural increase in general, and for proletarian increase in particular. Thus—to extend my argument to new ground—access to markets for the products of rural industry tended to heighten the effects of statemaking, taxation, and capital accumulation on the proletariat's growth.

Some habitués of social science history are now in for a shock. Despite some inexplicable wanderings; much of this book has followed the forms of a ritual that is readily recognizable within the trade: surveys and critiques of previous work, methodological disquisitions, introduction and elaboration of a limited number of critical variables by means of theoretically informed historical discussions. At this point in a densely historical book—one called, what's more, *As Sociology Meets History!* — the social science historians can reasonably expect a display of quantitative pyrotechnics. After all, the complex of arguments I have just built up amounts to a partial model of European social change, a model incorporating most of the major variables surveyed earlier in the book. Next step: Specify and estimate the model. Or so one might think.

Instead of a burst of fireworks, those observers will see a fizzle. In other contexts, I am meeting some of their expectations: trying hard to arrange confrontations between the more determinate hypotheses in the set and systematic evidence, conscientiously assembled. Here I am aiming at a different end. Two different ends, in fact. The first is to translate a general sense of connections among ostensibly independent political, economic, and demographic processes within the European experience of capitalism and statemaking into a set of concrete guides for detailed historical research. The second is to show—less by exhortation, this time, than by demonstration—that historically grounded sociological analysis has more bite and richness than any abstract, timeless model of social change. In that sense, I end up agreeing eagerly with the main message of Arthur Stinchcombe's *Theoretical Models in Social History*.

As the outcome of this discussion, then, I will be satisfied if we reach agreement on simple principles. First principle: The form and intensity of taxation had some independent importance in the political and economic histories of European states. Second principle: The growth of the proletariat in one part of Europe or another depended especially on the strategies of local capitalists but responded indirectly to state policies, including fiscal policies. Third principle: The delicate but enduring interdependence of statemakers and capitalists eventually worked, with many variations, to produce a world of capitalist institutions and proletarian workers. Fourth and final principle: The most effective way to elaborate, modify, and test these principles is through a sustained, detailed, systematic, and comparative confrontation with the abundant historical record.

Conclusion

9

Looking Forward . . .
Into a Rearview Mirror

Carr's Case

In his widely known Trevelyan Lectures, published as *What Is History?*, Russian historian Edward Hallett Carr unburdened himself on many topics, including the relations of sociology and history. "Sociology," he declared,

> if it is to become a fruitful field of study, must, like history, concern itself with the relation between the unique and the general. But it must also become dynamic—a study not of society at rest (for no such society exists), but of social change and development. For the rest, I would only say that the more sociological history becomes, and the more historical sociology becomes, the better for both [1963: 84].

Anyone who works in the borderland between sociology and history will take heart at encouragement from an outstanding historian. Yet I can only summon up two cheers, out of a possible three, for Carr's case. Integrating the unique and the general—right, especially if we understand by that the development of historically grounded theories. Analysis of change—certainly. As for the blending of history and sociology, it depends on which sociology, and which history. It would be fruitless to convert historians en masse to the Durkheimian analysis of social change and its consequences. It would be foolish to persuade sociologists that they should be applying their energies to the explanation of Napoleon, or Lenin . . . or Richard Nixon. When transferring between the disciplines, let us take account of the differences in their intellectual structures

211

and concentrate on problems, theories, and methods that fall clearly into their common ground.

Consider the enterprise called social history: the study of connections between large structural changes and alterations in the character of routine social life. Social history, in this sense, is the prime region of convergence between sociology and history. In the perspective of knowledge as a whole, social history has two fundamental callings. They are complementary. The first is retrospective: It takes certain features of our contemporary world as problematic and then moves back to trace the origins and transformations of those features. To my mind, the two features of our contemporary world which most distinguish it from other times and places are (a) the prevalence of work for wages under conditions of expropriation; and (b) the great power of national states. If those represent the most problematic features of our era, the retrospective program for social history should emphasize the study of proletarianization and of statemaking, as well as their interaction. Other observers consider industrial organization, dependence on inanimate sources of energy, personal alienation, or the scale and threat of war to be the problematic markers of our time. Each of those leads to a somewhat different retrospective program of inquiry for social history.

Social history's *prospective* calling, in contrast, consists of asking what could have happened to routine social life at major historical choice points, then considering how and why the outcomes that actually occurred won out over other possibilities. Any such analysis is bound to generate controversy, since it involves hypotheses about events and processes that did not, in fact, occur. Barrington Moore's thoughtful *Injustice*, for example, discusses "suppressed historical alternatives"—notably, the possibility that the leaders of the German Social Democrats, just after the First World War, could have fashioned a durable democratic solution for their country. Here is the crucial passage:

> In order to move toward a more stable liberal democracy, I have suggested, the government would have had to set to work at once to take control of the armed forces, the administrative bureaucracy, and the judiciary, remolding them as instruments loyal to the Republic. It would have had to adopt an economic policy that included a degree of government control over certain areas of heavy industry, with some concessions to the workers over conditions on the shop floor. In doing all that, the government would have had to be willing to forestall the National Assembly by taking a series of essentially irreversible decisions necessary as the foundation for a liberal and democratic version of capitalism [B. Moore 1978: 391–392].

Faced with such a speculation, many historians will protest the impossibility of one or another of the steps Moore enumerates, and other historians will reject the whole effort to replay the past. Any compelling account of the Social Democrats' actual course—temporization and compromise—implicitly assigns probabilities, nevertheless, to alternatives that did not occur.

Generalized, Moore's discussion of suppressed historical alternatives provides a model for the prospective task of social history. We identify choice points, lay out the alternative paths from those points, and consider the likely consequences of those paths for subsequent social life. The effort will produce more valuable results, it seems to me, to the extent that we employ an explicit theory to identify genuine choice points, concentrate on paths for whose possibility we have evidence, and constrain our enumeration of likely consequences by means of painstaking historical analogies. In the much-mooted case of Great Britain and Reform, for example, we have at least two explicit theories that easily identify 1831–1832 as a critical choice point: (a) the theory, built into much of modern British political historiography, that significant changes in the franchise ramify into extensive alterations of routine politics; and (b) that sort of theory of revolution—Leon Trotsky's, for instance—in which wide polarization of the polity constitutes a revolutionary situation. In the same case, we would surely want to consider at least three alternative outcomes:

1. The petty-bourgeois enfranchisement that actually occurred
2. The extension of national political rights to a significant part of the working class—at least to the organized artisans and skilled workers who formed part of the Reform coalition
3. The defeat of the whole campaign

The difficult part of the analysis proceeds from there. The enumeration of likely consequences requires the deployment of informed historical analogies, both with other segments of British experience and with the experience of other people outside of Britain. It requires something like the succession of deep analogies that Arthur Stinchcombe has urged as the essence of social—historical explanation.

Both the retrospective and the prospective callings of social history offer an important place to sociology, for sociologists spend a good deal of their time, now and then effectively, identifying features of the contemporary world as problematic; that will serve the retrospective enterprise. And sociologists collect analogies, some of them deep and some of them valid; that will serve the prospective enterprise. To the extent that we create a division of labor, it should not separate sociological "theories" from historical "facts." I prefer that there be no disciplinary division of labor: simply sociologists and historians, sensitized to different problems and opportunities by training and experience, doing social history. But if there must be a division, let it separate, not theory from fact, but types of theory from one another; let sociologists attempt to apply and improve the sorts of theory that prevail among their fellow sociologists, and let historians do the same for their fellow historians.

I deny, then, that history is, or ought to be, failed sociology—sociology with the theory left out. That historians can improve their theorizing, I have been at pains to say throughout this book. But they dare not leave the improvements to sociologists. That is because sociology is, to some degree, failed history. Not that sociologists have been pursuing the same agenda as historians, but they have done less well at it; sociologists have not, by and large, been attempting to decide whether the American Civil War was inevitable, whether the expansion of capitalism caused the European upheavals of the seventeenth century, and so on. The sociological failure resides in the building of models of industrialization, of bureaucratization, and of other large social processes in which time and place have no significant effects. Those models lack historical grounding.

No, that way of putting it is not quite correct. In fact, a hidden history roots most sociology in the present. Models of industrialization, bureaucratization, and so on, gain a measure of plausibility because they apply, more or less, to one piece of history: the piece their formulators are currently living. If differentiation models predominate in sociologists' gropings with the phenomenon of proletarianization, that is largely because the continuous subdivision of tasks plays so great a part in the occupational changes the sociologists of industrial countries can observe in their own strips of history. The mistake is to extrapolate backwards, without attempting to place the small contemporary strip of history into the broad band of social transformation to which it belongs. We need fewer general models of industrialization, however elegant and however well validated on the present. We need more general analyses of the historically specific processes by which capitalism came to be the world's dominant mode of production, and by which national states came to be the world's most powerful organizations.

Sociology Meets History

I do not claim for a moment that this book provides an adequate answer to that great challenge. Assembled from disparate materials, the book leaves many gaps and many uncertain connections. "Sociology, Meet History" raises far more issues than it resolves: It sketches American historical practice and characterizes the areas in which social scientists and historians are now self-consciously working together, but it offers no synthesis. "Computing History" contents itself with a checklist of the computer's advantages and limits in historical analysis. "Homans, Humans, and History" analyzes the *modus operandi* of a single important contributor to sociological history. "Useless Durkheim," in contrast, focuses on the drawbacks for historical analysis of one influential theoretical tradition within sociology. "War and Peasant Rebellion in Seventeenth-Century France" illustrates—but only in a preliminary, unsatisfactory way—the pursuit of a standard sociological problem within a specific historical setting. "How (And, to Some Extent, Why) to Study British Contention" does the same thing for a different problem and a different setting, and with a much larger emphasis on opportunities for research. "Proletarianization: Theory and Research" inverts the procedure of "Useless Durkheim," asking how it can be that existing sociological approaches deal so badly with such a pervasive and powerful process as proletarianization. Finally, "States, Taxes, and Proletarians" races past the processes taken up in several previous chapters, looking for connections among them. Measured against the challenge of building adequate, historically grounded sociological theory, the book is fragmentary, incomplete, much stronger on program and method than on results.

Where do we go from here? Two main classes of theoretical problems appear urgent to me. The first is the construction of historically grounded accounts of collective action—in particular the conditions under which ordinary people who share an interest act, or fail to act, together on that interest. The accounts require historical grounding, most obviously, because the known means of action that are available to people (a) vary significantly as a cumulative product of historical experience; and (b) strongly constrain the likelihood and the character of collective action. ("How . . . to Study British Contention" makes that point most explicitly, but several of the other chapters take it up as well.) The second urgent class of theoretical problems involves the historical reformulation of our ideas concerning very large structural changes, notably statemaking, the development of capitalism, proletarianization, and population growth. (Most of the book's later chapters point in that direction.) Properly articulated, the two classes of theoretical problems define the hopeless, absorbing project from which this book as a whole has grown: to understand how, in the Western experience of the last few hundred years, the growth of national states and the development of capitalism interacted to alter the ways in which ordinary people banded together to act on their interests.

Bibliography

Adams, Brooks
  1943   *The Law of Civilization and Decay*. New York: Knopf.
  [1896]
Adams, Henry
  1931   *The Education of Henry Adams*. New York: Modern Library.
  [1918]
  1933   *Mont-Saint Michel and Chartres*. Boston: Houghton Mifflin.
  [1905]
Agren, Kurt, *et al.*
  1973   *Aristocrats, Farmers, Proletarians: Essays in Swedish Demographic History*. Uppsala: Almqvist & Wiksell.
Agulhon, Maurice
  1966   *Pénitents et francs-maçons de l'ancienne Provence*. Paris: Fayard.
Allegre, Luciano, and Angelo Torre
  1977   *La Nascità della storia sociale in Francia: Dalla Comune alle "Annales."* Turin: Fondazione Luigi Einaudi.
Almond, Gabriel A.
  1973   "Approaches to developmental causation." In Gabriel A. Almond, Scott C. Flanagan, and Robert J. Mundt (eds.), *Crisis, Choice, and Change: Historical Studies of Political Development*. Boston: Little, Brown.
Annuaire Statistique
  1966   *Annuaire statistique de la France, 1966: Résumé rétrospectif*. Paris: Institut National de la Statistique et des Etudes Economiques.
Ardant, Gabriel
  1971   *Histoire de l'impôt*. 2 vols. Paris: Fayard.
Authén Blom, Grethe (ed.)
  1977   *Industrialiseringens første fase*. Urbaniseringsprosessen i Norden, 3. Oslo: Universitetsforlaget.
Aydelotte, William O.
  1971   *Quantification in History*. Reading, Mass.: Addison-Wesley.
  1977   (ed.) *The History of Parliamentary Behavior*. Princeton, N.J.: Princeton University Press.

Aydelotte, William O., Allan G. Bogue, and Robert William Fogel (eds.)
    1972   *The Dimensions of Quantitative Research in History.* Princeton, N.J.: Princeton
            University Press.
Bairoch, Paul
    1971   "La population active mondiale (1700 – 1970)." *Annales; Economies, Sociétés,*
            Civilisations 26: 960 – 976.
    1977   *Taille des villes, conditions de vie et développement economique.* Paris: Ecole
            des Hautes Etudes en Sciences Sociales.
Bairoch, Paul, and J.-M. Limbor
    1968   "Changes in the industrial distribution of the world labour force by region,
            1880 – 1960." *International Labor Review* 98: 311 – 336.
Barclay, George W.
    1958   *Techniques of Population Analysis.* New York: Wiley.
Barzun, Jacques
    1974   *Clio and the Doctors: Psycho-History, Quanto-History, and History.* Chicago:
            University of Chicago Press.
Baulant, Micheline
    1968   "Le prix des grains à Paris de 1431 à 1788." *Annales; Economies, Sociétés,*
            Civilisations 23: 520 – 540.
Beik, William H.
    1974   "Two intendants face a popular revolt: Social unrest and the structure of ab-
            solutism in 1645." *Canadian Journal of History* 243 – 262.
Bellerby, J. R.
    1958   "The distribution of manpower in agriculture and industry 1851 – 1951." *The*
            Farm Economist 9: 1 – 11.
Bendix, Reinhard
    1957   *Work and Authority in Industry: Ideologies of Management in the Course of*
            Industrialization. New York: Wiley.
    1964   *Nation-Building and Citizenship: Studies of Our Changing Social Order.* New
            York: Wiley.
Bercé, Yves-Marie
    1976   *Fête et révolte: Des mentalités populaires du XVIe au XVIIIe siècle.* Paris:
            Hachette.
Bergesen, Albert (ed.)
    1980   *Studies of the Modern World-System.* New York: Academic Press.
Best, Heinrich
    1980   *Interessenpolitik und nationale Integration 1848/49: Handelspolitische Konflikte*
            im frühindustriellen Deutschland. Göttingen: Vandenhoeck & Ruprecht.
Best, Heinrich, and Reinhard Mann (eds.)
    1977   *Quantitative Methoden in der historischsozialwissenshaftlichen Forschung.*
            Stuttgart: Klett-Cotta.
Blaschke, Karlheinz
    1967   *Bevölkerungsgeschichte von Sachsen bis zur industriellen Revolution.* Weimar:
            Böhlaus.
Bloch, Marc
    1952   *Les Caractères originaux de l'histoire rurale française.* Paris: Armand Colin.
    [1931]
Blum, Jerome
    1978   *The End of the Old Order in Rural Europe.* Princeton, N.J.: Princeton University
            Press.

Bogue, Allan G. (ed.)
   1973   *Emerging Theoretical Models in Social and Political History.* Sage
         Contemporary Social Science Issues, vol. 9. Beverly Hills, Calif.: Sage
         Publications.
Boislisle, A. M. de (ed.)
   1874— *Correspondance des contrôleurs généraux des finances avec les intendants des*
   1896   *provinces.* 3 vols. Paris: Imprimerie Nationale.
Bonney, Richard
   1978   *Political Change in France under Richelieu and Mazarin, 1624–1661.* Oxford:
         Oxford University Press.
Bourget, J.
   1954   "Prolétarisation d'une commune de l'agglomération parisienne: Colombes." *La
         Vie Urbaine: Urbanisme et Habitation,* n.s., nos. 3 and 4: 185–194.
Braudel, Fernand
   1958   "Histoire et sciences sociales: La longue durée." *Annales; Economies, Sociétés,
         Civilisations* 13: 725–753.
   1979   *Civilisation matérielle, économie, et capitalisme, XVe–XVIIIe siècle.* 3 vols.
         Paris: Colin.
Braun, Rudolf
   1960   *Industrialisierung und Volksleben.* Zurich: Rentsch.
   1965   *Sozialer und kultureller Wandel in einem ländlichen Industriegebiet.* Zurich:
         Rentsch.
   1978   "Early industrialization and demographic change in the canton of Zurich." In
         Charles Tilly (ed.), *Historical Studies of Changing Fertility.* Princeton, N.J.:
         Princeton University Press.
Brown, Brian R.
   1979   Lancashire Chartism and the mass strike of 1842: The political economy of
         working class contention. Center for Research on Social Organization, Univer-
         sity of Michigan, Working Paper 203.
Bukharin, Nicholas
   1928   *L'économie mondiale et l'impérialisme.* Paris: Editions Sociales Internation-
         ales.
Burguière, Andre
   1975   *Bretons de Plozévet.* Paris: Flammarion.
Carr, Edward Hallett
   1963   *What Is History?* New York: Knopf.
Castan, Yves
   1974   *Honnêteté et relations sociales en Languedoc (1715–1780).* Paris: Plon.
Chadwick, John
   1958   *The Decipherment of Linear B.* Cambridge: Cambridge University Press.
Chambers, J. D. and G. E. Mingay
   1966   *The Agricultural Revolution, 1750–1880.* London: Batsford.
Checkland, S. G., and E. O. A. Checkland (eds.)
   1974   *The Poor Law Report of 1834.* Harmondsworth: Penguin.
Chirot, Daniel
   1976   *Social Change in a Peripheral Society: The Creation of a Balkan Colony.* New
         York: Academic Press.
Clamagéran, J. J.
   1867— *Histoire de l'impôt en France.* 3 vols. Paris: Guillaumin.
   1876

Clubb, Jerome M., Erik W. Austin, and Michael W. Traugott
  1972   Computers in History and Political Science. Center for Political Studies, Insti-
          tute for Social Research, University of Michigan, Working Paper [originally pro-
          duced as a manual of International Business Machines, Inc.].
Coats, A. W.
  1967   "The classical economists and the labourer." In E. L. Jones and G. E. Mingay
          (eds.), Land, Labour, and Population in the Industrial Revolution: Essays Pre-
          sented to J. D. Chambers. London: Arnold.
Cobb, Richard
  1961 — Les armées révolutionnaires, instrument de la Terreur dans les départements. 2
  1963   vols. Paris: Mouton.
  1971   "Historians in white coats." Times Literary Supplement December 3:
          1527 — 1528.
Cohen, Jon S.
  1978   "The achievements of economic history: The Marxist school." Journal of Eco-
          nomic History 38: 29 — 57.
Cohen, Jon S., and Martin L. Weitzman
  1975   "Enclosure and depopulation: A Marxian analysis." In William N. Parker and
          Eric L. Jones (eds.), European Peasants and their Markets. Princeton, N.J.:
          Princeton University Press.
Coleman, James S.
  1973   The Mathematics of Collective Action. Chicago: Aldine.
Colloque de l'Ecole Normale Supérieure de Saint-Cloud
  1967   L'Histoire sociale: Sources et méthodes. Paris: Presses Universitaires de
          France.
Colquhoun, Patrick
  1806   A Treatise on Indigence. London: J. Hatchard.
  1815   Treatise on the Wealth, Power and Resources of the British Empire. London:
          Joseph Mawman.
Conrad, Alfred H., and John R. Meyer
  1958   "The economics of slavery in the ante bellum South." Journal of Political Econ-
          omy 56: 95 — 130.
Cooper, J. P.
  1967   "The social distribution of land and men in England, 1436 — 1700." Economic
          History Review, 2d ser. 20: 149 — 440.
Courturier, Marcel
  1969   Recherches sur les structures sociales de Châteaudun, 1525 — 1789. Paris:
          SEVPEN
Curtis, L P., Jr. (ed.)
  1970   The Historian's Workshop: Original Essays by Sixteen Historians. New York:
          Knopf.
Davis, Kingsley
  1959   "The myth of functional analysis as a special method in sociology and an-
          thropology." American Sociological Review 24: 757 — 773.
Davis, Natalie Zemon
  1975   Society and Culture in Early Modern France. Stanford, Calif.: Stanford Univer-
          sity Press.
Dawley, Alan
  1976   Class and Community: The Industrial Revolution in Lynn. Cambridge, Mass.:
          Harvard University Press.

Débidour, Antonin
　　1877　　La Fronde angevine: Tableau de la vie municipale au XVIIIe siècle. Paris: Thorin.
Delzell, Charles F. (ed.)
　　1977　　The Future of History. Essays in the Vanderbilt University Centennial Symposium. Nashville: Vanderbilt University Press.
Dupâquier, Jacques
　　1977　　"Histoire et démographie." Population, numéro special: 299 – 318.
Durkheim, Emile
　　1933　　The Division of Labor in Society. New York: Macmillan.
　　[1893]
　　1951　　Suicide: A Study in Sociology. Glencoe, Ill.: Free Press.
　　[1897]
　　1965　　The Elementary Forms of the Religious Life. New York: Free Press
　　[1912]
Eisenstadt, S. N.
　　1963　　The Political Systems of Empires: The Rise and Fall of the Historical Bureaucratic Societies. New York: Free Press of Glencoe.
Eley, Geoff, and Keith Nield
　　1980　　"Why does social history ignore politics?" Social History 5: 249 – 272.
Engerman, Stanley L.
　　1975　　"Comments on the study of race and slavery." In Stanley L. Engerman and Eugene D. Genovese (eds.), Race and Slavery in the Western Hemisphere: Quantitative Studies. Princeton, N.J.: Princeton University Press.
Erikson, Ingrid, and John Rogers
　　1978　　Rural Labor and Population Change: Social and Demographic Developments in East-Central during the Nineteenth Century. Stockholm: Almqvist & Wiksell.
Everitt, Alan
　　1967　　"Farm labourers." In H. P. R. Finberg (ed.), The Agrarian History of England and Wales: IV, 1500 – 1640. Cambridge: Cambridge University Press.
Eversley, David
　　1971　　"Populations and predictions." Times Literary Supplement September 24: 1151 – 1152.
Flick, Carlos
　　1978　　The Birmingham Political Union and the Movements for Reform in Britain, 1830 – 1839. Hamden, Conn.: Archon.
Flinn, M. W.
　　1970　　British Population Growth, 1700 – 1850. London: Macmillan.
Fogel, Robert William
　　1975　　"The limits of quantitative methods in history." American Historical Review 80: 329 – 350.
Fogel, Robert W., and Stanley L. Engerman
　　1974　　Time on the Cross. 2 vols. Boston: Little, Brown.
Forster, Robert
　　1978　　"Achievements of the annales school." Journal of Economic History 38: 58 – 76.
Foucault, Michel
　　1975　　Surveiller et punir: Naissance de la prison. Paris: Gallimard.
Fourastié, Jean
　　1969　　L'évolution des prix à long terme. Paris: Presses Universitaires de France.
Fox-Genovese, Elizabeth, and Eugene Genovese
　　1976　　"The political crisis of social history." Journal of Social History 10: 205 – 221.

Friedmann, Harriet
    1978   "World market, state, and family farm: Social bases of household production in
             the era of wage labor." *Comparative Studies in Society and History* 20: 545 – 586.
Gallie, Duncan
    1978   *In Search of the New Working Class: Automation and Social Integration within
             the Capitalist Enterprise.* Cambridge: Cambridge University Press.
Garlan, Yvon, and Claude Nières
    1975   *Les révoltes bretonnes de 1675: Papier timbré et Bonnets Rouges.* Paris: Edi-
             tions Sociales.
Gaunt, David
    1973   "Historisk demografi eller demografisk historia? En Oversikt och ett debattin-
             lagg om ett tvarventenskapligt dilemma." *Historisk Tidskrift* 1973: 382– 405.
    1977   "Pre-industrial economy and population structure: The elements of variance
             in early modern Sweden." *Scandinavian Journal of History* 2: 183 – 210.
Geertz, Clifford
    1973   *The Interpretation of Cultures.* New York: Basic Books.
Genet, J. P.
    1978   "L'Historien et l'ordinateur." *Historiens, Géographes* 270: 125 – 142.
Genovese, Eugene D.
    1975   "Concluding remarks." In Stanley L. Engerman and Eugene D. Genovese (eds.),
             Race and Slavery in the Western Hemisphere: Quantitative Studies. Princeton,
             N.J.: Princeton University Press.
George, C. H.
    1980   "The origins of capitalism: A Marxist epitome and a critique of Immanuel
             Wallerstein's modern world-system." *Marxist Perspectives* Summer 1980:
             70 – 101.
Gerschenkron, Alexander
    1962   *Economic Backwardness in Historial Perspective.* Cambridge, Mass.: Harvard
             University Press.
Gilbert, Felix
    1972   *Historical Studies Today.* New York: W. W. Norton
Gilmour-Bryson, A.
    1977   "Coding of the testimony of prisoners in the trial of the Templars in the papal
             states 1309 – 1310." In *Computing in the Humanities: Proceedings of the Third
             International Conference on Computing in the Humanities.* Waterloo, Ontario:
             University of Waterloo Press.
Goubert, Pierre
    1960   *Beauvais et le Beauvais de 1600 a 1730.* Paris: SEVPEN.
Great Britain, Census Office
    1833   Abstract of the Answers and Returns Made Pursuant to an Act, passed in the
             Eleventh Year of the Reign of His Majesty King George IV, intituled, "An Act for
             taking an Account of the Population of Great Britain, and of the Increase or
             Diminution thereof." Enumeration Abstract. Vol. I, 1831. [Westminster: House
             of Commons].
Gunder Frank, André
    1972   "The development of underdevelopment." In James D. Cockcroft *et al.* (eds.),
             Dependence and underdevelopment: Latin America's political economy. Garden
             City, N.Y.: Doubleday.
Hanham, H. J.
    1971   "Clio's weapons." *Daedalus* Spring 1971: 509 – 519.

Hechter, Michael
    1975   *Internal Colonialism: The Celtic Fringe in British National Development, 1536–1966.* Berkeley: University of California Press.

Henning, Friedrich-Wilhelm
    1977   "Der Beginn der modernen Welt im agrarischen Bereich." In Reinhart Koselleck (ed.), *Studien zum Beginn der modernen Welt.* Stuttgart: Klett-Cotta.

Henry, Louis
    1956   *Anciennes familles génévoises.* INED, Travaux et Documents, Cahier No. 26. Paris: Presses Universitaires de France.
    1967   *Manuel de démographie historique.* Geneva and Paris: Droz
    1968   "Historical demography." *Daedalus* Spring 1968: 385–396.

Herlihy, David
    1969   "Vieillir au quattrocento." *Annales; Economies, Sociétés, Civilisations* 24: 1338–1352.
    1978   "Computation in history: Styles and methods." *Computer* 8: 8–17.

Herlihy, David, and Christiane Klapisch-Zuber
    1978   *Les Toscans et leurs families: Une etude du catasto florentin de 1427.* Paris: Presses de la Fondation Nationale des Sciences Politiques and Editions de l'Ecole des Hautes Etudes en Sciences Sociales.

Hexter, J. H.
    1971   *The History Primer.* New York: Basic Books.

Higham, John
    1965   *History: The Development of Historical Studies in the United States.* Englewood Cliffs, N.J.: Prentice-Hall.

Hobsbawm, E. J.
    1959   *Primitive Rebels.* Manchester: Manchester University Press.
    1962   *The Age of Revolution: Europe 1789–1848.* London: Weidenfeld & Nicholson.
    1964   *Labouring Men: Studies in the History of Labour.* London: Weidenfeld & Nicolson.

Hobsbawm, E. J., and George Rudé
    1969   *Captain Swing.* London: Lawrence & Wishart.

Homans, George Caspar
    1941   *English Villagers of the Thirteenth Century.* Cambridge, Mass.: Harvard University Press.
    1961   *Social Behavior: Its Elementary Forms.* New York: Harcourt, Brace and World.
    1962   *Sentiments and Activities.* New York: Free Press.

Hoogvelt, Ankie M. M.
    1976   *The Sociology of Developing Societies.* London: Macmillan.

Hoselitz, Bert F., and Wilbert E. Moore (eds.)
    1966   *Industrialization and Society.* [Paris]: UNESCO/Mouton.

Huizer, Gerrit
    1973   *Peasant Rebellion in Latin America.* Harmondsworth: Penguin.

Jousselin, Mathurin
    1861   "Journal de M. Jousselin, curé de Sainte Croix de'Angers." In Célestin Port (ed.), *Inventaire analytique des archives anciennes de la Mairie d'Angers.* Paris: Dumoulin.

Judt, Tony
    1979   "A clown in regal purple: Social history and the historians." *History Workshop* 7: 66–94.
    1980   "The rules of the game." *The Historical Journal* 23: 181–192.

Kellenbenz, Hermann
 1976   *The Rise of the European Economy: An Economic History of Continental Europe from the Fifteenth to the Eighteenth Century.* London: Weidenfeld & Nicolson.
Klíma, Arnošt
 1974   "The role of rural domestic industry in Bohemia in the eighteenth century." *Economic History Review* 27: 48 – 56.
Kollmann, Wolfgang
 1974   *Bevölkerung in der industriellen Revolution.* Göttingen: Vandenhoeck & Ruprecht.
Kriedte, Peter, Hans Medick, and Jürgen Schlumbohm
 1977   *Industrialisierung vor der Industrialisierung: Gewerbliche Warenproducktion auf dem Land in der Formationsperiode des Kapitalismus.* Göttingen: Vandenhoeck & Ruprecht.
Kuznets, Simon
 1966   *Modern Economic Growth: Rate Structure, and Spread.* New Haven, Conn.: Yale University Press.
Landes, David, and Charles Tilly (eds.)
 1971   *History as Social Science.* Englewood Cliffs, N.J.: Prentice-Hall.
Landsberger, Henry A.
 1974   "Peasant unrest: Themes and variations." In Henry A. Landsburger (ed.), *Rural Protest: Peasant Movements and Social Change.* London: Macmillan.
Laslett, Barbara
 1980   "Beyond methodology: The place of theory in quantitative historical research." *American Sociological Review* 45: 214 – 228.
Laslett, Peter
 1965   *The World We Have Lost.* London: Methuen.
Lazonick, William
 1974   "Karl Marx and enclosures in England." *The Review of Radical Political Economy* 6(2): 1 – 59.
Lebrun, François
 1966   "Les soulèvements populaires à Angers aux XVIIe et XVIII siècles." 1: 119 – 140 in *Actes du quatre-vingt-dixieme Congrès national des Sociétés Savantes,* Nice, 1965. Paris: Bibliothèque Nationale.
Lefebvre, Georges
 1924   *Les paysans du Nord pendant la révolution française.* Lille: Robbe.
 1962 –   *Etudes orléanaises.* 2 vols. Paris: Commission d'Histoire Economique et Sociale
 1963   de la Révolution.
Le Goff, Jacques, and Pierre Nora (eds.)
 1974   *Faire de l'histoire.* 3 vols. Paris: Gallimard.
Lenski, Gerhard E.
 1966   *Power and Privilege: A Theory of Social Stratification.* New York: McGraw-Hill.
Le Play, Frederic
 1855   *Les ouvriers européens: Etudes sur les travaux, la vie domestique et la condition morale des populations ouvrières de l'Europe.* Paris: Imprimérie Imperiale.
Lequin, Yves
 1977   *Les ouvriers de la région lyonnaise (1848 – 1914).* 2 vols. Lyon: Presses Universitaires de Lyon.
Le Roy Ladurie, Emmanuel
 1966   *Les paysans de Languedoc.* 2 vols. Paris: SEVPEN.
 1975   *Montaillou, village occitan de 1294 à 1324.* Paris: Gallimard.

Levine, David
    1977   *Family Formation in an Age of Nascent Capitalism*. New York: Academic Press.

Liagre, Charles
    1934   "Les hostilités dans la région de Lille." *Revue du Nord* 20: 111–130.

Lichtman, Alan J., and Valerie French
    1978   *Historians and the Living Past*. Arlington Heights, Ill.: AHM Publishing Corp.

Lipset, Seymour Martin
    1968   "History and sociology: Some methodological considerations." In Seymour M. Lipset and Richard Hofstadter (eds.), *Sociology and History: Methods*. New York: Basic Books.

Lis, Catharina, and Hugo Soly
    1979   *Poverty and Capitalism in Pre-Industrial Europe*. Atlantic Highlands, N.J.: Humanities Press.

Liublinskaya, A. D.
    1966   *Vnutriennaia politika frantsuskovo absolutismo*. Moscow and Leningrad: Izdatel'stvo "Nauka."

Lofgren, Orvar
    1978   "The potato people: Household economy and family patterns among the rural proletariat in nineteenth century Sweden." In Sune Åkerman et al., *Chance and Change: Social and Economic Studies in Historical Demography in the Baltic Area*. Odense: Odense University Press.

Lorwin, Val R., and Jacob M. Price (eds.)
    1972   *The Dimensions of the Past: Materials, Problems and Opportunities for Quantitative Work in History*. New Haven, Conn.: Yale University Press.

Louvet, Jehan
    1854–   "Journal, ou récit véritable de tout ce qui est advenu digne de mémoire tant en
    1856   la ville d'Angers, pays d'Anjou et autres lieux (depuis l'an 1560 jusqu'à l'an 1634)." *Revue d'Anjou* 3 (1854): no. 1, 257–304, no. 2, 1–64, 129–192, 257–320; 4 (1855): no. 1, 1–65, 129–192, 257–320, no. 2, 1–64, 129–192, 257–320; 5 (1856): no. 1, 1–64, 129–192, 285–332, no. 2, 1–64, 133–196, 281–370.

Lowry, W. Kenneth
    1972   "Use of computers in information systems." *Science* 175: 841–846.

Ludz, Peter Christian
    1972   *Soziologie und Sozialgeschichte: Aspekte und Probleme*. Kölner Zeitschrift für Soziologie und Sozialpsychologie, Sonderheft 16. Opladen: Westdeutscher Verlag.

Luxemburg, Rosa
    1925   *Einführung in die Nationalökonomie*. Berlin: E. Lamb.

McClelland, Peter D.
    1975   *Causal Explanation and Model Building in History, Economics and the New Economic History*. Ithaca, N.Y.: Cornell University Press.

McCloskey, Donald N.
    1978   "The achievements of the cliometric school." *Journal of Economic History* 38: 13–28.

MacDonagh, Oliver
    1977   *Early Victorian Government, 1830–1970*. New York: Holmes & Meier.

Macfarlane, Alan
    1977   *Reconstructing Historical Communities*. Cambridge: Cambridge University Press.
    1978   *The Origins of English Individualism*. Cambridge: Cambridge University Press.

McKeown, Thomas
    1976   *The Modern Rise of Population.* New York: Academic Press.
Malowist, Marion
    1972   *Croissance et régression en Europe.* Cahiers des Annales, 34. Paris: Armand
             Colin.
Marrou, Henri-Irénée
    1967   "Comment comprendre le métier d'historien." In Charles Samaran (ed.), *L'His-*
             toire et ses méthodes. Encyclopédie de la Pléiade. Paris: Gallimard.
Marx, Karl
    1970   *Capital: A Critique of Political Economy.* 3 vols. London: Lawrence & Wishart.
    [1867]
Mathias, Peter
    1957   "The social structure in the eighteenth century: A calculation by Joseph Mas-
             sie." *Economic History Review,* 2d ser. 10: 30–45.
Mendels, Franklin
    1972   "Proto-industrialization: The first phase of the industrial process." *Journal of*
             Economic History 32: 241–261.
Montchrestien, Antoine
    1889   *Traité de l'économie politique.* Paris: Plon.
    [1615]
Montgomery, David
    1976   "Workers' control of machine production in the nineteenth century." *Labor*
             History Review 17: 485–509.
Moore, Barrington, Jr.
    1966   *Social Origins of Dictatorship and Democracy: Lord and Peasant in the Making*
             of the Modern World. Boston: Beacon Press.
    1978   *Injustice: The Social Bases of Obedience and Revolt.* White Plains, N.Y.: M. E.
             Sharpe
Moore, Wilbert E.
    1965   *The Impact of Industry.* Englewood Cliffs, N.J.: Prentice-Hall.
    1966   "Changes in occupational structures." In Neil J. Smelser and Seymour Martin
             Lipset (eds.), *Social Structure and Mobility in Economic Development.* Chicago:
             Aldine.
Moore, Wilbert E., and Arnold S. Feldman (eds.)
    1960   *Labor Commitment and Social Change in Developing Areas.* New York: Social
             Science Research Council.
Morrill, J. S.
    1978   "French absolutism as limited monarchy." *The Historical Journal* 21: 961–972.
Mottez, Bernard
    1966   *Systèmes de salaire et politiques patronales.* Paris: Centre National de la Re-
             cherche Scientifique.
Mousnier, Roland
    1964   (ed.) *Lettres et mémoires adressés au Chancelier Séguier (1633–1649).* 2 vols.
             Paris: Presses Universitaires de France.
    1978   *Paris capitale au temps de Richelieu et Mazarin.* Paris: Pédone.
Müller, Paul J. (ed.)
    1977   *Die Analyse prozess-produzierter Daten.* Stuttgart: Klett-Cotta
Munger, Frank W., Jr.
    1977   Popular protest and its suppression in early nineteenth century Lancashire,
             England: A study of historical models of protest and repression. Ph.D. disser-
             tation, University of Michigan.

National Research Council
    1978   *Science, Engineering, and Humanities Doctorates in the United States: 1977 Profile*. Washington, D.C.: National Academy of Sciences.

Ness, Gayl D. (ed.)
    1970   *The Sociology of Economic Development*. New York: Harper & Row.

Olsen, Steven L.
    1980   "Yankee city and the new urban history." *Journal of Urban History* 6:321 – 338.

Ozouf, Mona
    1971   "Le cortège et la ville: Les itinéraires parisiens des fêtes révolutionnaires." *Annales; Economies, Sociétés, Civilisations* 26: 889 – 916.
    1976   *La fête révolutionnaire, 1789 – 1799*. Paris: Gallimard.

Paige, Jeffery
    1975   *Agrarian Revolution: Social Movements and Export Agriculture in the Underdeveloped World.* New York: Free Press.

Palloix, Christian
    1971   *L'économie mondiale capitaliste*. 2 vols. "Economie et Socialisme," 16, 17. Paris: François Maspero.

Parsons, Talcott
    1960   "Durkheim's contribution to the theory of integration of social systems." In Kurt H. Wolff (ed.), *Essays on Sociology and Philosophy*. New York: Harper & Row.
    1971   *The System of Modern Societies*. Englewood Cliffs, N.J.: Prentice-Hall.

Patouillet, Xavier
    1971   "L'émeute des Lanturelus à Dijon en 1630." unpublished Mémoire de Maîtrise, U.E.R. Sciences Humaines, Dijon.

Pellicani, Luciano
    1973   "La rivoluzione industriale e il fenemeno della proletarizzazione." *Rassegna italiana di sociologia* 14: 63 – 84.

Henri Platelle
    1964   "Un village du Nord sous Louis XIV: Rumégies." *Revue du Nord* 46: 489 – 516.

Porchnev, Boris
    1963   *Les soulevements populaires en France de 1623 à 1648*. Paris: SEVPEN.

Portes, Alejandro, and John Walton
    1981   *Labor, Class, and the International System*. New York: Academic Press.

Reinhard, Marcel, André Armengaud, and Jacques Dupâquier
    1968   *Histoire générale de la population mondiale*. Paris: Editions Montchrestien.

Rogers, Alan
    1977   *Approaches to Local History*. 2d ed. London: Longman.

Rostow, W. W.
    1960   *The Stages of Economic Growth*. Cambridge: Cambridge University Press.

Rubin, Julius
    1972   "Expulsion from the garden" [review of Ester Boserup, *Conditions of Agricultural Growth*]. *Peasant Studies Newsletter* 1:35 – 39.

Rudé, George
    1959   *The Crowd in the French Revolution*. Oxford: Oxford University Press.

Sabean, David
    1976   "Aspects of kinship behavior and property in rural western Europe before 1800." In Jack Goody, Joan Thirsk, and E. P. Thompson (eds.), *Family and Inheritance: Rural Society in Western Europe, 1200 – 1800*. Cambridge: Cambridge University Press.

Saville, John
  1969   "Primitive accumulation and early industrialization in Britain." *Socialist Regis-
          ter* 1969: 247–271.
Schneider, Jane, and Peter Schneider
  1976   *Culture and Political Economy in Western Sicily.* New York: Academic
          Press.
Schofer, Lawrence
  1975   *The Formation of a Modern Labor Force: Upper Silesia, 1865–1914.* Berkeley:
          University of California Press.
Schon, Lennart
  1972   "Västernorrland in the middle of the nineteenth century: A study in the transi-
          tion from small-scale to capitalist production." *Economy and History* 15:
          82–111.
Schwartz, Michael
  1976   *Radical Protest and Social Structure: The Southern Farmers' Alliance and Cot-
          ton Tenancy, 1880–1890.* New York: Academic Press.
Schweitzer, R. A.
  1978   "Source reading for contentious gatherings in nineteenth-century British
          newspapers." Center for Research on Social Organization, University of Michi-
          gan, Working Paper 186.
  1979   "The study of contentious gatherings in early nineteenth-century Great Bri-
          tain." *Historical Methods* 12: 1–4.
Schweitzer, R. A., and Steven C. Simmons
  1978   "Interactive, direct-entry approaches to contentious gathering event files."
          Center for Research on Social Organization, University of Michigan, Working
          Paper 183.
Schweitzer, R. A., Charles Tilly, and John Boyd
  1980   "The texture of British contention in 1828 and 1829." Center for Research on
          Social Organization, University of Michigan, Working Paper 211.
Scott, Joan W.
  1974   *The Glassworkers of Carmaux: French Craftsmen and Political Action in a
          Nineteenth Century City.* Cambridge, Mass.: Harvard University Press.
Sedelow, Jr., Walter A., and Sally Yeates Sedelow
  1978,   "The history of sciences as discourse, the structure of scientific and literary
  1979   tests," Parts I and II. *Journal of the History of the Behavioral Sciences* 14:
          247–263; 15: 63–72.
Sharp, Buchanan
  1980   *In Contempt of All Authority: Rural Artisans and Riot in the West of England,
          1586–1660.* Berkeley: University of California Press.
Shorter, Edward
  1971   *The Historian and the Computer.* Englewood Cliffs, N.J.: Prentice-Hall.
Silbey, Joel H., Allan G. Bogue, and William H. Flanigan (eds.)
  1978   *The History of American Electoral Behavior.* Princeton, N.J.: Princeton Univer-
          sity Press.
Skinner, G. W.
  1964–   "Marketing and social structure in rural China." *Journal of Asian Studies* 24:
  1965   3–43, 195–228, 363–399.
Skocpol, Theda
  1979   *States and Social Revolutions: A Comparative Analysis of France, Russia, and
          China.* New York: Cambridge University Press.

Skolnick, M. H., *et al.*
    1971   "The reconstruction of genealogies from parish books." In *Mathematics in the Archeological and Historical Sciences: Proceedings of the Anglo-Romanian Conference, Mamaia 1970*. Edinburgh: University Press.

Smelser, Neil J.
    1959   *Social Change in the Industrial Revolution: An Application of Theory to the British Cotton Industry*. Chicago: University of Chicago Press.
    1963   *Theory of Collective Behavior*. New York: Free Press of Glencoe.
    1966   "Mechanisms of change and adjustment to change." In Bert F. Hoselitz and Wilbert E. Moore (eds.), *Industrialization and Society*. Paris: Mouton.
    1967   *Comparative Methods in the Social Sciences*. Englewood Cliffs, N.J.: Prentice-Hall.

Soboul, Albert
    1958   *Les sans-culottes parisiens en l'an II*. La Roche-sur-Yon: Potier.

Sorokin, Pitirim A.
    1962   *Social and Cultural Dynamics*. 4 vols. New York: Bedminster Press.
    [1937 – 1941]

Spengler, Oswald
    1932   *The Decline of the West*. London: George Allen and Unwin.
    [1926 – 1928]

Spufford, Margaret
    1976   "Peasant inheritance customs and land distribution in Cambridgeshire from the sixteenth to the eighteenth centuries." In Jack Goody, Joan Thirsk, and E. P. Thompson (eds.), *Family and Inheritance: Rural Society in Western Europe, 1200 – 1800*. Cambridge: Cambridge University Press.

Stedman Jones, Gareth
    1976   "From historical sociology to theoretical history." *British Journal of Sociology* 27: 295 – 305.

Stevenson, John
    1979   *Popular Disturbances in England, 1700 – 1870*. London: Longman.

Stinchcombe, Arthur L.
    1978   *Theoretical Methods in Social History*. New York: Academic Press.

Stoianovitch, Traian
    1976   *French Historical Method: The "Annales" Paradigm*. Ithaca, N.Y.: Cornell University Press.

Stone, Lawrence
    1977   "History and the social sciences in the twentieth century." In Charles F. Delzell (ed.), *The Future of History*. Nashville: Vanderbilt University Press.
    1979   "The revival of narrative." *Past and Present* 85: 3 – 24.

Swierenga, Robert P.
    1970   *Quantification in American History: Theory and Research*. New York: Atheneum.

Tate (Tate Gallery Publications Department)
    1974   *Turner 1775 – 1851*. London: Tate Gallery

Thernstrom, Stephan
    1964   *Poverty and Progress*. Cambridge, Mass.: Harvard University Press.
    1973   *The Other Bostonians: Poverty and Progress in the American Metropolis, 1880 – 1970*. Cambridge, Mass.: Harvard University Press.

Thirsk, Joan
    1961   "Industries in the countryside." In F. J. Fisher (ed.), *Essays in the Economic and*

Social History of Tudor and Stuart England in Honour of R. H. Tawney. Cambridge: Cambridge University Press.

Thomas, Keith
  1978   "The United Kingdom." In Raymond Grew (ed.), *Crises of Political Development in Europe and the United States*. Princeton, N.J.: Princeton University Press.

Thompson, E. P.
  1964   *The Making of the English Working Class*. London: Gollancz.
  1967   "Time, work-discipline, and industrial capitalism." *Past and Present* 38: 56 – 97.

Thompson, F. M. L.
  1966   "The social distribution of landed property in England since the sixteenth century." *Economic History Review*, 2d ser. 19: 505 – 517.
  1969   "Landownership and economic growth in England in the eighteenth century." In E. L. Jones and S. J. Woolf (eds.), *Agrarian Change and Economic Development: The Historical Problems*. London: Methuen.

Thompson, Paul
  1978   *The Voice of the Past: Oral History*. Oxford: Oxford University Press.

Thorner, Daniel *et al.*, (eds.)
  1966   *A. V. Chayanov on the Theory of Peasant Economy*. Homewood, Ill.: Richard D. Irwin.

Tilly, Charles
  1961   "Some problems in the history of the Vendée." *American Historical Review* 67: 19 – 33.
  1963   "The analysis of a counter-revolution." *History and Theory* 3: 30 – 58.
  1964   "Reflections on the revolutions of Paris: An essay on recent historical writing." *Social Problems* 12: 99 – 121.
  1966   "In defence of jargon." *Canadian Historical Association Record* 1966: 178 – 186.
  1970   "Clio and Minerva." In John C. McKinney and Edward A. Tiryakian (eds.), *Theoretical Sociology: Perspectives and Developments*. New York: Appleton-Century-Crofts.
  1972   "Quantification in history, as seen from France." In Val R. Lorwin and Jacob M. Price (eds.), *The Dimensions of the Past*. New Haven, Conn.: Yale University Press.
  1975   "Postscript: European statemaking and theories of political transformation." In Charles Tilly (ed.), *The Formation of National States in Western Europe*. Princeton, N.J.: Princeton University Press.
  1978a   *From Mobilization to Revolution*. Reading, Mass.: Addison-Wesley.
  1978b   "The historical study of vital processes." In Charles Tilly (ed.), *Historical Studies of Changing Fertility*. Princeton, N.J.: Princeton University Press.
  1978c   "Migration in modern European history." In William H. McNeill and Ruth Adams (eds.), *Human Migration: Patterns, Implications, Policies*. Bloomington, Ind.: Indiana University Press.
  1978d   "Anthropology, history, and the *Annales*." *Review* 1: 207 – 213.
  1979   Demographic origins of the European proletariat. Center for Research on Social Organization, University of Michigan, Working Paper 207.
  1980a   Charivaris, repertoires, and politics. Center for Research on Social Organization, University of Michigan, Working Paper 214.
  1980b   "Two callings of social history." *Theory and Society* 9: 679 – 681.
  1980c   The old new social history and the new old social history. Center for Research on Social Organization, University of Michigan, Working Paper 218.

1980d   Broad, broader . . . Braudel. Center for Research on Social Organization, University of Michigan, Working Paper 219.

1980e   "Historical sociology." In Scott G. McNall and Gary N. Howe (eds.), *Current Perspectives in Social Theory*. Greenwich, Conn.: JAI Press.

1981   "The web of contention in eighteenth-century cities." In Louise Tilly and Charles Tilly (eds.), *Class Conflict and Collective Action*. Beverly Hills, Calif.: Sage.

Tilly, Charles, and James Rule

1965   *Measuring Political Upheaval*. Princeton, N.J.: Center of International Studies, Princeton University.

1972   "1830 and the un-natural history of revolution." *Journal of Social Issues* 28: 49 — 76.

Tilly, Charles, and R. A. Schweitzer

1980   Enumerating and coding contentious gatherings in nineteenth-century Britain. Center for Research on Social Organization, University of Michigan, Working Paper 210.

Tilly, Louise A., and Joan W. Scott

1978   *Women, Work and Family*. New York: Holt, Rinehart & Winston.

Tilly, Richard, and Charles Tilly

1971   "An agenda for European economic history in the 1970s." *Journal of Economic History* 31: 184 — 197.

Tocqueville, Alexis de

1978   *Souvenirs*. Paris: Gallimard.

[1850]

Tønnesson, Käre

1959   *La défaite des sans-culottes*. Paris: Clavreuil.

Topolski, Jerzy

1976   *Methodology of History*. Warsaw: Polish Scientific Publishers; Dordrecht: D. Reidel.

Trotsky, Leon

1965   *History of the Russian Revolution*. 2 vols. London: Gollancz.

Vester, Michael

1970   *Die Enstehung des Proletariats als Lernprozess: Die Entstehung antikapitalistischer Theorie und Praxis in England, 1792 – 1848*. Frankfurt on the Main: Europaïsche Verlaganstalt.

Vovelle, Michel

1976   *Les métamorphoses de la fête en Provence de 1750 à 1820*. Paris: Aubier/ Flammarion.

Vries, Jan de

1976   *The Economy of Europe in an Age of Crisis, 1600 – 1750*. Cambridge: Cambridge University Press.

Wallerstein, Immanuel

1966   "Introduction" to Immanuel Wallerstein (ed.), *Social Change: The Colonial Situation*. New York: Wiley.

1974   *The Modern World-System: Capitalist Agriculture and the Origins of the European World-Economy in the Sixteenth Century*. New York: Academic Press.

1979   *The Capitalist World-Economy*. Cambridge: Cambridge University Press.

1980   *The Modern World System*. Vol. 2, *Mercantilism and the Consolidation of the European World-Economy, 1600 – 1750*. New York: Academic Press.

Weber, Max
    1950   *General Economic History.* Glencoe, Ill.: Free Press.
    [1927]
    1972   *Wirtschaft und Gesellschaft: Grundriss der verstehenden Soziologie.* 5th ed.
    [1921]   Tubigen: J. C. B. Mohr.

Wehler, Hans-Ulrich (ed.)
    1972   *Geschichte und Soziologie.* Cologne: Kiepenheuer & Witsch

Wemyss, Alice
    1961   *Les Protestants du Mas-d'Azil: Histoire d'une résistance 1680 – 1830.* Toulouse:
             Privat.

Winberg, Christer
    1978   "Population growth and proletarianization." In Sune Åkerman *et al., Chance
             and Change: Social and Economic Studies in Historical Demography in the
             Baltic Area.* Odense: Odense University Press.

Wolfe, Martin
    1972   *The Fiscal System of Renaissance France.* New Haven, Conn.: Yale University
             Press.

Wright, Gavin
    1978   *The Political Economy of the Cotton South: Households, Markets, and Wealth in
             the Nineteenth Century.* New York: W. W. Norton.

Wrightson, Keith, and David Levine
    1979   *Poverty and Piety in an English Village: Terling, 1525 – 1700.* New York: Academic
             Press.

Wrigley, E. A.
    1969   *Population and History.* New York: McGraw-Hill.

Zarri, G. P.
    1977   "Sur le traitement automatique de données biographiques médiévales: le pro-
             jet RESEDA." In *Computing in the Humanities: Proceedings of the Third Interna-
             tional Conference on Computing in the Humanities.* Waterloo, Ontario: Univer-
             sity of Waterloo Press.

Zimmerman, Carle C.
    1947   *Family and Civilization.* New York: Harper.

Index

A

Adams, Brooks, 86, 90
Adams family, 86
Adams, Henry, 86, 90
Africa, 40
Almond, Gabriel, 148
America, Latin, 39
America, North, 19, 22–23, 30–32, 58, 96, 99
American Historical Association, 15, 20
American War of Independence, 19
Anderson, Perry, 191
Anjou, 124
Anne of Austria, queen of France, 137
Annual Register, 95–96, 152
Anomie, 102, 104
Ardant, Gabriel, 202
Ariès, Philippe, 22
Armies, *see* Soldiers
Auden, W. H., 93
Audijos rebellion, 138, 204

B

Bairoch, Paul, 181–182
Baltazar, intendant of Languedoc, 133–134
Bandits, 2–3
Barclay, George, W., 67
Barzun, Jacques, 35
Beauregard, Sieur de, 131
Bendix, Reinhard, 9, 11, 148
Bergesen, Albert, 42

Best, Heinrich, 63–65
Biography, collective, 33
Birmingham Political Union, 174–175
Blaschke, Karlheinz, 198
Bloch, Marc, 92
Blum, Jerome, 191
Bonnets Rouges, 1675 rebellion in Brittany, 111–112, 138, 204
Boserup, Ester, 66
Boston Museum of Fine Arts, 91
Bouchu, intendant of Burgundy, 127
Bousquet, intendant of Languedoc, 133–134
Brandenburg-Prussia, *see* Prussia
Braudel, Fernand, 24, 42, 92, 191
Braun, Rudolf, 201
Briggs, Asa, 172
Brittany, 111–112
Brown, Brian, 172
Burgundy, 124, 129–132, 141
Bute, Lord, 99
Buxy, France, 130

C

Camisards, 138, 204, *see also* Protestants
Canada, 96
Capitalism, 4, 41, 46, 49, 72, 97, 100, 181–184, 191–210
Carr, Edward Hallett, 211
Catholic Association, 156
Catholic Emancipation, 79, 145–146, 156, 158–159, 164–165, 175

Cévennes, France, 136
Chambers, J. D., 196
Charenton, France, 134
Charleston (Charles Town), South Carolina, 96, 98, 107
Chartism, Chartists, 145, 172, 186
Chayanov, A. V., 186
Checkland, E.O.A., 176
Checkland, S. G., 176
China, 26, 58
Chirot, Daniel, 43
Civil War, American, 19, 30
Clamagéran, J. J., 119
Clapham, John, 18
Cliometrics, 66
Cobb, Richard, 33, 60–62, 70
Coding, 73–82
Colbert, Jean Baptiste, 111, 122, 204
Coleman, James, 101
Collective action, 4–5, 70–71, 100–101
Colquhoun, Patrick, 196
Computers, computing, 53–83, 166–168
Comte, Auguste, 38
Condé, France, 131
Condé, Prince of, 48, 116, 125
Conrad, Alfred, 30–31
Contention, 123–124, 150–151, 160–176
Contentious gatherings, 97, 114, 151, 153
   defined, 76
Cottage industry, 188
Crime, Criminals, 2–3, 107
Croquants rebellion, 138, 204

D

Demographic change, 208–209
Demographic transition, 67–68
Demography, historical, 25, 67–70
Denmark, 207
Development, see Theories, developmental
Dijon, France, 132–133
Disorganization, social, 106–107
Durkheim, Emile, 11–12, 37, 101–108,
   187–188

E

East Anglia, 86–89, 93
Eisenstadt, S. N., 43
Engerman, Stanley, 20, 30
England, 17–18, 86–90, 96–99, 192, 194–
   198, 201, 208, see also Great Britain

English Revolution (1640–1660), 12
Estrun, France, 128
Everitt, Alan, 195
Eversley, David, 68

F

Family reconstitution, 33, 68–70
Faultrier, intendant of Hainaut, 128–129
Fertility, 199–210
Flanders, 124, 141, 201
Florence, Italy, 59
Fogel, Robert, 20, 30
Food supply, 128, 165–166
Foster, John, 172
Fouquet, Nicolas, 117–118
Fourastié, Jean, 203
Fox-Genovese, Elizabeth, 35
France, 1–4, 34, 47–52, 60–61, 70–76, 96–
   98, 107, 109–144, 192, 194–195, 201–
   206, 207
Frank, André Gunder, 39, 41
Frankfurt Parliament (1848–1849), 63–65
French Revolution (1789–1799), 12, 49, 204
Friendly Societies, 158
Frisia, Frisians, 87–89, 93
Fronde, French rebellion (1648–1653), 50,
   119, 122–124, 135, 137, 204

G

Gabelle (salt tax), 131–132
Gardes des Gabelles (salt-tax guards), 128
Gazette de France, 126
Genovese, Eugene, 30–32, 35
Gentleman's Magazine, 107, 152
Gerschenkron, Alexander, 26
Gorant, Etienne, 131
Goubert, Pierre, 33–34
Great Britain, 26, 76–82, 98, 145–178, 207,
   213
Guilds, 122
Guilleri brothers, 2
Gutman, Herbert, 30

H

Hanham, Harry, 62
Hansard's Parliamentary Debates, 152
Harnel, Philippe, 131
Hechter, Michael, 43
Henry III, 47
Henry IV, 1, 3, 117

Henry, Louis, 33, 68–69
Herlihy, David, 59
Historiography, 16
History
    as a discipline, 1–52, 65–67, 211–215
    demographic, 29, 33
    economic, 29–32, 66–67
    social science, 27–37
Hobsbawm, E. J., 33, 36, 58, 112, 147–148,
    150, 154, 176
Holland, 195, 207–208, *see also* Nether-
    lands
Homans, George Caspar, 47, 85–94, 105–106
Home Office, Great Britain, 152–153, 170
Huguenots, *see* Protestants
Huizer, Gerrit, 110, 112
Hungary, 195

I
Idealism, historical, 103
Île-de-France, 124, 142
Industrialization, 106–107
*Institut National d'Études Démographi-
    ques* (INED), Paris 68
Inverness, Scotland, 162–163

J
Jones, Gareth Stedman, 5–6
Judt, Tony, 35

K
King, Gregory, 195–196
Kuznets, Simon, 6

L
Lancashire, England, 98, 159–160, 172, 201
Land reform, 194
Landsberger, Henry, 111
Languedoc, 124–125, 133, 143
La Rochelle, France, 135
Laslett, Peter, 33, 69
Lefebvre, Georges, 33
Le Mas d'Azil, France, 135–136
Lenski, Gerhard, 184
Le Play, Frédéric, 186
Le Tellier, Michel, 118
Levine, David, 196
Lille, France, 125
Linear B, 92
Lipset, Seymour Martin, 5

Liverpool, England, 146
London, England, 98, 146, 162–163, 172,
    204
Louis XIII, 47, 117, 119, 123, 134–135, 137,
    204
Louis XIV, 117, 120, 123, 137, 204
Louis Napoleon, French president and
    emperor, 61
Luddism, 186
Lustucru rebellion, 204

M
Macfarlane, Alan, 88–89
Malowist, Marion, 41
Malthus, T. R., 199
Manchester, England, 146
Maréchaussée (rural police), 128
Marie de Medici, 47
Marseilles, France, 98
Marx, Karl, 17, 37, 41, 66, 103, 179–181, 185,
    195, 197, 199
Marxism, Marxists, 41, 103, 150, 179, 186,
    189
Massie, Joseph, 196
Mayenne, duc de la, 134
Mazarin, Cardinal, 117, 119–120, 122, 137,
    204
McKeown, Thomas, 25
Mercure françois, 1–4, 13, 47–51
Meyer, John, 30–31
Michael Murphy Problem, 70
Milan, Italy, 98
Mill, John Stuart, 66, 103
Mirror of Parliament, 152
Modernization, 100, 183–184
Mons, Belgium, 131
Montauban, France, 134–135
Montchrestien, Antoine, 115
Montmorency, duc de, 127
Moore, Barrington, Jr., 43, 149–150, 191,
    212–213
Moore, Wilbert, 184
Morning Chronicle (newspaper), 77
Morrill, J. S., 205
Mousnier, Roland, 109
Munger, Frank, 159–160
Munitionnaires (military suppliers),
    129–130

N
Namier, Lewis, 16
Nantes, Edict of (1598), 116

Nation-states, national states, see State
Netherlands, 194, 207, see also Holland
New England, 87
Nimes, France, 132–133, 135
Northern Star, 172
Nu-Pieds rebellion, 138, 204

P
Paige, Jeffery, 109–110, 112
Palloix, Christian, 41
Pamiers, France, 135
Paris, France, 97–98, 134
Paris, Parlement of, 47
Parsons, Mr., 168–169
Parsons, Talcott, 101, 187–188
Particelli d'Emery, French minister, 137
Peasants, 193–202; see also Rebellion,
      peasant
Ph.D. degree, 14–15, 21
Place, Francis, 17–18
Political Register, Cobbett's, 152–154
Poor Law, 175
Poor Man's Guardian, 153
Portes, Alejandro, 42
Proletarianization, 179–210
Protestants, 116, 123–124, 134–137
Prussia, 201–202, 207–208
Pulitzer Prize, 19

Q
Quantification, 34–37, 59
Quercy (French province), 50–51

R
Ravaillac (assassin of Henry IV), 3
Rebellion, 1–3, 50, 204
      peasant, 109–144
Reconquista, 207
Reform Bill and campaign, 145, 149–150,
      159, 164–165, 174–175, 213
Repertoires of contention, 123–124, 151,
      160–176
Revolution, 17, 147–148, 178
Richelieu, Cardinal, 117, 119–120, 122, 137,
      204
Rohan, duc de, 125
Rostow, Walt Whitman, 65
Roure rebellion, 138, 204
Rubin, Julius, 66
Rudé, George, 18, 33, 36, 58, 154, 176

Rumégies, France, 125
Ruskin, John, 91–92
Russian Revolution (1917), 12

S
Sabotiers rebellion, 138, 204
Salt tax, see Gabelle
Saxby, George, 98
Saxony, 198
Schofield, R. S., 69
Schwartz, Michael, 43
Scotsman (newspaper), 153
Sharp, Buchanan, 197–198
Siebs, B. E., 87–88
Skinner, G. William, 58, 92
Skocpol, Theda, 43
Slavery, 9, 30
Smelser, Neil J., 9, 11, 18, 101, 105
Soboul, Albert, 33
Social science, historical, 29, 57–62
Social Science History (journal), 27
Social Science History Association, 28–29
Socialism, 41
Sociology
      as a discipline, 2–52, 100, 211–215
      historical, 100
Soldiers, armies, 2, 3, 126–129
Soly, Hugo, 191–192
Sorokin, P. A., 7
South Carolina Gazette, 95–96, 98, 107
Spain, 125, 207
Spencer, Herbert, 38
Spitalfields weavers, 172
Stamp Act, 98–99
State, national, 3 – 4, 44 – 47, 49, 72, 97,
      118 – 123, 191 – 210
Stevenson, John, 145, 150
Stinchcombe, Arthur, 7–12, 209, 213
Stone, Lawrence, 22, 36–37
Stouffer, Samuel, 53–54
Strikes, 73, 107
Suicide, 107
Sussex, England, 168
Sutch, Richard, 30
Swing Rebellion (1830), 154, 156–157, 159,
      166–169
Switzerland, 183, 201

T
Tardanizats rebellion, 138, 204
Tax rebellion, 3, 122, 132, 138

Taxes, 115–116, 118–123, 191–210
Test and Corporation Acts, 79, 158, 175
Thackeray, William Makepeace, 92
Theories, developmental, 38–40, 65–67, 180
Theory, historically grounded, 26, 46
Thernstrom, Stephan, 22–23, 58, 70
Thirty Years' War, 1, 126, 202
Thomas, Keith, 149
Thompson, E. P., 17–18, 33, 36, 148, 150, 173, 186
Thompson, F.M.L., 196–197
Times of London, 152
Tocqueville, Alexis de, 9, 11, 58
Tønnesson, Kåre, 33
Tönnies, Ferdinand, 37
Topolski, Jerzy, 16
Toulouse, France, 98, 132–133, 138
Trotsky, Leon, 9, 11–12, 213
Turner, J.M.W., 85, 91–92

U
Urbanization, 106–107
Ure, Andrew, 18
Utilitarianism, Utilitarians, 103

V
Vals, France, 136
Ventris, Michael, 92

Vernon, France, 130
Vester, Michael, 147–148
Vietnam, 183
Violence, collective, 71–76, 107
Vivarais, France, 136
Votes and Proceedings of Parliament, 152, 159
Vries, Jan de, 201

W
Wallerstein, Immanuel, 40–43, 45, 191, 194
Walton, John, 42
War, 45, 109–144, 204–207
War of Devolution, 125
Warner, W. Lloyd, 22
Wearmouth, R.F.W., 18
Weber, Max, 38, 103, 184–185
Wellington, duke of, 162
West Country, England, 87
Wilkes, John, 99
Wolf, Eric, 112
Wright, Gavin, 30–31
Wrightson, Keith, 196
Wrigley, E. A., 33, 69

Z
Zimmerman, Carle, 186

STUDIES IN SOCIAL DISCONTINUITY
(Continued from page ii)

Lucile H. Brockway. Science and Colonial Expansion: The Role of the British Royal Botanic Gardens

James Lang. Portuguese Brazil: The King's Plantation

Elizabeth Hafkin Pleck. Black Migration and Poverty: Boston 1865-1900

Harvey J. Graff. The Literacy Myth: Literacy and Social Structure in the Nineteenth-Century City

Michael Haines. Fertility and Occupation: Population Patterns in Industrialization

Keith Wrightson and David Levine. Poverty and Piety in an English Village: Terling, 1525-1700

Henry A. Gemery and Jan S. Hogendorn (Eds.). The Uncommon Market: Essays in the Economic History of the Atlantic Slave Trade

Tamara K. Hareven (Ed.). Transitions: The Family and the Life Course in Historical Perspective

Randolph Trumbach. The Rise of the Egalitarian Family: Aristocratic Kinship and Domestic Relations in Eighteenth-Century England

Arthur L. Stinchcombe. Theoretical Methods in Social History

Juan G. Espinosa and Andrew S. Zimbalist. Economic Democracy: Workers' Participation in Chilean Industry 1970-1973

Richard Maxwell Brown and Don E. Fehrenbacher (Eds.). Tradition, Conflict, and Modernization: Perspectives on the American Revolution

Harry W. Pearson. The Livelihood of Man by Karl Polanyi

Frederic L. Pryor. The Origins of the Economy: A Comparative Study of Distribution in Primitive and Peasant Economies

Charles P. Cell. Revolution at Work: Mobilization Campaigns in China

Dirk Hoerder. Crowd Action in Revolutionary Massachusetts, 1765-1780

David Levine. Family Formations in an Age of Nascent Capitalism

Ronald Demos Lee (Ed.). Population Patterns in the Past

Michael Schwartz. Radical Protest and Social Structure: The Southern Farmers' Alliance and Cotton Tenancy, 1880-1890

Jane Schneider and Peter Schneider. Culture and Political Economy in Western Sicily

Daniel Chirot. Social Change in a Peripheral Society: The Creation of a Balkan Colony

Stanley H. Brandes. Migration, Kinship, and Community: Tradition and Transition in a Spanish Village

James Lang. Conquest and Commerce: Spain and England in the Americas

Kristian Hvidt. Flight to America: The Social Background of 300,000 Danish Emigrants

STUDIES IN SOCIAL DISCONTINUITY

D. E. H. Russell. Rebellion, Revolution, and Armed Force: A Comparative Study of Fifteen Countries with Special Emphasis on Cuba and South Africa

John R. Gillis. Youth and History: Tradition and Change in European Age Relations 1770-Present

Immanuel Wallerstein. The Modern World-System I: Capitalist Agriculture and the Origins of the European World-Economy in the Sixteenth Century; II: Mercantilism and the Consolidation of the European World-Economy, 1600-1750

John W. Cole and Eric R. Wolf. The Hidden Frontier: Ecology and Ethnicity in an Alpine Valley

Joel Samaha. Law and Order in Historical Perspective: The Case of Elizabethan Essex

William A. Christian, Jr. Person and God in a Spanish Valley